Indiana Infantry. 79th Regiment

History of the Seventy-Ninth Rregiment Indiana Volunteer Infantry

In the Civil War of Eighteen Sixty-One in the United States

Indiana Infantry. 79th Regiment

History of the Seventy-Ninth Rregiment Indiana Volunteer Infantry
In the Civil War of Eighteen Sixty-One in the United States

ISBN/EAN: 9783337116125

Printed in Europe, USA, Canada, Australia, Japan

Cover: Foto ©ninafisch / pixelio.de

More available books at **www.hansebooks.com**

HISTORY

OF THE

SEVENTY-NINTH REGIMENT

INDIANA VOLUNTEER INFANTRY

IN THE CIVIL WAR OF EIGHTEEN SIXTY-ONE

IN THE

UNITED STATES

INDIANAPOLIS
THE HOLLENBECK PRESS
EIGHTEEN NINETY-NINE

PREFACE

The committee selected by the Regimental Association of the 79th Regiment of Indiana Volunteers to prepare the history of the regiment has completed its work, and submits it to the surviving members of the regiment and to the surviving representatives of our deceased comrades, and to all others who may be interested.

This has not been an easy task. The years of very active service of the regiment and the great events and battles in which it took a part make it difficult to write the history of the regiment without writing the history of the civil war of 1861.

After very careful consideration, the committee decided to limit its work to a narration of the experiences and service of the one regiment, so far as could possibly be done. One other question about which the committee was deeply concerned was to do justice to the individual men in the regiment in the record of honorable and dishonorable service. It was decided to present the muster-out roll of the field and staff and of each company, with the record as the officers of the companies had themselves made it at the time of the muster-out of the regiment.

The committee was impressed that there ought to be special mention made of the gallant and faithful service of many of the men who contributed to the honorable record of the regiment, and also special mention of a few men who deserved to have the facts stated which would go to their discredit. But there was danger, in the absence of any record made by company officers on the muster-out roll, that injustice might be done in condemnation, and words of praise might be made too strong in some cases and not strong enough in others to do exact justice where commendation should be expressed.

The officers, by the course pursued, are in exactly the same condition as the enlisted men. It was determined to make the history tell the truth, and give the account of each day from the muster-in of the regiment to the muster-out.

At the beginning of the work, a circular letter was sent to every man in the regiment, asking for any record or diary kept by him or any one else to his knowledge, and also for any incident, for the truth of which he could vouch. By these means we gathered some records, most of them fragmentary and concerning special occasions or short periods of time.

Many incidents were also received, given by members of the regiment. Some of these incidents were a little too highly colored to be put into history; many of them, however, were interesting and important, but it became apparent that we would have to limit this history as it has been done, in order to prevent a large and expensive book.

The committee must acknowledge the great service and assistance received in this work from the diary kept by William H. Huntsinger, of Company "I," who had kept a daily record most of the time the regiment was in the service. Though he had died before this work was undertaken, his widow, who now lives at Afton, Iowa, responded to our circular by sending us this record, which she had. It had been written with pencil mainly, and was so dim after thirty-four years that it was necessary to copy it, which was a very difficult thing to do.

The daily record, as given, is not an exact copy of that diary, but that was used and followed so far as it could be for information, and the work has been completed by resort to all the information and recollection of the committee and from members of the regiment.

It may appear to our comrades, individually, when they read this history, that they did not see some things that are recorded and did see other things of importance that are not recorded, but it should be borne in mind that no one of us saw everything, and each of us may be slightly mistaken in our recollection of some things occurring at the far-off days covered by this history.

The committee has given much time and great care to the preparation and presentation of this history. This they have done because parts of their own lives are in it, and their love for the 79th Regiment and their love for their dear old comrades has been in the work.

GEORGE W. PARKER,
JOHN G. DUNBAR,
DANIEL W. HOWE,
ELI F. RITTER,
AMOS C. BEESON,
CHARLES J. MANY,
JOSEPH O. PETTEGO,
Committee.

FIELD AND STAFF OFFICERS.

Name and Rank.	Place of Enlistment.	Date of Commission.	Present Residence.	Remarks.
COLONEL.				
Frederick Knefler	Indianapolis	Aug. 27, '62	Indianapolis	Mustered out with regiment.
LIEUTENANT-COLONEL.				
Samuel P. Oyler	Franklin	Aug. 26, '62	Franklin	Resigned Aug. 21, '64, cause disability.
George W. Parker	Indianapolis	Aug. 25, '64	Pendleton	Mustered out with regiment.
MAJOR.				
Perry M. Blankenship	Martinsville	Aug. 26, '62		Resigned Jan. 25, '63.
George E. Wallace	Indianapolis	Jan. 26, '63	Indianapolis	Discharged May 13, '63.
George W. Parker	Indianapolis	Oct. 11, '63	Pendleton	Promoted lieutenant-colonel.
John G. Dunbar	Greenfield	Aug. 25, '64	Greencastle	Mustered out with regiment.
ADJUTANT.				
Eli F. Ritter	Danville	Aug. 22, '62	Indianapolis	Promoted captain Co. "C," '62, '63.
Thompson Dunn	Indianapolis	May 9, '64		Killed in battle Lovejoy Station, Sept.
Leander W. Munhall	Indianapolis	Sept. 3, '64	Philadelphia	Mustered out with regiment.
QUARTERMASTER.				
William C. Shortridge	Kokomo	Aug. 11, '62		Resigned April 23, '63.
Jacob H. Coledazier	Indianapolis	April 24, '63		Mustered out with regiment.
CHAPLAIN.				
Love H. Jameson	Indianapolis	Dec. 6, '62		Resigned April 30, '63.
SURGEONS.				
Robert Charlton	Franklin	Aug. 26, '62		Resigned Dec. 18, '62.
Lewis Manker	Mooresville	Jan. 29, '63		Resigned June 11, '63.
William G. McFadden	London	June 12, '63	Shelbyville	Mustered out with regiment.
ASSISTANT SURGEON.				
William G. McFadden	London	Aug. 26, '62	Shelbyville	Promoted surgeon.
John H. Tilford	Indianapolis	Aug. 27, '62	Windom, Minn.	Mustered out with regiment.

ROSTER OF COMPANY "A."

Name and Rank.	Place of Enlistment.	Date of Enlistment.	Present Residence.	Remarks.
CAPTAINS.				
George F. Wallace	Indianapolis	July 30, '62	Indianapolis	Promoted to major.
James E. Harris	Madison	Jan. 31, '63	Hanover	Resigned Aug. 1, '63.
William A. Abbett	Indianapolis	Aug. 2, '63	Des Moines, Ia.	Mustered out with regiment.
FIRST LIEUTENANTS.				
John R. Cotton	Indianapolis	July 30, '62		Resigned Jan. 20, '63.
William A. Abbett	Indianapolis	Jan. 31, '63	Des Moines, Ia.	Promoted captain.
Frank H. Butterfield	Indianapolis	Aug. 2, '63		Declined.
William H. Hagerhorst	Indianapolis	March 1, '65	Indianapolis	Mustered out with regiment.
SECOND LIEUTENANTS.				
James A. Harris	Madison	July 30, '62	Hanover	Promoted captain.
George G. Earl	Indianapolis	Jan. 31, '63	Glendale, Mont	Promoted captain Co. "G."
FIRST SERGEANTS.				
Francis M. Severance	Indianapolis	July 18, '62	Franklin	Mustered out with regiment.
William B. Lewis	Indianapolis	July 23, '62	Indianapolis	Mustered out with regiment.
SERGEANTS.				
Edgar J. Foster	Indianapolis	July 28, '62	Indianapolis	Promoted 1st lieutenant Co. "K."
William A. Abbett	Indianapolis	July 18, '62	Des Moines, Ia.	Promoted 1st lieutenant.
Francis H. Butterfield	Indianapolis	July 23, '62		Promoted lieut. 15th U. S. colored.
Henry C. Earnest	Indianapolis	July 20, '62		Mustered out with regiment.
Adolph J. Many	Indianapolis	July 18, '62		Mustered out with regiment.
Arnold D. Lamb	Madison	July 30, '62	Lamb's P. O.	Mustered out with regiment.
CORPORALS.				
Arthur Rhouette	Indianapolis	July 23, '62		Discharged Jan. 27, '63.
James M. Caldwell	Quincy	July 24, '62		Mustered out with regiment.
Adam Hereth	Indianapolis	July 18, '62	Indianapolis	Mustered out with regiment.

James A. Pressley	Indianapolis	Aug. 6, '62	Indianapolis	Mustered out with regiment.
William B. Lewis	Indianapolis	Aug. 23, '62	Indianapolis	Promoted 1st sergeant.
Oliver Anthony	Indianapolis	Aug. 5, '62		Mustered out with regiment.
Julius Young	Indianapolis	Aug. 18, '62		Mustered out with regiment.
Robert C. Heizer	Indianapolis	Aug. 26, '62	Orlando, Fla.	Mustered out with regiment.
Herman Franer	Indianapolis	July 18, '62	Indianapolis	Discharged Feb. 2, '65, wounds.
Adolph J. Maury	Indianapolis	July 18, '62		Promoted to sergeant.
Samuel D. Lindsey	Indianapolis	July 19, '62		Deserted.
Charles D. Joslin	Indianapolis	July 18, '62	Anderson	Mustered out with regiment.
William J. Brattain	Indianapolis	July 18, '62		Transferred to engineer corps.
August Gregoire	Indianapolis	Aug. 12, '62		Mustered out with regiment.
MUSICIANS.				
Aruas P. Shauver	Indianapolis	Aug. 26, '62	Indianapolis	Mustered out with regiment.
WAGONER.				
Morris Sullivan	Indianapolis	July 20, '62		Discharged Mar. 11, '63.
PRIVATES.				
Anthony, Oliver	Cincinnati	Aug. 5, '62		Promoted corporal.
Arnold, Thomas	Indianapolis	July 18, '62		Died Jan. 7, '63, wounds.
Barton, Frederick	Cumberland	Aug. 16, '62		Discharged May 21, '65, wounds, '61.
Boehm, Philllip	Indianapolis	Aug. 10, '62		Died in Andersonville prison, Aug. 14.
Brademeyer, Henry	Indianapolis	Aug. 16, '62		Died at Georgetown,Tenn.,Dec.30,'63.
Brennan, Daniel	Indianapolis	Aug. 12, '62		Mustered out May 12, '65.
Brennan, Patrick	Indianapolis	July 20, '62	Indianapolis	Mustered out with regiment.
Bailey, William	Indianapolis	July 26, '62		Died Oct. 20, '62, wounds.
Caldwell, James M.	Indianapolis	July 24, '62		Promoted corporal.
Cerr, William	Indianapolis	July 24, '62		Discharged Mar. 26, '63, wounds.
Christian, Francis M.	Indianapolis	July 24, '62		Discharged Dec. '62.
Crigler, Benjamin	Indianapolis	July 26, '62		Killed at Stone River, Jan. 2, '63.
Delong, Isaac	Huntington	July 20, '62		Discharged Nov. 8, '62.
Delzell, Samuel	Indianapolis	July 26, '62		Mustered out with regiment.
Devine, John	Indianapolis	July 24, '62	Quincy, Ill.	Mustered out with regiment.
Downing, James P.	Indianapolis	July 18, '62		Deserted.
Ducker, John B.	Indianapolis	Aug. 5, '62		Died at Nashville, Sept. 30, '63.

ROSTER OF COMPANY "A."—CONTINUED.

Name and Rank.	Place of Enlistment.	Date of Enlistment.	Present Residence.	Remarks.
PRIVATES—Continued.				
Earl, George G.	Indianapolis	Aug. 9, '62	Glendale	Promoted second lieutenant.
Gaylord, Samuel B.	Indianapolis	Aug. 9, '62		Died Jan. 7, '63, wounds.
Grabhorn, Henry	Indianapolis	July 30, '62		Discharged March 17, '63.
Gregoire, August	Indianapolis	Aug. 12, '62		Promoted to corporal.
Haley, Timothy	Indianapolis	Aug. 12, '62		Died at Murfreesboro, Aug. 29, '63.
Hawkins, Samuel	Edinburg	Aug. 1, '62		Deserted.
Harper, Rufus	Indianapolis	July 26, '62		Killed at Chickamauga, Sept. 19, '63.
Hause, John	Indianapolis	July 29, '62		Discharged June 23, '63.
Hawthorn, James F.	Indianapolis	July 18, '62		Mustered out with regiment.
Heitzer, Robert C.	Indianapolis	July 26, '62	Orlando, Fla.	Promoted to corporal.
Hinsley, William	Indianapolis	July 21, '62		Mustered out with regiment.
Hoop, John W.	Indianapolis	July 18, '62		Mustered out with regiment.
Jameson, Benjamin	Indianapolis	Aug. 16, '62		Transferred to V. R. C. Nov. 1, '63.
Joslin, Charles D.	Indianapolis	July 18, '62		Promoted to corporal. ['64.]
Keeling, John C.	Cloverdale	July 28, '62	Anderson	Died in Andersonville Prison Dec. 31,
Kerlox, John	Indianapolis	July 25, '62	Sheridan	Transferred to 51st Ind.
Knodle, Sebastian	Indianapolis	Aug. 9, '62		Died at Nashville Dec. 21, '62.
Kuhn, Phillip	Indianapolis	July 20, '62	Lamb's P. O.	Mustered out with regiment.
Lamb, Arnold E.	Indianapolis	Aug. 7, '62		Promoted sergeant.
Lawson, Aaron	Indianapolis	Aug. 26, '62		Mustered out with regiment.
Lawson, James F.	Indianapolis	July 22, '62		Killed at Dallas, Ga. May 25, '64.
Lawson, Thomas S.	Indianapolis	Aug. 26, '62		Transferred to V. R. C., wounds.
Lawson, John S.	Indianapolis	July 29, '62		Discharged Dec. 15, '63.
Lang, Elijah	Indianapolis	Aug. 12, '62		Discharged April 7, '63.
Mann, Daniel	Indianapolis	Aug. 7, '62		Mustered out with regiment.
Metzger, George	Indianapolis			Deserted.

SEVENTY-NINTH INDIANA REGIMENT. 5

Medsker, Jacob	Indianapolis	Aug. 6, '62		Mustered out with regiment.
Moore, William P.	Indianapolis	Aug. 1, '62		Discharged April 9, '63, wounds.
McNeal, Alonzo	Indianapolis	July 20, '62	Green Springs, Mo.	Mustered out with regiment, died Jan. 17, '85.
Nelson, John H.	Indianapolis	July 21, '62		Died June 3, '63, wounds.
Nagle, William F.	Indianapolis	July 30, '62		Died at Nashville, Feb. 23, '63.
Ote, George	Indianapolis	July 18, '62		Deserted.
O'Connell, Dennis	Indianapolis	July 20, '62		Deserted.
O'Connell, Patrick	Indianapolis	July 12, '62		Mustered out with regiment.
O'Connor, Michael	Indianapolis	July 21, '62		Discharged June 21, '63.
Pearson, Abel B.	Indianapolis	July 26, '62		Died at New Albany, May 8, '63.
Pearson, David	Indianapolis	Aug. 5, '62		Died Nov. 8, '62.
Pearson, Jonas O.	Indianapolis	July 30, '62		Died June 20, '63, wounds.
Pettex, John M.	Indianapolis	Aug. 6, '62		Discharged Mar. 1, '65, wounds.
Pointer, Jesse S.	Indianapolis	Aug. 12, '62	Indianapolis	Promoted corporal.
Pressley, James A.	Indianapolis	July 29, '62		Discharged Dec. 1, '62.
Rafert, Frederick	Indianapolis	July 22, '62	Indianapolis	Mustered out with regiment.
Riester, John	Indianapolis	July 18, '62		Mustered out with regiment.
Renard, Emile	Indianapolis	July 14, '62	Indianapolis	Discharged Feb. 3, '63.
Ross, Robert	Indianapolis	July 18, '62	Dayton Home	Mustered out with regiment.
Seyfred, Phillip	Indianapolis	July 21, '62		Discharged Dec. 2, '62, wounds.
Steinman, George	Indianapolis	Aug. 20, '62	Strong, Kan	Transferred to engineer corps July 20, '64.
Watts, Wellington	Cincinnati	July 26, '62		Mustered out with regiment.
Weisenbach, John	Indianapolis	Aug. 6, '62	Cincinnati	Mustered out with regiment.
Werzner, William	Indianapolis	Aug. 11, '62		Mustered out with regiment.
Wortman, Charles	Indianapolis			Died at Louisville April, '63.
Williams, George				
Recruits.				
Kingsley, Royal	Indianapolis	Dec. 4, '63	Indianapolis	Transferred to 51st Ind.
McKinney, Andrew	Indianapolis	July 23, '63		Transferred to 51st Ind.
Stow, Sylvanus S.	Indianapolis	Dec. 15, '63		Mustered out May 29, '65.

ROSTER OF COMPANY "B."

Name and Rank.	Place of Enlistment.	Date of Enlistment.	Present Residence.	Remarks.
CAPTAINS.				
Louis Manker		Aug. 9, '62	Greencastle	Promoted surgeon.
John G. Dunbar		Aug. 9, '62	Greencastle	Promoted major.
William V. Burns		Aug. 9, '62		Discharged May 15, '65, disability.
FIRST LIEUTENANTS.				
John G. Dunbar		Aug. 9, '62	Greencastle	Promoted captain.
William V. Burns		Aug. 9, '62		Promoted captain.
Arthur St. Clair Vance		Aug. 9, '62	Smith Valley	Resigned June 20, '65.
Henry Magsam		Aug. 9, '62	Indianapolis	Mustered out with regiment.
William Hagerhorst		Aug. 9, '62		Promoted quartermaster.
SECOND LIEUTENANTS.				
Arthur St. Clair Vance		Aug. 9, '62		Promoted 1st lieutenant.
William V. Burns		Aug. 9, '62		Promoted 1st lieutenant.
Simeon J. Thompson		Aug. 9, '62	Shelbyville	Discharged Aug. 25, '64, leg amput'd.
FIRST SERGEANTS.				
Simeon J. Thompson		Aug. 9, '62	Shelbyville	Promoted 2d lieutenant.
Henry Magsam		Aug. 9, '62	Glenn Valley	Promoted 1st lieutenant.
SERGEANTS.				
Henry Magsam		Aug. 9, '62	Smith Valley	Promoted 1st Sergeant.
William H. H. Phillips		Aug. 9, '62	Indianapolis	Discharged May 12, '65, wounds.
Joseph B. Norman		Aug. 9, '62	Indianapolis	Discharged Jan. 3, '63.
James W. Catterson		Aug. 9, '62	Shoals, Ind.	Discharged Dec. 10, '62.
John W. Smith		Aug. 9, '62	Dundee, Ind.	Mustered out with regiment.
James T. Wright		Aug. 9, '62	Nora	Mustered out with regiment.
John R. Bellis		Aug. 9, '62	Indianapolis	Mustered out with regiment.
Thomas J. Carr		Aug. 9, '62	Greenfield	Mustered out with regiment.
Charles W. Killenbarger		Aug. 9, '62	Emerson, Iowa	Mustered out with regiment.

SEVENTY-NINTH INDIANA REGIMENT.

CORPORALS.				
Amos Neal	Aug.	9, '62		Died at Nashville, Dec. 18, '62.
John T. Hensley	Aug.	9, '62		Discharged May 13, '63.
Edward Arkbauer	Aug.	9, '62		Mustered out with regiment, private.
John W. Smith	Aug.	9, '62		Promoted sergeant.
John W. Miller	Aug.	9, '62		Discharged March 21, '63.
William Hagerthorst	Aug.	9, '62		Promoted first lieutenant.
James T. Wright	Aug.	9, '62	Nora	Promoted sergeant.
John Bardaery	Aug.	9, '62	Indianapolis	Transferred to V. R. C.
John T. Anderson	Aug.	9, '62	Lebanon	Mustered out with regiment.
Alfred G. Boyer	Aug.	9, '62	Frankfort	Mustered out with regiment.
George Hall	Aug.	9, '62	Trenton, Mo.	Mustered out with regiment.
Dudley D. Hudson	Aug.	9, '62	Greenfield	Mustered out with regiment.
John Pope	Aug.	9, '62		Mustered out with regiment.
George W. Robertson	Aug.	9, '62		Mustered out with regiment.
Isaac Stutesman	Aug.	9, '62		Mustered out with regiment.
PRIVATES.				
Anderson, John T	Aug.	9, '62	Lebanon	Promoted corporal.
Ashcraft, George W	Aug.	9, '62		Mustered out with regiment.
Bennett, John	Aug.	9, '62		Died at Nashville, Jan. 25, '63.
Berlin, John A	Aug.	9, '62		Mustered out with regiment.
Black, Jesse	Aug.	9, '62	Homer, Ill.	Mustered out with regiment.
Boyer, Alfred P	Aug.	9, '62	Frankfort	Promoted corporal.
Boyer, Nelson J	Aug.	9, '62		Died at Nashville, Dec. 3, '62.
Breese, Martin	Aug.	9, '62	Charleston, Ill	Discharged Feb. 15, '63.
Brock, Alfred	Aug.	9, '62		Discharged March 21, '63.
Brown, Theodore	Aug.	9, '62		Mustered out with regiment.
Burns, William V	Aug.	9, '62		Promoted second lieutenant.
Barton, Henry B	Aug.	9, '62		Died at Louisville, Oct. 11, '62.
Catterson, Robert W	Aug.	9, '62		Died at Nashville, Jan. 25, '63, wounds.
Carson, Joel	Aug.	9, '62		Died at Nashville, Dec. 7, '62.
Carr, Thomas J	Aug.	9, '62	Greenfield	Promoted sergeant.
Conger, Jonathan B	Aug.	9, '62	Rose Hill, Ill.	Mustered out with regiment.

ROSTER OF COMPANY "B"—Continued.

Name and Rank.	Place of Enlistment.	Date of Enlistment.	Present Residence.	Remarks.
PRIVATES Continued.				
Crail, Sylvester		Aug. 9, '62	Nora	Transferred to V. R. C.
Curry, Christopher		Aug. 9, '62		Died at Nashville Feb. 20, '63.
Culter, John W		Aug. 9, '62		Killed at Stone River, Jan. 2, '63.
Day, Humphrey M		Aug. 9, '62		Discharged Feb. 2, '63.
Dwyre, Michael W		Aug. 9, '62		Mustered out with regiment.
Elliott, James M		Aug. 9, '62	Gem	Transferred to V. R. C.
Gapen, James B		Aug. 9, '62	Greenfield	Mustered out with regiment.
Gapen, William		Aug. 9, '62	Hannibal, Mo.	Mustered out with regiment.
Glass, Thomas		Aug. 9, '62		Mustered out with regiment.
Ginand, John		Aug. 9, '62		Mustered out with regiment.
Hastings, James		Aug. 9, '62	Dallas, Ore.	Promoted corporal.
Hall, George		Aug. 9, '62	Trenton, Mo.	Discharged May 7, '63, wounds.
Hook, Samuel T		Aug. 9, '62	Ree's Mill	Discharged May 26, '63, wounds.
Hopper, John W		Aug. 9, '62	Greenfield	Promoted corporal.
Hudson, Dudley D		Aug. 9, '62		Died at Bowling Green, Nov. 16, '62.
Huff, Hanson		Aug. 9, '62		Deserted Oct. 16, '62.
Hoffman, Lewis		Aug. 9, '62	Greenfield	Discharged July 8, '63, wounds.
Hutton, William		Aug. 9, '62		Transferred to engineer corps.
Johnson, Charles W		Aug. 9, '62		Discharged Jan. 30, '63.
Johnson, Ashby		Aug. 9, '62		Mustered out with regiment.
Jones, Francis M		Aug. 9, '62	Indianapolis	Mustered out with regiment.
Jordan, Phineas G		Aug. 9, '62	Emerson, Ia	Promoted sergeant.
Killenberger, Charles W		Aug. 9, '62		Discharged April 25, '63.
Lawhan, Charles		Aug. 9, '62	Meridianville, Ala.	Mustered out with regiment.
Lawhan, Lewis M		Aug. 9, '62		Died Feb. 8, '63.
Leever, Felix F		Aug. 9, '62		

Leonard, Jacob		Aug. 9, '62	Gem	Discharged Mar. 28, '63, wounded.
Long, John K		Aug. 9, '62		Mustered out with regiment.
Lucas, William H		Aug. 9, '62		Died Dec. 18, '62.
Miller, James W		Aug. 9, '62		Mustered out with regiment.
Morgan, William M		Aug. 9, '62	Republic, Kan	Transferred to V. R. C.
Muth, David M		Aug. 9, '62		Mustered out with regiment.
Muth, Augustus W		Aug. 9, '62		Transferred to V. R. C.
Nutt, Thomas		Aug. 9, '62	Castleton	Mustered out with regiment.
Orpist, Isaac		Aug. 9, '62		Mustered out with regiment.
Palmer, James W		Aug. 9, '62		Deserted Sept. 25, '62.
Page, John		Aug. 9, '62		Promoted corporal.
Richey, Joseph G		Aug. 9, '62		Mustered out with regiment.
Rockey, Isaac		Aug. 9, '62		Deserted Nov. 6, '62.
Robbins, Francis M		Aug. 9, '62		Died April 7, '63.
Roberts, Thomas J		Aug. 9, '62	Gainesville, Mo.	Mustered out with regiment.
Robertson, Ralph		Aug. 9, '62	Carthage, Dak.	Mustered out with regiment.
Robertson, George		Aug. 9, '62		Promoted corporal.
Shaffer, William H		Aug. 9, '62		Deserted Nov. 5, '62.
Shaw, George		Aug. 9, '62	Wayne, Neb.	Mustered out with regiment.
Sheets, Benjamin C		Aug. 9, '62	Parsons, Kan	Mustered out with regiment.
Shuler, Anthony		Aug. 9, '62		Transferred to V. R. C.
Stewart, Hiram		Aug. 9, '62		Mustered out with regiment.
Swails, Alfred		Aug. 9, '62		Mustered out with regiment.
Spencer, James		Aug. 9, '62		Mustered out with regiment.
Statesman, Isaac		Aug. 9, '62	Gem	Promoted corporal.
Tague, William		Aug. 9, '62		Deserted Oct. 16, '62.
Tutewiler, Jacob W		Aug. 9, '62	Glenn Valley	Mustered out with regiment.
Turpin, David		Aug. 9, '62		Mustered out with regiment.
Watts, Jacob		Aug. 9, '62	Padonia, Kan	Deserted Mar. 25, '63.
Warintz, David		Aug. 9, '62	Powhatan, Kan	Mustered out with regiment.
Winkle, Henry		Aug. 9, '62	Indianapolis	Mustered out with regiment.
Winkle, Samuel		Aug. 9, '62		Mustered out with regiment.

ROSTER OF COMPANY "B"—CONTINUED.

Name and Rank.	Place of Enlistment.	Date of Enlistment.	Present Residence.	Remarks.
PRIVATES—(Continued.)				
Winters, William G.		Aug. 9, '62		Died Nov. 20, '62.
Williams, John W.		Aug. 9, '62		Discharged Oct. 1, '62.
Williams, Joseph W.		Aug. 9, '62		Transferred to engineer corps.
Willett, Clay		Aug. 9, '62		Discharged Dec. 23, '62.
York, William H.		Aug. 9, '62		Discharged April 7, '63.
RECRUITS.				
Beeson, Daniel W.		Aug. 26, '62		Discharged May 19, '63.
Banks, James K.		Feb. 16, '64	Greenfield	Transferred to 51st Indiana regiment.
Douglas, James		Aug. 26, '62		Discharged Jan. 23, '63.
Manker, Henry E.		Sept. 2, '62	Elliott, Ia	Mustered out with regiment.

ROSTER OF COMPANY "C."

Name and Rank.	Place of Enlistment.	Date of Enlistment.	Present Residence.	Remarks.
CAPTAINS.				
John G. Waters	Indianapolis	Aug. 19, '62	Rutland, Vt	Resigned Feb. 1, '63. [wounds.
Benjamin Valliquette	Indianapolis	Feb. 21, '63	Indianapolis	Honorably discharged Nov. 28, '63.
Eli F. Ritter	Danville	May 9, '64	Indianapolis	Mustered out with regiment.
FIRST LIEUTENANTS.				
Benjamin Valliquette	Indianapolis	Aug. 19, '62	Rutland, Vt	Promoted captain.
William S. Cardell	Indianapolis	Feb. 21, '63	Indianapolis	Promoted captain Co. "H."
Charles J. Many	Indianapolis	March 2, '65	Indianapolis	Mustered out with regiment.
SECOND LIEUTENANTS.				
William S. Cardell	Indianapolis	Aug. 19, '62	Indianapolis	Promoted 1st lieutenant.
Edwin M. Byrkit	Indianapolis	Feb. 21, '63	Michigan City	Promoted captain Co. "I."
FIRST SERGEANTS.				
Edwin M. Byrkit	Indianapolis	Aug. 15, '62	Michigan City	Promoted 2d lieutenant.
Charles J. Many	Indianapolis	Aug. 9, '62	Indianapolis	Promoted 1st lieutenant.
Edmond C. Boaz	Indianapolis	Aug. 11, '62	Brenham, Texas	Mustered out with regiment.
SERGEANTS.				
Charles J. Many	Indianapolis	Aug. 9, '62	Indianapolis	Promoted 1st sergeant Feb. 2, '63.
Charles Anderson	Indianapolis	Aug. 12, '62	Indianapolis	Mustered out with regiment.
Joseph Kline	Indianapolis	Aug. 15, '62	Springfield, Mo.	Promoted sergeant-major.
John Warner	Indianapolis	Aug. 15, '62		Killed at Atlanta July 21, '64.
Sidney Moore	Eden	Aug. 15, '62		Mustered out with regiment.
Henry A. Mittay	Indianapolis	Aug. 12, '62	Indianapolis	Mustered out with regiment.
Albert A. Chester	Indianapolis	Aug. 12, '62	Indianapolis	Mustered out with regiment.
Edmond C. Boaz	Indianapolis	Aug. 12, '62	Brenham, Texas	Promoted 1st sergeant.
William Reynolds	Eden	Aug. 15, '62	Maxwell	Promoted 1st sergeant.

ROSTER OF COMPANY "C"—CONTINUED.

Name and Rank.	Place of Enlistment.	Date of Enlistment.	Present Residence.	Remarks.
CORPORALS.				
Ransom R. Alvey	Walpole	Aug. 15, '62	Fortville	Mustered out as private with regiment.
John L. Monroe	Indianapolis	Aug. 25, '62	Indianapolis	Mustered out as private with regiment.
Henry A. Mittay	Indianapolis	Aug. 12, '62	Indianapolis	Promoted sergeant.
Leander W. Munhall	Indianapolis	Aug. 15, '62	Philadelphia	Promoted adjutant.
William R. Sullivan	Indianapolis	Aug. 15, '62	Indianapolis	Transferred to V. R. C. Sept. 1, '63.
Robert M. Hinds	Indianapolis	Aug. 15, '62		Deserted Oct. 1, '62.
Arthur L. Evans	Greencastle	Aug. 15, '62		Discharged Feb. 11, '63.
Albert A. Chester	Indianapolis	Aug. 12, '62	Indianapolis	Promoted sergeant.
Theodore R. Bryant	Indianapolis	Aug. 9, '62		Mustered out with regiment.
Edmond G. Boaz	Indianapolis	Aug. 12, '62	Brenham, Texas	Promoted sergeant.
Henry Anderson	Indianapolis	Aug. 10, '62	Indianapolis	Discharged Jan. 21, '63.
William Haggart	Indianapolis	Aug. 15, '62	Cabool, Texas	Mustered out with regiment.
John M. Bartlett	Cincinnati	Aug. 15, '62		Mustered out with regiment.
Cornelius Mingle	Eden	Aug. 15, '62	Glenwood	Mustered out with regiment.
George H. Jackson	Walpole	Aug. 15, '62	Fortville	Mustered out with reg'm't as private.
James M. Jarrett	Eden	Aug. 15, '62	Greenfield	Mustered out with regiment.
George A. Dresslar	Waverley	Aug. 11, '62	Banta	Mustered out with regiment.
Fleming B. Martin	Indianapolis	Aug. 22, '62		Mustered out with regiment.
James M. Martz	Arcadia	Aug. 13, '62	Arcadia	Mustered out with regiment.
MUSICIANS.				
John W. Hartgence	Indianapolis	Aug. 21, '62	Harrison, Ohio	Discharged July 26, '64, of wounds received in action.
George Frankenstein	Indianapolis	Aug. 13, '62	New Palestine	Discharged December 15, '62.
WAGONER.				
Oliver F. Long	Indianapolis	Aug. 12, '62	Chicago	Promoted quartermaster sergeant.
PRIVATES.				
Anderson, John	Indianapolis	Aug. 12, '62		Mustered out with regiment.

SEVENTY-NINTH INDIANA REGIMENT. 13

Name	Residence	Enlisted	Remarks
Ames, William	Indianapolis	Aug. 13, '62	Indianapolis	Mustered out with regiment.
Boaz, Edmond C	Indianapolis	Aug. 11, '62	Brenham, Texas	Promoted corporal.
Baugh, John	Indianapolis	Aug. 13, '62	Morgantown	Transferred to 51st Ind.
Bardwell, Thomas	Indianapolis	Aug. 14, '62		Deserted Oct. 10, '62.
Bardwell, Seth W	Indianapolis	Aug. 15, '62		Mustered out with regiment.
Bartlett, John M	Cincinnati	Aug. 15, '62		Promoted corporal.
Breninger, Thomas J	Woodberry	Aug. 15, '62		Died at Huntsville, Ala., Jan. 29, '65.
Blanton, John	Walpole	Aug. 15, '62	Fortville	Mustered out with regiment.
Burns, Condy	Indianapolis	Aug. 22, '62		Discharged March 26, '63.
Brown, Andrew	Walpole	Aug. 22, '62	Fortville	Mustered out with regiment.
Chester, Albert A	Indianapolis	Aug. 12, '62	Indianapolis	Promoted corporal.
Cox, Philander W	Eden	Aug. 15, '62		Died in Louisville, Ky., July 19, '63.
Chappel, Isaac	Walpole	Aug. 15, '62		Lost on steamer Sultana, April 27, '65.
Collins, Cornelius	Eden	Aug. 15, '62		Discharged Nov. 19, '63.
Cooper, John W	Eden	Aug. 15, '62		Deserted Nov. 18, '62.
Cooper, Benjamin T	Eden	Aug. 22, '62	Banta	Mustered out with regiment.
Dresslar, George A	Waverly	Aug. 11, '62		Promoted corporal.
Davis, David W	Indianapolis	Aug. 13, '62		Mustered out with regiment.
Denny, Enos	Walpole	Aug. 15, '62		Mustered out with regiment.
Dangler, Tunis	Eden	Aug. 22, '62	Leon, Kan.	Deserted Nov. 18, '62.
Eaton, Henry	Indianapolis	Aug. 13, '62		Transferred to 18th U. S. Infantry.
Edmonds, John C	Indianapolis	Aug. 15, '62	Indianapolis	Mustered out with regiment.
Eakes, Joseph R	Walpole	Aug. 15, '62	Fortville	Discharged April 18, '65. [65]
Eakes, Andrew J	Walpole	Aug. 15, '62		Died of wounds at Nashville, Jan. 25.
Foudray, James E	Indianapolis	Aug. 15, '62	Greencastle	Mustered out with regiment.
Foster, Richard	Greenfield	Aug. 15, '62		Discharged Sept. 1, '63.
Faussett, Robert	Walpole	Aug. 15, '62	Fortville	Mustered out with regiment.
Franklin, William	Eden	Aug. 22, '62		Discharged May 26, '63.
Frazier, James	Eden	Aug. 22, '62		Mustered out with regiment.
Green, Thomas	Indianapolis	Aug. 15, '62		Discharged April 21, '63.
Griffin, Timothy	Indianapolis	Sept. 4, '62	Indianapolis	Discharged May 2, '63.
Gwinn, Samuel	Cartersburg	Sept. 4, '62		Discharged May 2, '63.

ROSTER OF COMPANY "C"—CONTINUED.

Name and Rank.	Place of Enlistment.	Date of Enlistment.	Present Residence.	Remarks.
PRIVATES—Continued.				
Hall, William M	Indianapolis	Sept. 12, '62		Discharged Mar. 2, '63.
Hoover, Andrew	Indianapolis	Sept. 12, '62		Discharged April 18, '63.
Hunt, William H	Eden	Sept. 15, '62		Deserted Oct. 18, '62.
Hudson, Peter	Eden	Sept. 15, '62	Cumberland	Mustered out with regiment.
Harvey, Charles	Eden	Sept. 15, '62		Transferred to 18th U. S. Infantry.
Haggart, William	Indianapolis	Sept. 15, '62	Cabool, Texas	Promoted corporal.
Jackson, George H	Walpole	Sept. 15, '62	Fortville	Promoted corporal.
Jackson, Huanders	Walpole	Sept. 15, '62		Discharged Jan. 26, '63.
Jarrett, James M	Eden	Sept. 15, '62	Greenfield	Promoted corporal.
Jacobs, William	Indianapolis	Sept. 22, '62		Killed by accident June 13, '63.
Leonard, Hiram L	Walpole	Sept. 15, '62		Died at McMinnville, July 25, '63. ('63.)
Loomis, John G	Eden	Sept. 15, '62	Cincinnati	Missing in action Stone River, Jan. 2,
Loomis, Benjamin	Eden	Sept. 15, '62	Eden	Transferred to engineer corps July 11, '63.
Munsell, Newton	Indianapolis	Sept. 26, '62		Discharged April 9, '63.
Mittay, Henry A	Indianapolis	Sept. 12, '62	Indianapolis	Promoted corporal.
Martz, James M	Arcadia	Sept. 13, '62	Arcadia	Promoted corporal.
McClain, Neal	Indianapolis	Aug. 14, '62		Transferred to 51st Ind.
Marple, Howard	Indianapolis	Aug. 15, '62		Discharged Feb. 7, '63.
Moore, Sidney	Eden	Aug. 15, '62		Promoted to corporal.
McMannis, John	Indianapolis	Sept. 4, '62		Died of wounds Jan. 21, '63.
Mingle, Cornelius	Indianapolis	Sept. 4, '62	Glenwood	Promoted corporal.
McCole, Neal	Indianapolis	Sept. 4, '62		Left in hospital, Louisville, Oct. 1, '62.
Martin, Fleming B	Indianapolis	Sept. 22, '62		Promoted corporal, (never heard from.)
Merryman, Edward F	Indianapolis	Sept. 22, '62		Mustered out with regiment.
Montgomery, James	Indianapolis	Sept. 20, '62		Died at Louisville, Dec. 20, '62.

SEVENTY-NINTH INDIANA REGIMENT. 45

Poppino, John S.	Indianapolis	Sept. 15, '62		Transferred V. R. C. Sept. 1, '63.
Pardue, Francis M.	Eden	Sept. 15, '62		Mustered out with regiment.
Price, Lewis	Eden	Sept. 15, '62		Transf'd to engineer corps July 11, '63.
Rochester, Robert	Indianapolis	Sept. 15, '62		Discharged April 29, '63.
Reynolds, William	Eden	Sept. 15, '62	Maxwell	Promoted corporal.
Ryan, John	Indianapolis	Sept. 14, '62		Killed at Kennesaw June 8, '64.
Roberts, William H.	Eden	Sept. 22, '62		Mustered out with regiment.
Stumph, Henry	Indianapolis	Sept. 15, '62		Died at Murfreesboro, March 5, '63.
Steel, Samuel	Walpole	Sept. 15, '62	Fortville	Mustered out with regiment.
Torrence, William	Walpole	Sept. 15, '62	Fortville	Transferred to V. R. C. Jan. 14, '64.
Valentine, William	Walpole	Sept. 15, '62	Fortville	Mustered out with regiment.
Welsh, James	Eden	Sept. 15, '62		Deserted Dec. 31, '62.
Walker, James S.	Indianapolis	Sept. 9, '62		Discharged Jan. 26, '63.
Wallsmith, William	Walpole	Sept. 15, '62	Trenton, Tenn	Mustered out with regiment.
Walpole	Sept. 15, '62			Mustered out with regiment.
Ward, Benjamin Lester	Indianapolis	Sept. 14, '62	Cambridge, N. Y.	Mustered out with regiment.

RECRUITS.

Dunn, Thompson	Indianapolis	Sept. 4, '62		Promoted adjutant.
Stewart, Joseph	Indianapolis	Sept. 1, '62		Discharged July 3, '63.

ROSTER OF COMPANY "D."

Name and Rank.	Place of Enlistment.	Date of Enlistment.	Present Residence.	Remarks.
CAPTAINS.				
James M. Buchanan	Indianapolis	Aug. 20, '62		Honorably discharged Feb. 5, '64.
John T. Newland	Indianapolis	Aug. 20, '62	Chehalis, Wash.	Mustered out with regiment.
FIRST LIEUTENANTS.				
John T. Newland	Indianapolis	Aug. 20, '62	Chehalis, Wash.	Promoted captain.
Ezra Buchanan	Indianapolis	Aug. 20, '62		Mustered out with regiment.
SECOND LIEUTENANTS.				
John S. McDaniel	Indianapolis	Aug. 20, '62		Died Dec. 26, '62.
George Harris	Indianapolis	Aug. 20, '62	Vincennes	Mustered out with regiment.
FIRST SERGEANTS.				
William M. Johnson		Aug. 13, '62		Killed at Kenesaw, June 23, '65.
Frederick Hartman		Aug. 17, '62	Indianapolis	Mustered out with regiment.
SERGEANTS.				
David Buchanan		Aug. 18, '62	Holden, Mo.	Transferred to V. R. C.
George Harris		Aug. 18, '62	Vincennes	Promoted to second lieutenant.
Ezra Buchanan		Aug. 7, '62		Promoted to first lieutenant.
Thomas Barnett		Aug. 6, '62	Indianapolis	Discharged Dec. 26, '62.
Frederick Hartman		Aug. 17, '62	Indianapolis	Promoted first sergeant.
William Richman		Aug. 15, '62	Cumberland	Mustered out with regiment.
Francis M. Eastes		Aug. 8, '62	Great Bend, Kan.	Mustered out with regiment.
Henry W. Sunawalt		Aug. 18, '62	Green Fork	Mustered out with regiment.
Leroy Vanlaningham		Aug. 4, '62	Knightstown	Mustered out with regiment.
CORPORALS.				
Henry F. Wilson		Aug. 12, '62	Indianapolis	Died Feb. 13, '63.
Henry C. Smothers		Aug. 6, '62	Indianapolis	Discharged Nov. 10, '62.
William Steele		Aug. 8, '62	Indianapolis	Died Dec. 31, '62.
Frederick Hartman		Aug. 17, '62	Indianapolis	Promoted sergeant.

SEVENTY-NINTH INDIANA REGIMENT.

Name	Date	Place	Remarks
William Richman	Aug. 15, '62	Cumberland	Promoted sergeant.
Charles A. Vansickle	Aug. 13, '62		Died Nov. 30, '62.
George W. Ray	Aug. 8, '62		Died Nov. 9, '62.
Henry C. Monroe	Aug. 11, '62		Discharged.
Christian Brewer	Aug. 25, '62	Brinkley, Ark.	Mustered out with regiment.
William Collins	Aug. 8, '62	Shelburn	Mustered out with regiment.
Henry W. Eichman	Aug. 16, '62	New Palestine	Mustered out with regiment.
William Knoop	Aug. 16, '62		Mustered out with regiment.
John L. Lynch	Aug. 13, '62	Marion	Mustered out with regiment.
John P. Murphy	Aug. 12, '62	Mohawk	Mustered out with regiment.
Anthony Raabe	Aug. 16, '62	New Palestine	Mustered out with regiment.
Henry Philpot	Aug. 12, '62	Bentonville	Mustered out with regiment.
MUSICIANS.			
Charles Hole	Aug. 18, '62		Mustered out with regiment.
William E. Herron	Aug. 11, '62	Swazee	Mustered out with regiment.
WAGONER.			
Levi B. Rogers	Aug. 24, '62	Ben Davis	Mustered out with regiment.
PRIVATES.			
Brewer, Christian	Aug. 25, '62	Brinkley, Ark	Mustered out with regiment.
Burris, Charles H	Aug. 14, '62	Madison, Kan	Mustered out with regiment.
Church, Henry H	Aug. 18, '62	Mexico, Mo.	Discharged Feb. 6, '63.
Cotton, James H	Aug. 13, '62		Died at Nashville Sept. 28, '64, wounds
Collins, William	Aug. 8, '62	Shelburn	Promoted corporal.
Crumbaugh, John	Aug. 8, '62		Died Jan. 13, '63.
Colelazer, Jacob H	Aug. 26, '62		Promoted quartermaster.
Deshong, Amos	Aug. 12, '62		Mustered out with regiment.
Dillman, James	Aug. 18, '62		Died Nov. 30, '63.
Downing, Charles L	Aug. 12, '62	Westville, Ill	Mustered out with regiment.
Dunn, Michael N	Aug. 25, '62		Died Nov. 30, '62.
Eastes, James A	Aug. 8, '62	Andover, Kan	Discharged March 25, '63.
Eastes, Francis M	Aug. 8, '62	Great Bend, Kan	Promoted sergeant.
Eickman, Henry W	Aug. 16, '62	New Palestine	Promoted corporal.
Eller, Thomas J	Aug. 16, '62		Killed at Stone River, Jan. 2, '63.

ROSTER OF COMPANY "D"—CONTINUED.

Name and Rank.	Place of Enlistment.	Date of Enlistment.	Present Residence.	Remarks.
PRIVATES—(Continued.)				
Eller, Andrew J.		Aug. 16, '62		Died Feb. 12, '63.
Eller, David		Aug. 16, '62		Died April 8, '64.
Eaves, Samuel		Aug. 25, '62	Indianapolis	Transferred to V. R. C.
Groves, Archibald		Aug. 11, '62	Mahott Park	Died Nov. 4, '63.
Gibson, John W.		Aug. 8, '62		Mustered out with regiment.
Harvey, Joseph N.		Aug. 12, '62		Discharged Dec. 5, '63.
Harvey, William H.		Aug. 14, '62		Mustered out with regiment.
Herron, Noah D.		Aug. 11, '62		Killed at Stone River, Jan. 2, '63.
Hinds, William H.		Aug. 9, '62		Transferred to V. R. C.
Hole, Horatio M.		Aug. 13, '62	Chanute, Kan.	Discharged May 15, '63.
Hiff, Charles E.		Aug. 26, '62	Indianapolis	Discharged Dec. '62.
King, Darius A.		Aug. 16, '62		Killed at Stone River, Jan. 2, '63.
Knoop, Frederick		Aug. 16, '62		Mustered out with regiment.
Knoop, William		Aug. 16, '62		Promoted corporal.
Kuntz, George		Aug. 24, '62		Discharged Oct. 22, '63.
Langemeyer, George T.		Aug. 16, '62		Died Nov. 21, '62.
Lynch, John L.		Aug. 13, '62	Marion	Promoted corporal.
Meyer, Christian F.		Aug. 16, '62		Mustered out with regiment.
McDuffey, Samuel		Aug. 8, '62	Boston	Mustered out with regiment.
McChoney, John L.		Aug. 16, '62		Died April 13, '63.
McConnell, James H.		Aug. 14, '62	Noblesville	Discharged April 6, '63.
McDaniels, James R.		Aug. 20, '62		Mustered out with regiment.
Miller, William		Aug. 16, '62	Indianapolis	Mustered out with regiment.
McCord, Cyrus F.		Aug. 17, '62		Died Jan. 21, '63, wounds.
Mason, William		Aug. 24, '62		Transferred to V. R. C.
Murphy, John P.		Aug. 12, '62	Mohawk	Promoted corporal.

SEVENTY-NINTH INDIANA REGIMENT.

Name	Date	Place	Remarks
Northway, William J.	Aug. 14, '62		Died July 24, '64, wounds.
Philpot, Henry	Aug. 12, '62	Bentonville	Promoted corporal.
Plummer, Stephen C.	Aug. 16, '62	Carlisle	Discharged April 15, '63.
Pricket, Jasper	Aug. 12, '62		Discharged May 2, '63.
Pyles, William	Aug. 7, '62		Mustered out with regiment.
Ray, Asbury W.	Aug. 8, '62		Died Dec. 12, '62.
Rabe, Anthony	Aug. 16, '62	New Palestine	Mustered out with regiment.
Roney, Samuel	Aug. 8, '62	Mohawk	Promoted corporal.
Russell, James W.	Aug. 16, '62	Indianapolis	Transferred to Pioneer corps.
Stanley, John W.	Aug. 8, '62	Brightwood	Mustered out with regiment.
Stanley, Martin V.	Aug. 10, '62		Mustered out with regiment.
Stanley, Thomas B.	Aug. 21, '62		Killed at Stone River, Jan. 2, '63.
Sewel, Jacob	Aug. 11, '62	Mohawk	Killed at Kenesaw, June 23, '64.
Seely, Jesse	Aug. 18, '62		Mustered out with regiment.
Sheerer, William H.	Aug. 13, '62		Transferred to V. R. C.
Smith, Thomas J.	Aug. 8, '62	Geneva	Killed at Stone River, Dec. 31, '62.
Smith, Samuel	Aug. 13, '62		Mustered out with regiment.
Smith, Aaron C.	Aug. 16, '62		Died Feb. 18, '63.
Snyder, Joseph H.	Aug. 8, '62		Died July 12, '63.
Spliker, Christian	Aug. 16, '62	Cumberland	Transferred to marine corps.
Stockwell, Tillman	Aug. 23, '62	Indianapolis	Mustered out with regiment.
Stockwell, Daniel	Aug. 23, '62		Mustered out with regiment.
Sumwalt, Henry	Aug. 18, '62	Greenfork	Discharged Feb. 6, '63.
Vanlaningham, Leroy	Aug. 4, '62	Knightstown	Promoted sergeant.
Wiley, John W.	Aug. 16, '62	Versailles, Ill	Promoted sergeant.
Wilson, Andrew J.	Aug. 12, '62		Mustered out with regiment.
Wilson, Charles	Aug. 12, '62		Died Feb. 13, '63.
Wishmeyer, Anthony	Aug. 13, '62		Discharged Sept. 23, '63.
Wright, William C.	Aug. 16, '62		Mustered out with regiment.
			Died Oct. 28, '62.

RECRUITS.

Name	Date	Place	Remarks
Cavanaugh, Thomas	Sept. 24, '62	Vincennes	Mustered out with regiment.
Harkness, Thomas	Sept. 24, '62		Deserted Sept. 27, '62.
Jones, Francis P.	Dec. 9, '63		Transferred to 51st Ind.
Tigard, James	Feb. 26, '64		Transferred to 51st Ind.

ROSTER OF COMPANY "E."

Name and Rank.	Place of Enlistment.	Date of Enlistment.	Present Residence.	Remarks.
CAPTAIN.				
John N. Scott	Shelbyville	Aug. 22, '62	Port Townsend, Wash.	Honorably discharged April 7, '64; appointed maj. and paymaster, U.S.A.
Loman Jones	Marietta	April 8, '64		Mustered out with regiment.
FIRST LIEUTENANT.				
Loman Jones	Marietta	April 22, '62		Promoted captain.
John W. Gosney	Indianapolis	July 1, '64	Blackburn, Okla.	Mustered out with regiment.
SECOND LIEUTENANT.				
James I. Robinson	Davisville	Aug. 22, '62		Resigned November 3, '63.
FIRST SERGEANT.				
Henry Slusher	Indianapolis	Sept. 2, '62	Danville, Ill.	Discharged June 30, '63.
Charles H. Eaton	Indianapolis	Sept. 2, '62	Cincinnati	Discharged Feb. 1, '65, wounds.
SERGEANTS.				
Charles H. Eaton	Indianapolis	Sept. 2, '62	Cincinnati	Promoted first sergeant.
Phillip L. Bartsch	Marietta	Sept. 2, '62	Kokomo	Discharged May 25, '65.
Joseph Bishop	Marietta	Sept. 2, '62	Red Oak, Iowa	Mustered out with regiment.
David F. Campbell	Shelbyville	Sept. 2, '62		Mustered out with regiment.
James M. Hanes	Carmel	Sept. 2, '62	Lowther, Mo.	Mustered out with regiment.
CORPORALS.				
William Buckingham	Davisville	Sept. 2, '62		Died at Nashville, Dec. 10, '62.
Samuel Dick	Marietta	Sept. 2, '62		Died at Nashville, Nov. 7, '63.
Harry J. Clark	Shelbyville	Sept. 2, '62		Discharged Jan. 30, '63.
John H. White	Fairland	Sept. 2, '62		Mustered out with regiment.
William A. Curson	Shelbyville	Sept. 2, '62	Indianapolis	Mustered out with regiment.
James H. Lourey	Swanville	Sept. 2, '62	Chelsey	Mustered out with regiment.
Joseph K. Hardy	Davisville	Sept. 2, '62	Blue Mound, Ill.	Discharged March 6, '65.
Joseph Bishop	Marietta	Sept. 2, '62	Red Oak, Iowa	Promoted sergeant.

SEVENTY-NINTH INDIANA REGIMENT. 21

Zaddock M. Carey	Carmel		'62	Lansing, Kan	Mustered out with regiment.
MUSICIANS.					
Thomas F. Chafee	Shelbyville	Sept.	'62	Shelbyville	Transferred V. R. C.
John McNeely	Davisville	Sept.	'62		Deserted Sept. 15, '62.
WAGONER.					
John W. Heuk	Shelbyville	Sept.	'62		Transferred to V. R. C.
PRIVATES.					
Allenthorpe, Joseph P	Shelbyville	Sept.	'62	Shelbyville	Discharged March 16, '63.
Ayers, Marion	Daviesville	Sept.	'62		Transferred to V. R. C.
Applegate, Jeremiah	Freeport	Sept.	'62	Fountaintown	Transferred to V. R. C.
Anderson, Perry	Marietta	Sept.	'62	Tipton	Mustered out with regiment.
Burk, Edmund	Shelbyville	Sept.	'62		Killed at Louisville, Sept. 5, '62.
Baxley, Thomas	Fairland	Sept.	'62		Transferred to V. R. C.
Berry, George W	Indianapolis	Sept.	'62		Mustered out with regiment.
Clark, Richard M	Shelbyville	Sept.	'62	Shelbyville	Discharged March 16, '63.
Camren, Joseph	Edinburg	Sept.	'62		Discharged Oct. 5, '63.
Copeland, George	Daviesville	Sept.	'62	Indianapolis	Mustered out with regiment.
Carey, Zaddock M	Carmel	Sept.	'62	Lansing, Kan	Promoted corporal.
Campbell, David F	Shelbyville	Sept.	'62		Promoted sergeant.
Bill, Joshua F	Indianapolis	Sept.	'62	Clermont	Discharged Jan. 29, '65.
Davis, George W	Smithland	Sept.	'62		Killed at Atlanta July 21, '64.
Beret, William B	Fairland	Sept.	'62	Buffalo, Kan	Discharged Feb. 20, '63.
Fox, Daniel	Shelbyville	Sept.	'62		Killed at Stone River, Jan. 2, '63.
Fountain, Edwin M	Daviesville	Sept.	'62		Died at Nashville, May 6, '63.
Fogarty, John	Fairland	Sept.	'62	London	Mustered out with regiment.
Golding, William B	Shelbyville	Sept.	'62		Died at Nashville Dec. 5, '62.
Golding, James E	Shelbyville	Sept.	'62	Shelbyville	Mustered out with regiment.
Gibson, Alfred	Carmel	Sept.	'62	Erie, Kan	Mustered out with regiment.
Gibson, Andrew L	Carmel	Sept.	'62		Mustered out with regiment.
Griffin, Timothy	Indianapolis	Sept.	'62	Indianapolis	Transferred to Co. "C."
Hardy, William F	Daviesville	Sept.	'62		Mustered out with regiment.
Hodge, Robert	Shelbyville	Sept.	'62		Transferred to V. R. C.
Henderson, James W	Shelbyville	Sept.	'62	Shelbyville	Transferred to V. R. C.

ROSTER OF COMPANY "E"—CONTINUED.

Name and Rank.	Place of Enlistment.	Date of Enlistment.	Present Residence.	Remarks.
PRIVATES—Continued.				
Henry, Moses	Marietta	Sept. '62		Mustered out with regiment.
Hill, Milton	Freeport	Sept. '62		Died at Louisville, Dec. 30, '62.
Hadden, George W	Fairland	Sept. '62		Discharged May 25, '63.
Hinshaw, William H	Carmel	Sept. '62		Mustered out with regiment.
Hanes, James M	Carmel	Sept. '62	Emporia, Kan	Promoted sergeant.
Jacobs, Vanransaleer	Carmel	Sept. '62	Lauther, Mo	Deserted.
Jessup, Sylvester M	Carmel	Sept. '62		Killed at Picket Mills, May 27, '64.
Kendall, John E	Shelbyville	Sept. '62		Killed at Stone River, Jan. 2, '63.
Kitchell, Percy S	Davisville	Sept. '62	Fountaintown	Mustered out with regiment.
Little, Azar	Shelbyville	Sept. '62	Duracheow, Kan	Mustered out with regiment.
Little, John	Marietta	Sept. '62	Elwood	Discharged April 1, '63.
Larmer, Oliver P	Marietta	Sept. '62		Died at Lebanon, Ky., Nov. 15, '62.
Laird, Robert	Fairland	Sept. '62	Hymera	Discharged May 20, '63.
Martin, Mathias	Davisville	Sept. '62	Fountaintown	Mustered out with regiment.
Moore, William H	Davisville	Sept. '62	Morristown	Mustered out with regiment.
Miller, John	Davisville	Sept. '62	Alto	Mustered out with regiment.
Miller, Lewis	Davisville	Sept. '62		Mustered out with regiment.
McFadden, John B	Fairland	Sept. '62		Discharged March 25, '63, wounds.
McFadden, Louis L	Fairland	Sept. '62		Transferred to Co. "C."
McManus, John	Indianapolis	Sept. '62		Discharged March 26, '63.
McLaughlin, John	Shelbyville	Sept. '62		Discharged May 20, '63.
Martyn, Peter W	Davisville	Sept. '62		Mustered out with regiment.
Morgan, Henry A	Tampico	Sept. '62	Walnut	Mustered out with regiment.
Newton, John M	Shelbyville	Sept. '62		Killed at Chickamauga, Sept. 19, '63.
Nicely, Michael	Franklin	Sept. '62		Deserted.
Price, Anderson	Indianapolis	Sept. '62		

SEVENTY-NINTH INDIANA REGIMENT.

Reed, James	Marietta	Sept.	'62	Died at Cave Springs, Ky., Nov. 21, '62
Reed, William	Marietta	Sept.	'62	Mustered out with regiment.
Reese, Ferdinand M	Marietta	Sept.	'62	Transferred to V. R. C.
Rogers, William C	Marietta	Sept.	'62	Mustered out with regiment.
Roseberry, Levy	Indianapolis	Sept.	'62	Discharged May 20, '63.
Smith, Henry	Shelbyville	Sept.	'62	Died at Nashville, Dec. 15, '62.
Smith, Paul H	Davisville	Sept.	'62	Killed at Marietta June 23, '64.
Toney, James	Shelbyville	Sept.	'62	Mustered out with regiment.
Tull, Edward N	Fairland	Sept.	'62	Transferred to V. R. C.
Tucker, Benjamin	Marietta	Sept.	'62	Died in Shelby county, Nov. 21, '62
Wheatley, Joseph N	Shelbyville	Sept.	'62	Mustered out with regiment.
West, Allison	Freeport	Sept.	'62	Missing in action June 25, '64.
Wilhier, Thomas E	Franklin	Sept.	'62	Killed at Marietta, June 23, '64.
Yeager, Jacob	Shelbyville	Sept.	'62	Transferred to V. R. C.
RECRUITS.				
Johnson, William C	Lincoln, Neb	Dec. 14,	'63	Transferred to 51st Ind.
Shoemaker, Charles		Dec. 9,	'63	Transferred to 51st Ind.
Troup, Andrew J		Dec. 9,	'63	Transferred to 51st Ind.

ROSTER OF COMPANY "F."

Name and Rank.	Place of Enlistment.	Date of Enlistment.	Present Residence.	Remarks.
CAPTAINS.				
Andrew W. Furqua	Indianapolis	Aug. 23, '62		Resigned Dec. 30, '62.
James P. Catterson	Indianapolis	Dec. 21, '62	Brownsburg	Resigned March 22, '64.
Isaac W. Stubbs	Indianapolis	Mar. 23, '64		Mustered out with regiment.
FIRST LIEUTENANTS.				
John B. Johnson	Indianapolis	Aug. 23, '62		Resigned Nov. 16, '62.
James P. Catterson	Indianapolis	Nov. 17, '62	Brownsburg	Promoted captain.
Isaac W. Stubbs	Indianapolis	Dec. 21, '62		Promoted captain.
William J. Carter	Indianapolis	Dec. 23, '63	Indianapolis	Honorably discharged Oct. 14, '64.
John B. W. Parker	Indianapolis	Mar. 1, '65	Catlin, Ill	Mustered out with regiment.
SECOND LIEUTENANTS.				
James P. Catterson	Indianapolis	Aug. 22, '62	Brownsburg	Promoted first lieutenant.
Benjamin T. Poynter	Danville	Nov. 17, '62		Killed at Stone River, Jan. 2, '62.
Richard E. Parrott	Indianapolis	Jan. 5, '63		Resigned for the good of the service [Sept. 2, '63.]
FIRST SERGEANTS.				
Benjamin F. Riley	Indianapolis	Aug. 7, '62	Indianapolis	Discharged Oct. 18, '62.
James Bailey	Indianapolis	Aug. 12, '62		Mustered out with regiment.
SERGEANTS.				
Edward P. Thomas	Indianapolis	Aug. 7, '62		Died at Nashville Dec. 18, '62.
Richard E. Parrott	Indianapolis	Aug. 7, '62		Promoted second lieutenant.
Benjamin T. Poynter	Danville	Aug. 7, '62		Promoted second lieutenant.
Boswell C. Chapman	Indianapolis	Aug. 7, '62		Discharged Jan. 19, '63.
Robert M. Dunham	Ninevah	Aug. 12, '62	Greenridge, Mo.	Mustered out with regiment.
Joshua W. Langsdale	Indianapolis	Aug. 7, '62	Rising Sun	Mustered out with regiment.
CORPORALS.				
William H. Blackwell	Indianapolis	Aug. 7, '62	Indianapolis	Discharged Feb. 11, '63.

SEVENTY-NINTH INDIANA REGIMENT.

Name	Residence			Remarks
John J. Murdock	Indianapolis	Aug.	'62		Mustered out with regiment as private.
John W. McKee	Brownsburg	Aug.	'62		Mustered out with regiment as private.
Samuel Redman	Indianapolis	Aug.	'62	Kokomo	Discharged Jan. 19, '63.
Charles Hayes	Indianapolis	Aug.	'62		Discharged Feb. 6, '63.
John E. Alexander	Indianapolis	Aug.	'62		Discharged Jan. 30, '63.
Joseph Roberts	Martinsville	Aug.	'62		Died at Chattanooga, Mar. 25, '63.
John Decker	Indianapolis	Aug.	'62		Mustered out with regiment.
Job M. Dunham	Nineveh	Aug.	'62	White-Rabbit, Neb.	Mustered out with regiment.
Adam Hess	Indianapolis	Aug.	'62		Mustered out with regiment.
John W. James	Indianapolis	Aug.	'62	New Cambria, Mo.	Mustered out with regiment.
Daniel Pritchard	Nineveh	Aug.	'62	Normandie	Mustered out with regiment.
John J. Stormer	Indianapolis	Aug.	'62		Mustered out with regiment.
MUSICIANS.					
William S. Robinson		Aug.	'62		Discharged Feb. 10, '63. ['64.]
Henry E. Smith	Brownsburg	Aug.	'62		Died in Andersonville prison, July 27.
WAGONER.					
Caleb L. Thomas	Indianapolis	Aug.	'62		Mustered out with regiment.
PRIVATES.					
Arnold, Taylor	Indianapolis	Aug.	'62	Redman, Ill.	Mustered out with regiment.
Brooks, Nathan	Indianapolis	Aug.	'62		Transferred to V. R. C.
Buckley, Jeremiah M	Indianapolis	Aug.	'62		Discharged May 13, '63. [10, '63.
Beats, Bartus	Brownsburg	Aug.	'62		Missing in action (Chickamauga, Sept.
Beomfetter, John	Indianapolis	Aug.	'62		Mustered out with regiment.
Bailey, James	Indianapolis	Aug.	'62		Promoted 1st sergeant.
Burnworth, Thomas	Martinsville	Aug.	'62		Discharged Jan. 29, '63.
Cowgill, Elijah	Indianapolis	Aug.	'62		Deserted.
Carter, William J	Indianapolis	Aug.	'62		Promoted 1st lieutenant.
Champain, William S		Aug.	'62		Died at Louisville, Sept. 28, '62.
Chapman, James S. M	Nineveh	Aug.	'62		Died Feb. 28, '63, wounds.
Clements, James A	Indianapolis	Aug.	'62	Abingdon, Ill.	Mustered out with regiment.
Decker, John	Indianapolis	Aug.	'62		Mustered out with regiment.
Doughty, Lafayette	Indianapolis	Aug.	'62		Discharged Sept. 11, '63.
Doughty, Severe	Indianapolis	Aug.	'62		Discharged Feb. 11, '63.

ROSTER OF COMPANY "F"—Continued.

Name and Rank.	Place of Enlistment.	Date of Enlistment.	Present Residence.	Remarks.
PRIVATES—(Continued).				
Dunnagan, William	Hall	Aug. 12, '62		Died at Knoxville, April 7, '64.
Dean, Joseph	Nineveh	Aug. 12, '62		Died at Nashville, Feb. 15, '63.
Dunham, Robert M	Nineveh	Aug. 12, '62	Greenridge, Mo	Mustered out with regiment.
Dunham, Job M	Nineveh	Aug. 12, '62	White Rabbit, Neb	Mustered out with regiment.
Elliott, John K	Indianapolis	Aug. 12, '62		Deserted.
Eck, Teterick	Indianapolis	Aug. 12, '62	Indianapolis	Mustered out with regiment.
Edgington, John F	Indianapolis	Aug. 12, '62		Discharged Feb. 28, '63.
Earley, Alfred	Franklin	Aug. 12, '62		Discharged April 2, '63.
Fort, James	Indianapolis	Aug. 12, '62		Killed at Kenesaw, June 18, '64.
Francis, William H	Bridgeport	Aug. 12, '62		Mustered out with regiment.
Fink, Andrew J	Indianapolis	Aug. 12, '62		Deserted.
Fink, Daniel	Indianapolis	Aug. 12, '62		Transferred to V. R. C.
Gosney, John W	Hall	Aug. 12, '62	Blackburn, Okla	Promoted 2d lieutenant Co. "E."
Gosney, Thomas	Nineveh	Aug. 12, '62		Transferred to V. R. C.
Gordon, Edward	Indianapolis	Aug. 12, '62		Mustered out with regiment.
Garvey, Thomas	Indianapolis	Aug. 12, '62	Indianapolis	Mustered out with regiment.
Holderman, Joseph	Indianapolis	Aug. 12, '62		Mustered out with regiment.
Hanlin, Francis	Indianapolis	Aug. 12, '62		Deserted.
Holmes, Uriah M	Indianapolis	Aug. 12, '62		Discharged March 8, '63.
Hess, Adam	Indianapolis	Aug. 12, '62		Promoted corporal.
James, Henry	Indianapolis	Aug. 12, '62		Died at Nashville, Dec. 26, '62.
James, John W	Indianapolis	Aug. 12, '62		Promoted corporal.
Ketrow, Joseph	Indianapolis	Aug. 12, '62		Mustered out with regiment.
Ketrow, George W	Indianapolis	Aug. 12, '62	Ben Davis	Mustered out with regiment.
Kocher, Edward	Indianapolis	Aug. 12, '62		Discharged April 12, '63.
Lynn, Robert	Indianapolis	Aug. 12, '62		Mustered out with regiment.

SEVENTY-NINTH INDIANA REGIMENT.

Name	Residence	Date	Year	Birthplace	Remarks
Lynn, John	Indianapolis	Aug.	12	'62		Mustered out with regiment.
Long, Samuel	Indianapolis	Aug.	12	'62		Transferred to U. S. engineers.
Langsdale, Joshua W	Indianapolis	Aug.	7	'62	Mt. Jackson	Promoted sergeant.
Landon, Joseph	Byrket's Corner	Aug.	7	'62	Rising Sun	Mustered out with regiment.
Middough, John	Indianapolis	Aug.	12	'62		Died at Scottville, Ky., Nov. 16, '62.
Mathews, Jacob	Nineveh	Aug.	12	'62		Died at Murfreesboro, March 31, '63.
Mattox, Tobias	Indianapolis	Aug.	7	'62	Greely, Colo	Mustered out with regiment.
Pressel, Thomas G	Indianapolis	Aug.	12	'62		Deserted.
Potter, Robert	Indianapolis	Aug.	12	'62		Killed at Stone River, Jan. 2, '63.
Probons, Jeremiah	Indianapolis	Aug.	12	'62		Died at Knoxville Jan. 16, '64.
Prichard, Daniel	Nineveh	Aug.	12	'62	Normandie	Mustered out with regiment.
Randolph, Reuben	Indianapolis	Aug.	12	'62	Indianapolis	Mustered out with regiment.
Randolph, David A	Indianapolis	Aug.	12	'62		Died at Marietta, Aug. 1, '64, wounds.
Robinson, John S	Sugar Grove	Aug.	7	'62		Mustered out with regiment.
Reed, Nathaniel B	Indianapolis	Aug.	12	'62		Deserted.
Stout, Harmon	Indianapolis	Aug.	12	'63		Discharged Aug. 31, '63.
Stewart, Joseph B	Indianapolis	Aug.	7	'62		Transferred to Co. " C."
Stubbs, Isaac W	Indianapolis	Aug.	12	'62		Promoted 1st lieutenant.
Scott, William H	Indianapolis	Aug.	12	'62		Deserted.
Scott, Samuel T	Indianapolis	Aug.	12	'62		Discharged March 1, '63.
Southern, Christopher	Indianapolis	Aug.	12	'62		Mustered out with regiment.
Shafer, John	Indianapolis	Aug.	7	'62		Mustered out with regiment.
Stormer, John J	Indianapolis	Aug.	12	'62		Mustered out with regiment.
Vanhariettum, Benjamin	Indianapolis	Aug.	12	'62		Discharged May 5, '63.
Walker, John H	Monrovia	Aug.	12	'62		Died at Murfreesboro, Jan. 16, '63.
Walz, Frank	Indianapolis	Aug.	12	'62		Transferred to V. R. C.
Ward, Stephen	Indianapolis	Aug.	12	'62		Mustered out with regiment.
Ward, Joseph	Indianapolis	Aug.	7	'62		Died at Chattanooga, Sept. 19, '62.
Wood, Rosin H	Indianapolis	Aug.	7	'62		Deserted.
RECRUITS.						
Hardin, Shelton M		Sept.	1	'62		Died at Murfreesboro March 5, '63.
Smith, James		Sept.	1	'62		Discharged Feb. 10, '63.

ROSTER OF COMPANY "G."

Name and Rank.	Place of Enlistment.	Date of Enlistment.	Present Residence.	Remarks.
CAPTAINS.				
George W. Parker	Indianapolis	Aug. 23, '62	Pendleton	Promoted major.
William H. H. Sheets	Indianapolis	Aug. 14, '63		Declined.
George G. Earl	Indianapolis	Mar. 1, '65	Glendale, Mont	Mustered out with regiment.
FIRST LIEUTENANTS.				
William H. H. Sheets	Indianapolis	Aug. 21, '62		Mustered out with regiment.
George W. Clark	Indianapolis	Oct. 14, '63		Died of wounds, Sept. 29, '63.
SECOND LIEUTENANTS.				
James Comstock	Indianapolis	Aug. 23, '62		Resigned Sept. 21, '62.
George W. Clark	Indianapolis	Nov. 25, '62		Promoted 1st lieutenant.
FIRST SERGEANTS.				
George W. Clark	Indianapolis	Aug. 12, '62		Promoted 2d lieutenant.
John B. W. Parker		Aug. 9, '62	Catlin	Promoted 1st lieutenant Co. F.
SERGEANTS.				
Stephen H. Evans		Aug. 11, '62		Mustered out with regiment as private.
Henry C. Lawrence		Aug. 14, '62	Reese's Mill	Mustered out with regiment. [poral.
Solomon R. Richardson		Aug. 11, '62	Marco	Mustered out with regiment as cor-
Elza T. Pedigo		Aug. 13, '62	White Lick	Mustered out with regiment as private
Jacob H. Gibbons		Aug. 12, '62	McCordsville	Mustered out with regiment.
Silas M. Girt		Aug. 20, '62	White Lick	Mustered out with regiment.
Fielding J. Affrey		Aug. 18, '62	Crawfordsville	Mustered out with regiment.
John H. Scott		Aug. 22, '62	Greenfield	Mustered out with regiment.
CORPORALS.				
James H. Lewis		Aug. 13, '62		Discharged April 9, '63.
Henry E. Talbott		Aug. 12, '62		Discharged Nov. 25, '62.
Harman W. Boles		Aug. 12, '62	Fountaintown	Mustered out with regiment.
Jacob H. Gibbons		Aug. 12, '62	McCordsville	Promoted sergeant.

SEVENTY-NINTH INDIANA REGIMENT. 29

Name				
John Allen		Aug. 11, '62		Died at Murfreesboro, April 3, '63.
Cornelius Louks		Aug. 14, '62	Crestline, Kan.	Transferred to V. R. C.
George W. Johnson		Aug. 15, '62		Died at Nashville, April 12, '63.
Silas M. Girt		Aug. 20, '62	White Lick	Promoted sergeant.
William Faulkner		Aug. 21, '62	White Lick	Discharged with regiment.
John Shoman		Aug. 12, '62	Irvington	Discharged with regiment.
MUSICIANS.				
James P. Weaver		Aug. 22, '62		Transferred to V. R. C.
WAGONER.				
Nimrod Low		Aug. 22, '62	Indianapolis	Discharged June 15, '63.
PRIVATES.				
Abrams, William J.		Aug. 9, '62	Crawfordsville	Mustered out with regiment.
Alfrey, Fielding J.		Aug. 18, '62	Indianapolis	Promoted sergeant.
Baker, Aaron		Aug. 16, '62	Indianapolis	Mustered out with regiment.
Ball, Edward		Aug. 12, '62	Westfield	Mustered out with regiment.
Barrett, Sylvester W.		Aug. 11, '62	Winchester	Died at Nashville, Feb. 2, '63.
Beeson, Amos C.		Aug. 12, '62	Greenfield	Discharged Feb. 7, '65, wounds.
Bolen, Andrew J.		Aug. 12, '62	Indianapolis	Transferred to engineer corps.
Boles, John W.		Aug. 12, '62	Greenfield	Mustered out with regiment.
Boswell, John		Aug. 12, '62		Mustered out with regiment.
Cassidy, John S.		Aug. 22, '62		Discharged April 20, '63.
Catt, Nathan		Aug. 15, '62		Died at Nashville, June 8, '63.
Cline, John H.		Aug. 19, '62	Greenfield	Died at Murfreesboro, June 30, '63.
Collin, Eleazer		Aug. 19, '62		Discharged Jan. 7, '65.
Conner, Benjamin F.		Aug. 21, '62	Indianapolis	Discharged March 20, '63.
Cook, Charles W.		Aug. 12, '62	Greenfield	Promoted first lieutenant 90th cavalry.
Coomlus, Levy C.		Aug. 18, '62		Mustered out with regiment.
Copeland, Daniel		Aug. 21, '62	Monrovia	Mustered out with regiment.
Crabb, Abraham J.		Aug. 15, '62	Morgantown	Mustered out with regiment.
Cross, Warren		Aug. 21, '62		Transferred to V. R. C.
Davis, Speer B.		Aug. 22, '62		Discharged Feb. 2, '63.
Faulkner, William		Aug. 21, '62	White Lick	Mustered out with regiment.

ROSTER OF COMPANY "G"—CONTINUED.

Name and Rank.	Place of Enlistment.	Date of Enlistment.	Present Residence.	Remarks.
PRIVATES—(Continued.)				
Fonty, John H. H.		Aug. 21, '62	Fountaintown	Mustered out with regiment.
Glass, Fleming		Aug. 21, '62	Bird's P. O., Ill.	Mustered out with regiment.
Green, Ebenezer D.		Aug. 19, '62		Sent to Dry Tortugas.
Harrison, David A.		Aug. 11, '62		Died at Nashville, March 13, '63.
Heizer, Cyrus C.		Aug. 13, '62	Indianapolis	Discharged Feb. 19, '63, wounds.
Heizer, Thomas G.		Aug. 13, '62		Transferred to V. R. C.
Helton, Joshua S.		Aug. 16, '62	Law, Okla	Mustered out with regiment.
Hardin, Marion S.		Aug. 15, '62		Died at Nashville, Feb. 18, '63.
Harper, John H. H.		Aug. 20, '62	Marion	Mustered out with regiment.
Hollingsworth, Francis		Aug. 9, '62		Mustered out with regiment.
Johnson, John L.		Aug. 12, '62		Discharged July 26, '64.
Johnson, Robert		Aug. 13, '62		Mustered out with regiment.
Kelly, Hampton		Aug. 15, '62	Lebanon	Discharged May 22, '65.
King, Francis M.		Aug. 21, '62	Indianapolis	Mustered out with regiment.
Kise, Elisha		Aug. 9, '62	Reese's Mills	Mustered out with regiment.
Lace, Edward		Aug. 13, '62		Discharged Dec. 7, '63.
Langford, William		Aug. 13, '62		Transferred to engineer corps, '64.
Marshall, Richard F.		Aug. 20, '62		Missing in action Kenesaw, June 28.
Marshall, Benjamin F.		Aug. 18, '62	Lawrence	Mustered out with regiment.
Miller, William T.		Aug. 13, '62		Died at Murfreesboro, April 17, '63.
Moore, John W.		Aug. 21, '62		Deserted Oct. 25, '62.
McManus, John		Aug. 21, '62		Deserted Sept. 2, '62.
McLain, John S.		Aug. 22, '62	Indianapolis	Mustered out with regiment.
McLain, Jacob		Aug. 9, '62	Catlin, Ill	Discharged Feb. 21, '63.
Parker, John B. W.		Aug. 14, '62	Lebanon	Promoted Co. F. 1st lieutenant.
Pedigo, Joseph O.		Aug. 13, '62		Promoted lieutenant 28th U. S. C. T.

Pedigo, James A		Aug. 29, '62		Discharged July 8, '63.
Pennington, William		Aug. 21, '62		Mustered out with regiment.
Pherson, John H		Aug. 9, '62		Died in the field, June 3, '64.
Pool, Daniel		Aug. 20, '62		Transferred to V. R. C.
Rice, Nathaniel		Aug. 21, '62		Deserted.
Richey, John W		Aug. 13, '62	Greenfield	Mustered out with regiment.
Richey, Samuel		Aug. 13, '62		Died at Louisville, Dec. 2, '62.
Scott, John H		Aug. 22, '62	Greenfield	Mustered out with regiment.
Shuman, John		Aug. 12, '62	Irvington	Promoted corporal.
Shirley, William D		Aug. 13, '62		Mustered out with regiment.
Smith, Jacob T		Aug. 16, '62	White Lick	Discharged Aug. 14, '63.
Swinehart, Daniel		Aug. 15, '62		Deserted Sept. 2, '62.
Smith, Milton		Aug. 16, '62		Died January 8, '63.
Sopher, Abijah		Aug. 11, '62		Discharged April 1, '63.
Stewart, Richard		Aug. 22, '62		Deserted Sept. 28, '62.
St. John, Edward M		Aug. 22, '62		Discharged March 28, '63.
Tanner, John L		Aug. 22, '62		Mustered out with regiment.
Watson, James W		Aug. 20, '62		Mustered out with regiment.
White, Thomas J		Aug. 22, '62		Mustered out with regiment.
Wood, John W		Aug. 15, '62		Deserted Sept. 2, '62.
RECRUITS.				
Schlinker, George W		March 8, '65		Transferred to 51st Ind.

ROSTER OF COMPANY "H."

Name and Rank.	Place of Enlistment.	Date of Enlistment.	Present Residence.	Remarks.
CAPTAINS.				
Edwin M. Byrkit	Indianapolis	Aug. 8, '62	Michigan City	Promoted capt. Co. I, assigned Co. H.
Perry M. Blankenship	Martinsville	Aug. 27, '62		Promoted major. [Must. out with reg.
Sandford C. Pruit	Martinsville	Aug. 15, '62		Resigned Dec. 12, '62.
John L. Hadin	Indianapolis	Nov. 17, '64		Resigned Nov. 17, '64; wounds.
FIRST LIEUTENANTS.				
Sandford C. Pruit	Martinsville	Aug. 15, '62		Promoted captain.
Francis Hedderick	Martinsville	Aug. 15, '62		Mustered out with regiment.
Henry H. Newton	Martinsville	Aug. 15, '62		Resigned Oct. 4, '62.
William P. Mounts	Indianapolis			Dishonorably dismissed Dec. 15, '64.
SECOND LIEUTENANTS.				
William A. Guy	Martinsville	Aug. 15, '62		Resigned Nov. 28, '62.
FIRST SERGEANTS.				
William A. Guy	Martinsville	Aug. 15, '62		Promoted 2d lieutenant.
Francis Hedderick	Martinsville	Aug. 15, '62		Promoted 1st lieutenant.
Martin Kenworthy	Martinsville	Aug. 15, '62	Heelsment	Mustered out with regiment.
SERGEANTS.				
Martin Kenworthy	Martinsville	Aug. 15, '62	Heelsment	Promoted 1st sergeant.
Abraham Stierwalt	Martinsville	Aug. 15, '62		Transferred to V. R. C.
Francis Hedderick	Martinsville	Aug. 15, '62		Promoted 1st sergeant.
Joseph Hodges	Martinsville	Aug. 15, '62	Paragon	Mustered out with regiment.
William Whitesett	Martinsville	Aug. 15, '62	Paragon	Mustered out with regiment.
Nathan Hedderick	Martinsville	Aug. 15, '62	Eiuta	Mustered out with regiment.
William M. Baker	Martinsville	Aug. 15, '62		Died Nov. 30, '64.
Isaiah B. Worthan	Martinsville	Aug. 15, '62		Discharged Dec. 1, '63.
George Evans	Martinsville	Aug. 15, '62		Discharged Sept. 4, '63.
William Langford	Martinsville	Aug. 15, '62		Discharged Aug. 1, '63.

SEVENTY-NINTH INDIANA REGIMENT.

Name	Residence	Date		Remarks
William Secrest	Martinsville	Aug. 15, '62		Discharged Dec. 26, '62.
CORPORALS.				
George W. Bass	Martinsville	Aug. 15, '62	Crown Point, Kan.	Mustered out with regiment.
Jesse L. Harper	Martinsville	Aug. 15, '62	Wakeland	Mustered out with regiment.
Ephraim R. Knox	Martinsville	Aug. 15, '62	Herbemont	Mustered out with regiment.
Charles Griffith	Martinsville	Aug. 15, '62		Mustered out with regiment.
Nathan Hedderick	Martinsville	Aug. 15, '62	Banta	Promoted sergeant.
Samuel Kennedy	Martinsville	Aug. 15, '62		Died March 6, '63.
William H. Tout	Martinsville	Aug. 15, '62		Died Jan. 4, '63.
Andrew J. Baker	Martinsville	Aug. 15, '62		Deserted Nov. 18, '62.
William Wilson	Martinsville	Aug. 15, '62		Discharged Dec. 26, '62.
Walker W. Cavendiss	Martinsville	Aug. 15, '62		Discharged April 23, '63.
John C. Duncan	Martinsville	Aug. 15, '62		Discharged Sept. 4, '63.
John Wingler	Martinsville	Aug. 15, '62	Indianapolis	Discharged Jan. 21, '63.
Henry Sutherland	Martinsville	Aug. 15, '62		Discharged May 25, '63.
PRIVATES.				
Adkins, William	Martinsville	Aug. 15, '62		Died Feb. 4, '63.
Asher, Henry	Martinsville	Aug. 15, '62	Wakeland	Discharged May 26, '65.
Baker, William M	Martinsville	Aug. 15, '62		Promoted sergeant.
Baker, Jesse R	Martinsville	Aug. 15, '62		Died at home.
Barnes, Joseph	Martinsville	Aug. 15, '62		Died Jan. 24, '63.
Bass, John H	Martinsville	Aug. 15, '62		Died Dec. 9, '63.
Baker, Andrew J	Martinsville	Aug. 15, '62		Promoted corporal.
Bray, Josiah	Martinsville	Aug. 15, '62		Discharged Dec. 17, '62.
Barton, William H	Martinsville	Aug. 15, '62		Discharged May 29, '65.
Baker, Isaac C	Martinsville	Aug. 15, '62	Martinsville	Discharged Aug. 11, '63.
Bass, George W	Martinsville	Aug. 15, '62	Crown Point, Kan.	Promoted corporal.
Cavendiss, Walker W	Martinsville	Aug. 15, '62		
Chandler, Joshua D	Martinsville	Aug. 15, '62	Martinsville	Discharged May 15, '65.
Crow, Henry	Martinsville	Aug. 15, '62		Transferred to V. R. C.
Coston, John	Martinsville	Aug. 16, '62		Transferred to V. R. C.
Collins, John W	Martinsville	Aug. 15, '62		Mustered out with regiment.
Dangler, Daniel	Martinsville	Aug. 15, '62		Deserted Nov. 18, '62.

ROSTER OF COMPANY "H"—CONTINUED.

Name and Rank.	Place of Enlistment.	Date of Enlistment.	Present Residence.	Remarks.
PRIVATES (Continued.)				
Duncan, John C.	Martinsville	Aug. 15, '62	Indianapolis	Promoted corporal.
Delap, William	Martinsville	Aug. 15, '62		Discharged March 25, '63.
Evans, George	Martinsville	Aug. 15, '62		Promoted sergeant.
Fincham, William	Martinsville	Aug. 15, '62		Died in rebel prison, Jan. 7, '63.
Fincham, Robert	Martinsville	Aug. 15, '62		Deserted Nov. 18, '62.
Fincham, Elijah	Martinsville	Aug. 15, '62		Deserted Nov. 18, '62.
Gatbright, Eli	Martinsville	Aug. 15, '62		Discharged Jan. 16, '63.
Guy, William A.	Martinsville	Aug. 15, '62		Promoted sergeant.
Griffith, Charles	Martinsville	Aug. 15, '62		Promoted corporal.
Pleasant, C. Gass	Martinsville	Aug. 15, '62		Died March 28, '63.
Hodges, Joseph	Martinsville	Aug. 15, '62	Paragon	Promoted sergeant.
Hedderick, Nathan	Martinsville	Aug. 15, '62	Banta	Promoted sergeant.
Harper, Jesse L.	Martinsville	Aug. 15, '62	Wakeland	Promoted corporal.
Hodges, William N.	Martinsville	Aug. 15, '62	Paragon	Mustered out with regiment.
Hedderick, Jacob	Martinsville	Aug. 15, '62		Died at home.
Hedderick, Francis	Martinsville	Aug. 15, '62		Promoted sergeant.
Hodges, Thomas F.	Martinsville	Aug. 15, '62		Discharged Sept. 22, '63.
Hancock, John W.	Martinsville	Aug. 15, '62		Transferred to V. R. C.
Hagy, Jacob	Martinsville	Aug. 15, '62		Transferred to V. R. C.
Johnson, Daniel	Martinsville	Aug. 15, '62		Discharged March 25, '63.
Jones, Henry	Martinsville	Aug. 15, '62		Died at home.
Kenworthy, Martin	Martinsville	Aug. 15, '62	Herbemont	Promoted sergeant.
Knox, Ephraim R.	Martinsville	Aug. 15, '62	Martinsville	Promoted corporal.
Kennedy, James C.	Martinsville	Aug. 15, '62	Liquet	Mustered out with regiment.
Kennedy, Samuel	Martinsville	Aug. 15, '62		Promoted corporal.
Langford, William	Martinsville	Aug. 15, '62	Martinsville	Promoted sergeant.

SEVENTY-NINTH INDIANA REGIMENT. 35

Miller, Robert	Martinsville	Aug. 15, '62		Mustered out with regiment.
Merriwether, Robert F	Martinsville	Aug. 15, '62		Died Feb. 15, '63.
McDaniel, Eli R	Martinsville	Aug. 15, '62		Died April 13, '63.
Murphy, Alexander	Martinsville	Aug. 15, '62		Died April 10, '63.
Mosier, James R	Martinsville	Aug. 15, '62	Martinsville	Discharged Feb. 25, '63.
Newton, Marion J	Martinsville	Aug. 15, '62		Discharged Jan. 25, '63.
O'Neal, Willis	Martinsville	Aug. 15, '62		Discharged Dec. 31, '62.
Pierson, John M	Martinsville	Aug. 15, '62	Paragon	Discharged May 24, '65.
Peyton, Harrison	Martinsville	Aug. 15, '62	Paragon	Discharged May 6, '63, of wounds.
Peyton, Anderson	Martinsville	Aug. 15, '62		Deserted Nov. 29, '62.
Peyton, William H	Martinsville	Aug. 15, '62		Deserted Nov. 29, '62.
Pettit, John	Martinsville	Aug. 15, '62		Died Jan. 26, '63, of wounds.
Pettit, Thomas	Martinsville	Aug. 15, '62		Mustered out with regiment.
Robinson, Thomas	Martinsville	Aug. 15, '62		Mustered out with regiment.
Reeves, James S	Martinsville	Aug. 15, '62		Discharged May 18, '62.
Roe, Milton	Martinsville	Aug. 15, '62		Discharged Jan. 21, '63.
Stierwalt, Daniel	Martinsville	Aug. 15, '62	Silver Lake, Minn.	Transferred to V. R. C.
Stierwalt, James L	Martinsville	Aug. 15, '62	W. Indianapolis	Transferred to V. R. C.
Stierwalt, Abraham	Martinsville	Aug. 15, '62	Winslow, Ill	Transferred to V. R. C.
Stierwalt, George W	Martinsville	Aug. 15, '62		Mustered out with regiment.
Shetters, John	Martinsville	Aug. 15, '62		Mustered out with regiment.
Stiles, John B	Martinsville	Aug. 15, '62		Mustered out with regiment.
Snavely, David	Martinsville	Aug. 15, '62	Concordia, Kan.	Discharged Jan. 1, '63.
Secrest, Pleasant	Martinsville	Aug. 15, '62		Discharged Aug. 24, '63.
Sebastian, William	Martinsville	Aug. 15, '62		Discharged Feb. 2, '63.
Sutherland, Henry A	Martinsville	Aug. 15, '62		Promoted corporal.
Seerest, William	Martinsville	Aug. 15, '62		Discharged Sept. 2, '63, of wounds.
Sebastian, James S	Martinsville	Aug. 15, '62		Deserted Oct. 12, '62.
Stout, Ira	Martinsville	Aug. 15, '62		Died Nov. 28, '62.
Stout, Ambrose	Martinsville	Aug. 15, '62		Died Nov. 30, '62.
Secrest, Parker	Martinsville	Aug. 15, '62		Died Jan. 25, '63.
Secrest, Ira W	Martinsville	Aug. 15, '62		Died Jan. 10, '63.
Scotten, James L	Martinsville	Aug. 15, '62		Killed in battle, Sept. 19, '63.

ROSTER OF COMPANY "H"—CONTINUED.

Name and Rank.	Place of Enlistment.	Date of Enlistment.	Present Residence.	Remarks.
PRIVATES—Continued.				
Thompson, William B.	Martinsville	Aug. 15, '62	Tuscola, Ill.	Mustered out with regiment.
Tout, William H.	Martinsville	Aug. 15, '62		Promoted corporal.
Tout, Benjamin	Martinsville	Aug. 15, '62		Discharged Nov. 17, '62.
Vashell, Ephraim	Martinsville	Aug. 15, '62	Wakeland	Mustered out with regiment.
Witson, Nathan	Martinsville	Aug. 15, '62		Discharged Sept. 14, '63.
Way, Alfred	Martinsville	Aug. 15, '62		Discharged April 15, '63.
Warthan, Ira S.	Martinsville	Aug. 15, '62		Discharged March 10, '63.
Wingler, John	Martinsville	Aug. 15, '62	Wakeland	Promoted corporal.
Wilson, William	Martinsville	Aug. 15, '62		Promoted corporal.
Worthan, Isaiah B.	Martinsville	Aug. 15, '62	Melrose, Kan	Promoted sergeant.
Worthan, James I.	Martinsville	Aug. 15, '62	Paragon	Mustered out with regiment.
Whitesett, William	Martinsville	Aug. 15, '62	Paragon	Promoted sergeant.
Yount, James	Martinsville	Aug. 15, '62		Died Dec. 24, '62.
Yount, Miles W.	Martinsville	Aug. 15, '62		Mustered out with regiment.
Yount, George A.	Martinsville	Aug. 15, '62		Mustered out with regiment.

ROSTER OF COMPANY "I."

Name and Rank.	Place of Enlistment.	Date of Enlistment.	Present Residence.	Remarks.
CAPTAINS.				
Samuel P. Oyler	Franklin	Aug. 8, '62	Franklin	Promoted lieutenant-colonel.
William B. Ellis	Franklin	Aug. 27, '62	Franklin	Resigned July 16, '63. [wounds.
Daniel W. Howe	Franklin	July 17, '63	Indianapolis	Honorably discharged Nov. 10, '64;
Edwin M. Byrkit	Indianapolis	Mar. 1, '65	Michigan City	Mustered out with regiment.
FIRST LIEUTENANTS.				
Daniel W. Howe	Franklin	Aug. 27, '62	Indianapolis	Promoted captain. [wounds.
Thomas C. Batchelor	Franklin	July 15, '63	Vernon	Honorably discharged Oct. 4, '64;
William H. Huntzinger	Franklin	Mar. 1, '65		Mustered out with regiment.
SECOND LIEUTENANTS.				
James B. Bell	Franklin	Aug. 8, '62		Resigned Nov. 6, '62.
George C. Whitlock	Franklin	Nov. 27, '62		Resigned June 20, '63.
Thomas C. Batchelor	Franklin	June 21, '63	Vernon	Promoted 1st lieutenant.
FIRST SERGEANTS.				
Henry C. Branham		Aug. 14, '62		Discharged Dec. 6, '62.
James C. Dunlap		Aug. 14, '62		Mustered out with regiment.
SERGEANTS.				
Henry C. Whitlock		Aug. 14, '62		Mustered out with regiment (private).
Joseph J. Calvin		Aug. 14, '62	Albuquerque, Mex.	
Thomas McIlvain		Aug. 14, '62	Taylorsville	Mustered out with regiment (private).
William F. McIlvain		Aug. 14, '62	Wellsville, Mo.	Mustered out with regiment.
Vincent F. Browning		Aug. 14, '62	Danville, Ill.	Mustered out with regiment.
Matthew Chandler		Aug. 14, '62		Mustered out with regiment.
William D. Mitchell		Aug. 14, '62		Mustered out with regiment.
John Shoemaker		Aug. 14, '62		Mustered out with regiment.
CORPORALS.				
Henry B. Moffatt		Aug. 14, '62		Died at Nashville, Dec. 25, '62.

ROSTER OF COMPANY "I"—CONTINUED.

Name and Rank.	Place of Enlistment.	Date of Enlistment.	Present Residence.	Remarks.
CORPORALS—Continued.				
John T. Mitchell		Aug. 14, '62		Transferred to V. R. C.
Richard M. Gosney		Aug. 14, '62		Promoted Q. M. 28th U. S. Col.
William Skidmore		Aug. 14, '62		Discharged Oct. 1, '62.
John W. Israel		Aug. 14, '62		Mustered out with regiment.
Walter H. Hunter		Aug. 14, '62		Missing in action, June 7, '63.
William A. Richardson		Aug. 14, '62	Franklin	Mustered out with regiment.
William M. Robbins		Aug. 14, '62		Discharged May 9, '63.
James Cotton		Aug. 14, '62	Edinburg	Mustered out with regiment.
James Hague		Aug. 14, '62	Trafalgar	Mustered out with regiment.
Ezra J. Hicks		Aug. 14, '62	Eagle Cove, Texas	Mustered out with regiment.
James P. Johnson		Aug. 14, '62		Mustered out with regiment.
WAGONER.				
Meredy G. Wilkinson		Aug. 14, '62		Mustered out with regiment.
PRIVATES.				
Anderson, George W		Aug. 14, '62		Died at Knoxville, March 25, '64.
Anderson, Elijah		Aug. 14, '62	New Hartford, Mo.	Mustered out with regiment.
Anderson, John		Aug. 14, '62		Mustered out with regiment.
Anderson, George W		Aug. 14, '62		Mustered out with regiment.
Applegate, Richard S		Aug. 14, '62		Deserted.
Batchelor, Thomas C		Aug. 14, '62	Vernon	Promoted second lieutenant.
Beatty, Joseph		Aug. 14, '62	Indianapolis	Discharged Jan. 12, '63.
Bennett, Joseph P		Aug. 14, '62		Died at Nashville, Dec. 4, '62.
Bryant, Pearson		Aug. 14, '62		Died at Murfreesboro, April 18, '63.
Browning, Vincent F		Aug. 14, '62	Taylorsville	Promoted sergeant.
Bridges, Benjamin		Aug. 14, '62		Died at Nashville, Jan. 14, '63.
Bennett, John		Aug. 14, '62		Died at Nashville, Dec. 4, '62.

SEVENTY-NINTH INDIANA REGIMENT.

Name				Remarks
Butler, Michael B		Aug.	14, '62	Died at Chattanooga, Dec. 9, '63.
Byers, James		Aug.	14, '62	Died at Nashville, Dec. 28, '62.
Callon, William A	Middletown, Mo.	Aug.	14, '62	Died Jan. 23, '63.
Chandler, Matthew	Wellsville	Aug.	14, '62	Promoted sergeant.
Chandler, Thomas C	Edinburg	Aug.	14, '62	Mustered out with regiment.
Clark, James E	Morgantown	Aug.	11, '62	Mustered out with regiment.
Clark, Henry S		Aug.	14, '62	Mustered out with regiment as hospital steward.
Coy, James		Aug.	14, '62	Discharged May 30, '63.
Cotton, James	Edinburg	Aug.	14, '62	Died at Nashville, Jan. 3, '63.
Critester, William	Edinburg	Aug.	14, '62	Promoted corporal.
Downing, Elias M	Paris, Ill.	Aug.	14, '62	Mustered out with regiment.
Dodd, Tilman		Aug.	14, '62	Mustered out with regiment.
Drake, Wesley		Aug.	14, '62	Died.
Drybread, Joseph M	Franklin	Aug.	14, '62	Transferred to engineer corps.
Dunlap, James C	Nineveh	Aug.	14, '62	Mustered out with regiment.
Ellis, William B		Aug.	14, '62	Promoted 1st sergeant.
Fitzpatrick, George W		Aug.	14, '62	Promoted captain.
Foley, Jeremiah		Aug.	14, '62	Died at Nashville, Dec. 23, '63.
Gillaspie, Milton G	Franklin	Aug.	14, '62	Mustered out with regiment. (thority.)
Hague, Smith		Aug.	14, '62	Discharged May 12, '63, by civil au-
Hague, James	Trafalgar	Aug.	14, '62	Discharged March 23, '63.
Hancock, Columbus		Aug.	14, '62	Promoted corporal.
Hill, Wesley A	Cincinnati, O.	Aug.	14, '62	Mustered out with regiment.
Hicks, Ezra J	Eagle Cove	Aug.	14, '62	Promoted corporal.
Holecraft, William	Nineveh	Aug.	14, '62	Mustered out with regiment.
Holecraft, Edmond		Aug.	14, '62	Killed at Kenesaw, June 23, '64.
Huntzinger, William H		Aug.	14, '62	Promoted 1st lieutenant.
Irwin, Alexander E	Lebanon, Neb.	Aug.	14, '62	Transferred to V. R. C.
Johnson, Preston	Denver	Aug.	14, '62	Mustered out with regiment.
Johnson, James P		Aug.	14, '62	Died at Kansas, Ind., Dec. 6, '62.
Kittle, Josiah H		Aug.	14, '62	Promoted corporal.
		Aug.	14, '62	Transferred to V. R. C.

ROSTER OF COMPANY "I"—Continued.

Name and Rank.	Place of Enlistment.	Date of Enlistment.	Present Residence.	Remarks.
PRIVATES—Continued.				
Long, Benjamin F		Aug. 14, '62	Bartlett, Iowa	Mustered out with regiment.
Martin, Silas		Aug. 14, '62		Mustered out with regiment.
McIlvain, Thomas		Aug. 14, '62	Albuquerque, N. M.	Mustered out with regiment.
McKain, William		Aug. 14, '62		Died Jan. 10, '63.
McMillon, James A		Aug. 14, '62		Transferred to marine corps.
Mitchell, William D		Aug. 14, '62	Danville, Ill	Promoted sergeant.
Mitchell, Peter A		Aug. 14, '62	Danville, Ill	Discharged Feb. 16, '63.
Middleton, John T		Aug. 14, '62		Transferred to marine corps.
Miller, Benjamin R		Aug. 14, '62		Mustered out with regiment.
Neidy, Abraham		Aug. 14, '62		Died at Nashville, Dec. 31, '62.
Parks, Billip		Aug. 14, '62	Indianapolis	Discharged April 20, '63.
Reeves Enoch		Aug. 14, '62	Jamestown	Transferred to V. R. C.
Robinson, Alexander		Aug. 14, '62		Killed at Pickets Mills, May 27, '64.
Robbins, Daniel		Aug. 14, '62	Franklin	Discharged Feb. 26, '63.
Robbins, Ralph		Aug. 14, '62	Union Village	Mustered out with regiment.
Roberts, John R		Aug. 14, '62		Died at Nashville, Dec. 25, '62.
Stewart, Alexander		Aug. 14, '62		Transferred to V. R. C.
Shipman, Hiram		Aug. 14, '62	New Corner	Mustered out with regiment.
Sheppard, Wesley S		Aug. 14, '62	Franklin	Mustered out with regiment.
Shoemaker, John		Aug. 14, '62		Promoted sergeant.
Stultz, William		Aug. 14, '62		Died at Nashville, Jan. 29, '63.
Stinnett, Linsey		Aug. 14, '62	Franklin	Mustered out with regiment.
Schoonmeyer, Philip		Aug. 14, '62		Died at Nashville, Jan. 5, '63.
Swan, Thomas		Aug. 14, '62		Mustered out with regiment.
Taylor, John W		Aug. 14, '62		Transferred to V. R. C.
Tully, Thomas C		Aug. 14, '62		Died at Nashville, Dec. 17, '63.

SEVENTY-NINTH INDIANA REGIMENT.

Terhune, Abraham H.	Aug. 14, '62	Stilesville	Mustered out with regiment.
Tyler, John A.	Aug. 14, '62		Discharged Feb. 10, '63.
Tyler, Thomas M.	Aug. 14, '62		Died at Nashville, March 9, '63.
Tyler, William A.	Aug. 14, '62		Died at Nashville, Jan. 8, '63.
Vaught, Harrison	Aug. 14, '62		Died at Chattanooga, Nov. 11, '63.
Watson, David M.	Aug. 14, '62		Died at Nashville, Dec. 25, '62.
Wheatley, Charles H.	Aug. 14, '62		Died at McMinnville, July 31, '63.
Wheaton, Fielding	Aug. 14, '62	Nineveh	Discharged April 18, '63.
Wilson, Samuel	Aug. 14, '62	Edinburg	Mustered out with regiment.
RECRUITS.			
Samuel Swan	Aug. 14, '62	Muncie	Discharged March 18, '63.

ROSTER OF COMPANY "K."

Name and Rank.	Place of Enlistment.	Date of Enlistment.	Present Residence.	Remarks.
CAPTAINS.				
Joseph W. Jordan	Brownsburg	Aug. 25, '62		Honorably discharged July 16, '64.
Daniel W. Hoadley	Plainfield	Jan. 1, '65		Mustered out with regiment.
FIRST LIEUTENANTS.				
Tyra Montgomery	Brownsburg	Aug. 25, '62		Resigned Nov. 12, '62.
Edgar J. Foster	Indianapolis	Nov. 13, '62	Indianapolis	Resigned Feb. 22, '64.
Daniel W. Hoadley	Plainfield	Feb. 23, '64		Promoted captain.
Henry J. Brattain	Indianapolis	Mar. 13, '65		Mustered out with regiment.
SECOND LIEUTENANT.				
Augustine T. Stone	Plainfield	Aug. 25, '62		Resigned Aug. 15, '64.
FIRST SERGEANTS.				
William H. Toute		Aug. 11, '62	Archie, Mo.	Transferred to V. R. C.
Gilbert D. McClain		Aug. 22, '62	Plainfield	Mustered out with regiment.
SERGEANTS.				
Reuben Patterson		Aug. 15, '62	Pendleton	Mustered out with regiment (private).
Lotan W. Jenkins		Aug. 26, '62	Avon	Mustered out with regiment, [wounds.
Henry N. Osborn		Aug. 18, '62		Died at Chattanooga, Dec. 1, '63.
Nelson R. Woods		Aug. 22, '62		Mustered out with regiment, musician.
Patrick H. Crafton		Aug. 28, '62	Butler, Mo.	Mustered out with regiment.
Robert V. Franklin		Aug. 22, '62	Lincoln, Neb.	Mustered out with regiment.
Isaac W. Gray		Aug. 31, '62	Brownsburg	Mustered out with regiment.
CORPORALS.				
William Hulsizer		Aug. 15, '62	Clermont	Transferred to V. R. C.
William F. Dinwiddie		Aug. 14, '62	Brownsburg	Discharged March 26, '63.
Gilbert D. McClain		Aug. 22, '62	Plainfield	Promoted first sergeant.
William Logan		Aug. 15, '62	Toledo, Ill.	Mustered out with regiment (private).
Daniel Sanders		Aug. 22, '62	Bridgeport	Transferred to V. R. C.

SEVENTY-NINTH INDIANA REGIMENT.

Name	Residence	Date of enlistment	Remarks
Henry J. Brattain		Aug. 15, '62	Promoted 1st lieutenant.
Urban T. Stone		Aug. 22, '62	Discharged Feb. 10, '63.
George R. Simms		Aug. 22, '62	Transferred to engineer corps.
William T. Eudaly		Aug. 19, '62	Hutchings, Kan. Mustered out with regiment.
Asberry S. Hollingsworth	Plainfield	Aug. 22, '62	Mustered out with regiment.
John W. Ray		Aug. 22, '62	Mustered out with regiment.
Henry C. Ratliff		Aug. 26, '62	Mustered out with regiment.
James A. Snyder	Gall	Aug. 12, '62	Mustered out with regiment.
James White	Truckers' Point	Aug. 20, '62	Mustered out with regiment.
MUSICIANS.			
George W. Brown		Aug. 14, '62	Discharged April 8, '62.
Obed M. Dennis		Aug. 22, '62	Discharged April 22, '63.
WAGONER.			
John H. Manley		Aug. 14, '62	Discharged Feb. 10, '63.
PRIVATES.			
Ayers, Horatio W.	Royalton	Aug. 14, '62	Transferred to V. R. C.
Annick, Isaac	New Castle, Neb.	Aug. 22, '62	Mustered out with regiment.
Annick, William C.	Elmwood, Neb.	Aug. 22, '62	Mustered out with regiment.
Barsott, David O.		Aug. 14, '62	Died Dec. 27, '62.
Barsott, Tilman F.		Aug. 14, '62	Discharged March 7, '63.
Brown, James W.		Aug. 22, '62	Died Jan. 6, '63.
Bly, William C.	Plainfield	Aug. 22, '62	Discharged March 8, '63.
Bly, John F.		Aug. 22, '62	Discharged April 29, '63.
Bennett, Joseph T.		Aug. 22, '62	Transferred to engineer corps.
Bray, Tilman E.		Aug. 22, '62	Died in Andersonville prison, Sept. 27, '64.
Crafton, Patrick H.	Butler, Mo.	Aug. 28, '62	Promoted sergeant.
Caywood, Henry V.	Butler, Mo.	Aug. 14, '62	Mustered out with regiment.
Courtney, Wallace	Whitestown	Aug. 14, '62	Transferred to V. R. C.
Crafton, Aleyette R.	Butler, Mo.	Aug. 31, '62	Discharged May 29, '65.
Davis, Lewis	Pittsboro	Aug. 14, '62	Mustered out with regiment.
Dobson, James A. C.		Aug. 13, '62	Transferred to V. R. C.
Douglass, David	Plainfield	Aug. 18, '62	Mustered out with regiment.
Eaton, Harrison	Butler, Mo.	Aug. 15, '62	Discharged March 30, '63.

ROSTER OF COMPANY "K"—Continued.

Name and Rank.	Place of Enlistment.	Date of Enlistment.	Present Residence.	Remarks.
PRIVATES—Continued.				
Ellingwood, Hiram		Aug. 15, '62		Died Sept. 24, '64, wounds.
Evans, George I.		Aug. 19, '62	Chetopa, Kan	Discharged Feb. 4, '63.
Endaly, William T.		Aug. 19, '62	Hutchings, Kan.	Promoted corporal.
Fitch, Daniel B.		Aug. 14, '62	Haughville	Discharged Jan. 1, '63.
Fitch, James W.		Aug. 14, '62	Haughville	Discharged Feb. 21, '63.
Franklin, Robert V.		Aug. 22, '62	Lincoln, Neb.	Promoted sergeant.
Gorrell, James.		Aug. 15, '62	Royalton	Mustered out with regiment.
Graham, Ebenezer W		Aug. 15, '62		Died Feb. 12, '63.
Gray, Isaac W.		Aug. 31, '62	Brownsburg	Promoted sergeant.
Hoadly, Daniel W.		Aug. 22, '62		Promoted first lieutenant.
Hethcoat, William A.		Aug. 22, '62		Discharged April 19, '63.
Hollingsworth, Asbury		Aug. 22, '62	Plainfield	Promoted corporal.
Hendricks, Milton		Aug. 22, '62	Clermont	Discharged Feb. 28, '63, wounds.
Hartley, George B.		Aug. 14, '62	Dundee	Mustered out with regiment.
Hollett, Mark		Aug. 15, '62		Died April 1, '63.
Herring, Elias E.		Aug. 15, '62		Died March 20, '63.
Hultz, John		Aug. 14, '62		Died March 30, '63.
Hollett, John A.		Aug. 14, '62		Killed at Kenesaw, June 18, '64.
Jones, William M.		Aug. 22, '62		Mustered out with regiment.
Kite, Isaiah		Aug. 22, '62	Greenfield	Transferred to V. R. C.
Leach, Ezra S.		Aug. 19, '62		Died at Murfreesboro, March 2, '63.
Loy, Tobias		Aug. 22, '62	Ben Davis	Mustered out with regiment.
Leonard, Frederick		Aug. 14, '62	Pittsboro	Discharged March 8, '63.
Lacy, William H.		Aug. 16, '62		Died at Chattanooga, March 18, '63.
Manker, Henry E.		Aug. 20, '62		Transferred to Co. B.
Myers, John S.		Aug. 12, '62		Died at Nashville, Dec. 24, '63.

SEVENTY-NINTH INDIANA REGIMENT. 45

Name			Residence	Remarks
McNeely, Samuel	Aug.	21, '62		Died at Murfreesboro, Feb. 14, '63.
Maxwell, David I	Aug.	21, '62		Discharged Aug. 31, '64.
McDaniel, Mahlon	Aug.	22, '62		Discharged April 28, '63.
Mann, Noah K	Aug.	22, '62	Monrovia	Discharged May 16, '65.
McKee, Allen	Aug.	28, '62		Died at Nashville, Jan. 27, '63.
McLain, Bascom S	Aug.	30, '62	Avon	Discharged May 17, '65.
Morgan, John S	Aug.	31, '62		Discharged March 6, '63; wounds.
Olney, John R	Aug.	13, '62		Died at Knoxville, March 13, '64.
Pearcy, Isaac	Aug.	22, '62	Millcdgeville	Mustered out with regiment.
Patterson, William	Aug.	22, '62	Avon	Discharged April 6, '63.
Parnell, George	Aug.	22, '62	Bridgeport	Transferred to engineer corps.
Pulliam, Jesse F	Aug.	22, '62		Discharged Jan. 31, '63.
Perkins, Samuel H	Aug.	22, '62		Mustered out with regiment.
Ray, John W	Aug.	22, '62		Died at Indianapolis, March 12, '63.
Ray, Doctor F	Aug.	26, '62		Promoted corporal.
Ratliff, Henry C	Aug.	15, '62	Gall	Discharged March 7, '65.
Rice, George E	Aug.	12, '62	Indianapolis	Mustered out with regiment.
Ramsey, Francis M	Aug.	15, '62		Promoted corporal.
Snyder, James A	Aug.	15, '62	Whitestown	Died Jan. 28, '64; wounds.
South, Archibald	Aug.	22, '62	Shoals	Mustered out with regiment.
Smith, Levy	Aug.	22, '62	Danville	Transferred to V. R. C.
Sherrill, Leonard	Aug.	12, '62	Brownsburg	Mustered out with regiment.
Sears, William R	Aug.	15, '62	Allen, Ohio.	Discharged Feb. 28, '63.
Tyler, Charles W	Aug.	15, '62		Mustered out with regiment.
Wirt, Francis M	Aug.	15, '62		Died at Nashville, Dec. 24, '62.
Wells, Simon R	Aug.	20, '62	Traders' Point	Mustered out with regiment.
Wells, George W	Aug.	22, '62		Promoted corporal.
White, James				Died at Chattanooga, March 20, '64.
Worrell, Legrand				
RECRUITS.				
Moore, William P	Aug.	12, '63		Transferred to 51st Indiana.
Patterson, Eli	Sept.	10, '62		Mustered out with regiment.
Rice, Warren	Nov.	23, '63		Transferred to 51st Indiana.

HISTORY

OF THE

Seventy-Ninth Indiana Regiment

Regiment Mustered in August 27, 1862

AUGUST, 1862.

27. Fred Knefler appointed colonel of regiment. Six companies left Indianapolis at 2 A. M.

28. Arrived at Jeffersonville at 12 M.. Lieutenant-Colonel S. P. Oyler in command. Crossed river to Louisville, Ky. Camped near L. & N. R. R. depot.

29. In camp at Louisville, Ky. Drilling, etc.

30. Part of the regiment at Louisville at 2 A. M. Was ordered to be ready to march. Marched at 5 A. M. a short distance and was ordered back to camp.

31. In camp near Louisville. Drilling.

SEPTEMBER, 1862.

1. In camp near Louisville. Drilling and routine duties.

2. Colonel Knefler at Indianapolis mustered into service of United States. Part of regiment in camp. Drilling, etc.

3. Marched at 7 A. M. without striking camp. Marched to camp three miles from fair grounds. The other four companies and Colonel Knefler joined regiment. Sergeant-Major Burns reduced to the ranks and Corporal Ed J. Foster, of Company A, appointed sergeant-major of regiment.

4. Marched toward Shelbyville about twelve miles.

Camped on the side of a hill. Regiment assigned to provisional brigade, General Sill commanding.

5. At 4 A. M. received orders to march to cover troops retreating from Richmond. The regiment fell in the rear of passing troops and covered the retreat. Marched to camp. Tents had not been taken down.

6. In camp. Routine duties. Company and squad drills.

7. In camp. Routine duties. Company officers drilled by Colonel Kneffer. Company and squad drills superintended by colonel all day.

8. In camp. Routine duties. Company officers drilled by Colonel Kneffer. Company and squad drills superintended by colonel all day.

9. Formed in line. Tents struck. Wagons loaded. Marched at 6 A. M. to Louisville. Lay in the streets in the hottest time of day. Many of the boys became overheated and were prostrated. Orders were received to return to the old camp, arriving there at about 4 P. M. Put up tents again.

10. In camp. Routine duties. Company and squad drills. Company officers drilled and instructed in guard duties.

11. In camp. Routine duties. Company and squad drills. Company officers drilled and instructed in guard duties.

12. In camp. Routine duties. Company and squad drills. Company officers drilled and instructed in guard duties.

13. In camp. Routine duties. Company and squad drills. Company officers drilled and instructed in guard duties.

14. In camp. Routine duties. Company and squad drills. Company officers drilled and instructed in guard duties.

15. Awakened early to be ready to move. Marched at 6 A. M. to Louisville. Seventy-ninth in front. Lay in Broadway two or three hours in scorching sun. Many prostrated from heat. Several sent to hospital in ambulances. Marched southeast of city about two miles and pitched camp in a delightful, shady place.

16. In camp. Routine duties. Commissioned officers' drill. Non-commissioned officers instructed in guard duties by Colonel Knefler.

17. In camp. Routine duties. Commissioned officers' drill. Non-commissioned officers instructed in guard duties by Colonel Knefler.

18. Marched at 6 A. M. to Louisville. Worked on entrenchment south of city. Marched back to camp at 7 P. M.

19. In camp. Routine duties and drill.

20. Marched southeast of the city. Went in camp about ten miles from old camp.

21. In camp. Routine duties and drills.

22. Marched back to the camp left two days before.

23. Ordered to march. Struck tents. Left camp about 6 A. M. Marched to Louisville. Great excitement. Women and children leaving city by hundreds, by order of General Nelson. Bragg is expected to attack the city. Regiment marched south of the city about one mile, where trenches had been dug, and manned the trenches.

24. Second Lieutenant James Comstock, "G" company, resigned. Regiment on picket for the first time.

25. In line in trenches from 3 A. M. until morning.

26. Marched to Jefferson street; out on that street about a mile or more to another street and camped in a public garden. Good camping ground for the regiment.

27. Exchanged Austrian guns for the sword-bayonet Vincennes rifles.

28. In camp. Routine duties and drills.

29. In camp. General Nelson was shot and killed by General J. C. Davis. Excitement in the city and the camps.

30. In camp. Assigned to 3d Brigade, 3d Division, 21st Army Corps. Colonel Samuel Beatty, 19th Ohio Volunteers, commanding brigade. Brigadier-General H. P. Van Cleve commanding 3d Division. Major-General S. L. Crittenden commanding 21st Corps. Regiment ordered to be ready to march next day and join 3d Brigade as soon as practicable. The 3d Brigade to be composed of 19th Ohio Volunteers, Lieutenant-Colonel Manderson; 9th Kentucky Volunteers, Colonel B. F. Grider; 11th Kentucky Volunteers, Major Motley; 79th Indiana Volunteers, Colonel Fred Knefler.

OCTOBER, 1862.

1. The army of General Buell started in pursuit of Bragg's rebel army. Marched out on the Bardstown pike and camped about 10 P. M. Joined the 3d Brigade of Colonel Sam Beatty on arrival in the camp.

2. At Mount Washington in support of cavalry. Battery on hill first cannonading.

3. At Salt river bridge.

4. At Bardstown. Camped in the fair grounds.

5. At Beach Fork, on the Springfield road.

6. To Springfield. Much suffering for water.

7. Marched to South Rollens Ford. Very hard marching. Camped at 10 P. M. Marched thirty miles.

8. Marched to near Perryville and formed in line of battle in reserve, unslung knapsacks and piled them. Hard battle in the line to our left.

9. On picket near Perryville on the Harrisburgh

pike. Many dead rebels discovered on the field. A large rebel field hospital within picket line.

10. Marched six miles and countermarched double-quick three miles to guard a train reported attacked by rebel cavalry. Marched four miles. Camped at 11 o'clock p. m. Raining.

11. In line of battle. Cavalry in action. Skirmishing.

12. Marched seven miles and formed in line of battle.

13. Marched to Danville. Formed in line of battle on the Lexington pike, near the town, and bivouacked.

14. Sergeant George W. Clark, of "G" company, appointed first lieutenant of company, vice Comstock, resigned. Marched through Danville on the Stanton pike and camped near Stanton. Called up at 11 p. m. and marched six miles. The rebels are shelled.

15. Marched to Crab Orchard and formed in line of battle near the town. The rebels shelled us. One man of "A" company killed, and some of our men wounded. The regiment on the skirmish line, Company "C" on the flank. Drew rations. Rebel rear guard in retreat.

16. Marched five miles. Camped near Big Springs.

17. Marched six miles and returned to Big Springs to camp.

18. Marched to Rock Castle river and three miles beyond the mountain to the Wild Cat battle ground. Marched back four miles. Bivouacked by the road side.

19. Sunday Marched at 1 p. m. to the battle ground and beyond it eight miles. Camped at London cross-roads.

20. Marched at 1 p. m. one mile. Bivouacked,

waiting for the provision train, which is much delayed by bad roads.

21. In camp same place. Drilled twice per day.

22. Ordered to be ready to march at 4 p. m. Company drills. Rations scarce; crackers wormy; water very hard to find. Worst experience up to date.

23. Drilled in the forenoon. Marched at 2 p. m. over the mountains, twelve miles to Rockcastle, then on to the big springs. The march was a hard one. Roads very bad. Many stragglers.

24. Marched to Mount Vernon, turned to left and marched six miles in direction of Somerset and bivouacked.

25. Marched to Somerset. The colonel ordered tents put up. Marched eighteen miles. Snowed in the night. Six inches deep in the morning.

26. Sunday. Snowed nearly all of the day.

27. Weather cleared up some. Dress parade at 5 p. m.

28. Marched early. The roads very bad. Marched but four miles by evening. Then marched eight miles and bivouacked.

29. Marched until nearly night. Bivouacked.

30. Marched at daylight, sixteen miles.

31. Marched until 1 p. m. Went into bivouack near Columbia, the county-seat of Adair county, Kentucky.

NOVEMBER, 1862.

1. Marched until night. Went into bivouack. Regiment detailed for picket.

2. On picket. Ate breakfast before daylight. Marched to Edmunton and went in camp, five miles from Glasgow.

3. Marched to Glasgow and through the town on the Louisville pike, about two miles, to Beaver creek. Camped near plenty of water.

4. In camp all day. In the evening the regiment is formed in front of the colonel's headquarters, and an elegant stand of colors presented to the regiment by Miss Sheets and other ladies of Indianapolis. The presentation speech was made by Miss Sheets, a sister of First Lieutenant Harry Sheets, of Company "G." Lieutenant-Colonel Oyler accepted the colors with very appropriate remarks, returning the thanks of the regiment to the ladies for the magnificent stand of colors, assuring them that the men of the regiment would return them to the great state of Indiana unsullied and victorious. Three cheers and a tiger were given for the ladies.

5. Marched through Glasgow to Barren river and camped for the night.

6. Reveille before day. Marched to Scottville, Allen county, Kentucky, and camped for the night.

7. Up early. Snowing some. Marched at 12 M. Crossed into Tennessee at about 4 P. M. Snowing and raining. Camped in the woods, having marched twelve miles.

8. Up early. Marched after sun-up to Gallatin, Tenn., marched through town and three miles beyond and camped in a field of cedar, having marched twenty-five miles.

9. Sunday. Rested and cleaned up. Sunday morning inspection. Water and wood had to be carried a good distance.

10. Up early. Marched and crossed the Cumberland river on the Nashville pike. Formed in line of battle. Sent out skirmishers. Marched to Silver Springs. Camped.

11. Remained in camp. It is raining.

12. Up before day and in line of battle. It is rain-

ing. First Lieutenant Tyra Montgomery, of "K" company, resigned.

13. Up early. Policed the quarters. Companies drilled.

14. Up very early. Had breakfast; ordered to have dinner cooked and in haversack by 5 A. M., and be ready to fall in. Marched about one and one-half mile to a field and drilled all day. Returned to camp at sundown.

15. Up early. Marched to the same place, had company and battalion drill and returned to camp at sundown.

16. Up early. It is raining. The regiment is ordered in line to march out on picket. Went about three miles. Rained all night.

17. Relieved at 4 P. M. and marched to camp. It is still raining some. Second Lieutenant James P. Catterson mustered as first lieutenant company "F," vice Johnson resigned. Rev. Love H. Jameson mustered as chaplain of the regiment.

18. Up early. Drew clothing. Struck tents at 10 A. M. Marched at 10:30 A. M. eight miles without halting for rest. Passed near the Hermitage of General Jackson and gave three cheers as we passed. Camped at dark.

19. Up early. A detail is made from each company to work the road near the bridge burned by the rebels over Stone river. Rain all day.

20. Up early. Ordered to clean guns and accoutrements for general inspection. At 2 P. M. the regiment is formed and marched on picket.

21. Relieved from picket early and marched to camp. Ordered to get ready to march. Marched toward Nashville, turned to the left six miles from Nashville and went in camp on a high and dry place.

22. In camp near Nashville. Nothing important.
23. In camp near Nashville. Nothing important.
24. In camp near Nashville. Had battalion drill.
25. Up early, ready to march. Marched toward Nashville and camped two miles from town. First Sergeant Benjamin G. Poynter, "F" company, mustered as 2d lieutenant "F" company.
26. Up early. Cleaned up camp. Skirmish drill by companies and battalion drill.
27. Thanksgiving day; a day of rest for the soldier. The battalion attended divine services by Major Blankenship in the afternoon.
28. Up early. Drilled all forenoon. Ordered to get ready to march after dinner. Marched on the Murfreesboro pike about six miles, marching very fast, and camped near the state institution for the insane. It is a beautiful place for a camp.
29. Up early and policed camp in morning. Marched out some distance on picket after dinner.
30. Sunday. Relieved from picket and marched to camp before dark. Ordered to be ready for general review on to-morrow at 9 A. M.

DECEMBER, 1862.

1. Up early, prepared for review. Marched a mile from camp into a large field. Cloudy and cold. The general did not put in an appearance. Troops returned to camps.
2. Up early and marched to same place for review. Reviewed by Generals Rosencrans and Van Cleve. Marched in review and to camp just before dark. The regiment ordered on picket. Sergeant Geo. W. Clark, "G" company, mustered as 2d lieutenant of "G" company.

3. Relieved from picket in the afternoon. Policed camp and cleaned up.

4. Up early. Skirmish drill by company, then battalion drill. Continued drill all day.

5. Up early and ordered to get ready to go on picket. Snowing. Marched out on picket. Very cold. There was an eclipse of the moon.

6. Relieved from picket before dinner. Marched to camp. The men made flues in their tents. Stick chimneys.

7. Sunday. Up early. Very cold. Had company inspection. Drew rations at midnight.

8. Up early. Ordered to have three days' rations in our haversacks and be ready to move at any time. The order countermanded. Drilled all afternoon.

9. Up early. Drilled all morning. Dress parade at 4.30 P. M. Ordered out on the pike with brigade and marched about three miles to guard a forage train that had been attacked by the rebels. Marched back to camp. Ordered to be ready to march at a moment's notice and to sleep with arms by our side. Drew three days' rations.

10. Up early. Ordered to get ready for picket. Marched to the picket line, half mile out. An attack is expected.

11. Relieved from picket. Marched to camp before dark. The camp had been moved back three miles. The men who were not on picket put up tents.

12. Up very early. Ordered to escort forage train. Marched out with the brigade to the Hermitage, about ten miles. Found no rebels. Returned to camp by dark. Marched very fast.

13. Up early. Had company drills, battalion drill and dress parade.

14. Sunday. Up early. Cleaned up. Had inspec-

tion at 10 A. M. Attended divine services at 11 A. M., by the new chaplain, Love H. Jameson.

15. In camp. Nothing of importance. Raining.

16. Up early and in line, expecting attack. The regiment is ordered on picket.

17. Relieved from picket in the afternoon. Marched to camp. Captain Sanford C. Pruit, of "H" company, resigned.

18. Company and battalion drills. Dress parade. Major Robert Charlton, surgeon of the regiment, resigned.

19. Company and battalion drills. Dress parade.

20. Up early. Very cold. Company and battalion drills and dress parade. The rebels attacked the picket line after night. Captain Andrew W. Fuqua, "F" company, resigned. Disability.

21. Sunday. Policed camp. Inspection at 10 A. M. Divine services at 11 A. M. Dress parade 4:30 P. M.

22. Up early. Ordered to be ready for picket. Marched to the outposts. First Lieutenant James P. Catterson, "F" company, mustered as captain of "F" company, vice Fuqua, resigned.

23. Relieved from picket. Marched to camp.

24. In camp. Drills and routine duties.

25. Christmas. No difference between this and other days for soldiers. Cannonading is heard on the right.

26. Marched at 2 P. M. Cheers after cheers went up as we left camp. Cannonading in front. Marched late into the night. Camped one mile from Lavergne. Rain all day. Second Lieutenant John S. McDaniel, "D" company, died in hospital at Nashville.

27. Marched, at 10 A. M., beyond Lavergne about two miles. Ordered to countermarch back to the rear, and left to support some troops building a bridge over

Stewart creek. Reached the position late in the night. Camped.

28. In camp at this same place.

29. Monday. Ordered to march down the creek. Joined the division. Marched toward Murfreesboro. Crossed the bridge and arrived on the pike in a half hour. Reached the battlefield, within a mile of the rebel breastworks, and bivouacked.

30. The whole army was aroused at 5 A. M. Lines were formed, batteries placed in position commanding roads and the cavalry pushed forward on the flanks. There was slight firing on the outpost lines. During the day heavy skirmish lines, covering the front of the whole army, advanced and pressed forward, engaging the enemy's outposts. Reconnaissances found the enemy in force across Stone river. The fire of the skirmishers increased rapidly, and the artillery along the front opened fire occasionally, but there was no serious engagement. Dark, at 5 P. M., when the firing ceased. The casualties were few, and camp-rumors circulated that there were indications that the rebels were abandoning their position at Murfreesboro, retreating southward. The whole army bivouacked in line of battle. The weather cold, raw and intensely disagreeable. There was firing on the outposts during the night but no artillery firing. The night passed quietly.

31. The whole army was aroused at 5 A. M. and ordered into line. Arms were stacked and breakfast was cooked behind the stacks. The men were ordered to fill their canteens and be in readiness to march at any moment. The lines in reserve joined their respective commands. Immediately after daylight the 3d Division was ordered to move to the left. The other two divisions of the corps to follow at proper in-

tervals. The order of battle was for the 21st Army Corps to march to the left, crossing Stone's river; to advance until opposite and left of Murfreesboro, then by a turning movement to the right attack the enemy's right wing, double up his lines and push him on to his center. During this operation the center and right wing to remain in position until the turning movement on the left was executed, when the lines were to advance, attacking the enemy along his front. There was very little firing during the march to the left, and very little resistance by the enemy. When the position was reached from which the attack was to be made, the lines were formed, and strong skirmish lines pushed forward; heavy firing was heard, apparently on the right and rear of the Union lines, increasing every moment in intensity, and rapidly extending toward the left. In front of the left, facing the enemy's position in Murfreesboro there was no movement or action of any kind, not even a reply to the fire of the advancing skirmishes. At this time orders were received to countermarch by divisions and march rapidly to the right in the most expeditious manner possible. As soon as Stone's river was recrossed the brigades spread out, taking advantage of short cuts across fields to hurry forward. Where it was possible without interfering, or breaking up formations, the advance was made in double quick time. The distance to the right from Stone's river was fully three miles; such was the zeal of the troops that this distance was made very quickly, with the columns well closed up ready to form lines to move to the front. As the troops approached the right unmistakable signs of disaster became visible every moment. Artillery, ambulances, teams and groups of retreating soldiers flying in every direction to the rear. It then appeared, from what could be ascertained, that the right wing, General A. D. McCook commanding, while eating breakfast, and while the artillery teams, unhitched and going to water, with no disposition to receive an attack or resist an advance, was surprised by the enemy in strong force and driven to the rear in great confusion, exposing the right flank of the army. The unexpected attack came with such suddenness and vigor that it was impossible to form lines to resist, and the enemy penetrated the position, capturing a large number of officers and men and much of the artillery, and driving the confused masses to the rear with irresistible force. Surrounded by the debris of McCook's corps streaming to the rear, Beatty's 3d Brigade, 19th Ohio, 79th Indiana, 9th Kentucky, and 11th Kentucky reached a point where the railroad intersecting the pike formed a triangle. Being the first to arrive, the 3d Brigade was placed in position, where it was intended to form the right of the new line. During this formation there was danger of the forming line being swept away by the retreating troops of McCook, and the lines had to be opened for their passage. As soon as the lines could be reformed, the pursuing enemy came in sight, debouching out of the cedar woods. The front line of the 3d Brigade, the 19th Ohio and 9th Kentucky, supported by the 79th Indiana and 11th Kentucky, in second line, opened fire upon the approaching enemy, firing volley after volley with such effect as not only to stop the advance, but bringing the enemy to a halt, struggling in vain to advance out of the cedar woods, which combat was vigorously continued until the ammunition of the front line was nearly exhausted, when the second line was ordered forward to relieve it. The front line opened ranks, and the second line passed to the front, where, after firing a few volleys, it was ordered by General Rosencrans, who had been a spectator of the fight, to fix bayonets and drive back the enemy, promising support on the flanks. The advance was rapidly made, and prisoners were taken along the line, the enemy falling back to his original position. In the meantime, owing to a change of plan, the line was recalled and directed to a point on the right, where the Chicago Board of Trade Battery was in position on a slight elevation on a knoll, which became the center of the new line formed on the right of the center. Repeated charges were made upon this part of the line during the day, which were successfully beaten off by the infantry and artillery until night-fall, when the whole army reformed bivouacked in line of battle during the night. The night was bitter cold, and there was much suffering until the troops were allowed to kindle fires, when the army could cook its rations and the men warm themselves. There was very little firing during the night. The troops of both sides were willing to rest after the exhausting labors of the preceding day.

JANUARY, 1863.

1. Cold and gloomy. The 21st Army Corps was ordered to cross Stone's river and form on the left. Line of battle was formed, the artillery of the corps placed in position and strong skirmish lines pushed forward, but no advance ordered. During the day changes were made in the position, and the 1st and 2d Divisions of the corps were withdrawn across Stone's river to make closer connection with the left center. There was only slight skirmishing, with occasional cannon shots during the day, as the armies confronted each other. There was no serious move-

ment on either side. Ammunition was replenished and rations were issued. There was an alarm toward midnight, and lines were promptly formed. It was ascertained that the alarm was false, and the troops returned to their bivouacs.

2. Cold, cloudy and windy. Quiet all along the lines of both armies. After breakfast orders were issued for rigid inspection, and to put everything in serviceable condition. The whole forenoon passed away without any change of position of the 3d Division except that the 79th Indiana about noon was taken from its position and moved forward to fill a gap in the front line between the brigades of Fife and Price. No orders were given to Colonel Kneffer of any kind, nor was he ordered to report for orders to either of the brigade commanders of the front line of the division. The afternoon until 3 o'clock passed without any other change of position or change in the formation of the 3d Division. There was slight firing occasionally on the right but no movement of a serious nature. At 3 o'clock the batteries of the 3d Division, one after another, were withdrawn from their positions and moved back across Stone's river to the rear and the division remained apparently dangerously exposed on both flanks, without artillery. It remained very quiet until about 4 o'clock when indications of a movement by the enemy forming in front became visible. The skirmishers in front opened fire, which gradually extended along the whole front, increasing rapidly in violence. The skirmishers began falling back on their lines and reported the advance of a large column of the enemy, seven lines deep and supported by many batteries. The skirmishers attempted to retard the enemy's advance, but were rapidly pressed back by the front line of the advancing column, composed of

the whole Breckenridge corps and its artillery. When the front became cleared of the skirmishers the whole 3d Division opened fire upon the enemy, but after a few well directed volleys, which inflicted severe loss upon the front line, the rebels brought the second line to the front which rapidly forced the 3d Division into retreat to Stone's river, pursued by overwhelming numbers of the enemy. As the 3d Division descended the banks of the stream and was crossing it, thus uncovering the pursuing enemy, a fearful discharge of many batteries, massed on the high bank commanding the entire position of the 3d Division and its line of retreat, swept the front clear of the pursuing enemy, who in turn fell back rapidly, this time pursued by the 3d Division under cover of the artillery on the bluffs and a heavy column of infantry on the right which had remained concealed until this time—Negley's Division. The enemy quickly rallied and the whole line retreated again to the banks of Stone's river pursued by the enemy whose advance was again stopped by the concentrated fire of the massed artillery and pursued again to the original position of attack. This maneuver was repeated the third time, when the whole line, reinforced by heavy bodies of infantry on the right and left, and batteries of artillery, drove the enemy from the field, who retreated into his defensive works on the right of Murfreesboro. When darkness came and the fight ceased, the 3d Division occupied about the same threatening position from which it was recalled to the right on the morning of the 31st of December, 1862.

3. Up early and in line. Heavy cannonading and musketry is heard on the right.

4. Up early. Heavy rains. Mud is very deep in camp. It is rumored that the rebels have evacuated

Murfreesboro and that the Union troops are marching into the town. The report is confirmed at night, occasioning great rejoicing. Missing men are reporting to the regiment. The loss to the regiment is 124—killed, wounded and missing.

5. Up early and ready for duty. The battlefield indicates a great loss of life. Will probably reach nine or ten thousand on Union side in killed, wounded and missing. Trees twelve inches in diameter are cut off in places, where fighting was hot. Horses are laying around killed in every possible manner. Details busy burying the dead. Rained hard all night.

6. Up early. A detail is made from the regiment to guard a bridge in process of construction across Stone river. Weather pleasant, but cold.

7. Up early. Marched at 6 A. M. toward Murfreesboro. Marched about two miles and arrived at the town. Marched through the lower part of town, then out on the Lebanon pike about two miles and went in camp in a wood near the road on rebel General Maney's place, Murfreesboro. Presents a very desolate appearance now, all business houses being closed and many private houses turned into hospitals.

8. Wagons came up to-day with our camp equipage and tents are put up. Volunteer surgeons came from Indianapolis, to attend on the wounded. The weather is damp and disagreeable. Men are recovering from their fatigue.

9. Up early. Men are taking it easy, resting and writing home.

10. In camp. Men are cleaning up their clothing, first time in two weeks they have had an opportunity.

11. In camp. Lieutenant Howe, of Company "I," detailed to command Company "E," the captain and

first lieutenant being wounded in the battle of Stone river. The second lieutenant is in hospital at Nashville.

12. In camp. Men are taking time easy and are ready for active duty.

13. Up early. Laid off camp and policed quarters. Regiment camped in a convenient and beautiful location; water and wood convenient; easily drained; guards are stationed about the camp, which is quiet and lonesome. It is observed that the battle had the effect of increasing sociability and good feeling among the men and officers.

14. Up at reveille. Camp guards are relieved on account of very hard rain. At 3 P. M. it rained harder than any time since the regiment marched into Tennessee; a dismal sleet followed in the morning. Several ladies came from Indianapolis as volunteer nurses.

15. Up at reveille. Had roll-call. It is very cold to-day, so cold it is almost impossible to keep warm. The ladies can not have a good opinion of soldiering, taking the weather as a specimen. Colonel Knefler does not approve of the presence of ladies in camp.

16. Reveille. Roll-call. The regiment detailed for picket. Marched out to the line. Company "E" is stationed at an elegant house, formerly occupied by a man now in the rebel army. The house was at one time luxuriously furnished. It is now stripped of everything, such as books, furniture, pictures, etc.; nothing is left but the bare walls.

17. Relieved from picket duty at 2 P. M. Marched to camp. The weather still very cold.

18. Reveille. Roll called. The men are building fire-places in their tents. The bricks were appropriated from some brick kilns near by camp, the property of some rebel.

19. Up at reveille. Roll-call at 5 P. M. Men are

5

busy completing chimneys in tents and making themselves comfortable generally. Preparing to take things easy.

20. Reveille at 5 A. M. Roll called. Camp guards stationed this morning. Raining. Very muddy.

21. Reveille at 5 A. M. and roll-call. Ordinary routine duties of camp resumed, policing and company drills as in former times. Men do not take much interest in company drills. Weather pleasant, but muddy.

22. Reveille at 5 A. M. and roll called. Mail very irregular, owing to a break on the L. & N. R. R. Cloudy and looks like rain. In Tennessee at this season it rains on an average every other day.

23. Reveille at 5 A. M. Roll called. Rumors of good news from the east. Grand victory by General Burnside reported.

24. Reveille at 5 A. M. Roll called. Camp guard is taken off. Regiment is detailed for picket and marched out to the line. The picket line is extended to the identical ground occupied by the rebels during the battle of Stone river. Broken guns, pieces of shells, etc., are laying around in abundance. Rained nearly all night.

25. Relieved at 2 P. M. Marched to camp. Weather damp and disagreeable. Men are anxious to go home. Desertions are reported quite frequent all over the army. Major Perry M. Blankenship resigned.

26. Reveille at 5 A. M. and roll called. Company drills and rest is all the men have to do. The sad diminution of the regiment does not tend to create cheerfulness. The hospitals are crowded with men who have succumbed to hardships, greatly reducing the effective strength of the army.

27. Reveille at 5 A. M. Roll called. The regiment is detailed for picket. Marched out to the line. The reason that the regiment is detailed for picket duty so often is on account of most of the division working on the fortifications around Murfreesboro.

28. Relieved at 2 P. M. and marched to camp.

29. Reveille at 5 A. M. Roll called. All quiet in camp.

30. Reveille at 5 A. M. Roll called. The regiment is detailed for picket. Marched out to the line. All quiet on the line. First Lieutenant John R. Cotton, "A" company, resigned.

31. Relieved at 1 P. M. Marched to camp. Weather is mild. Roads are very muddy and almost impassable. There is much sickness in camp. Many men are despondent and homesick. James A. Harris appointed and mustered in as captain of "A" company.

FEBRUARY, 1863.

1. Ordered in line and marched about a mile and worked on a fort. The earthwork is sixteen feet thick and six feet high. The ditch in front is twelve feet wide and six feet deep.

2. In camp. Very cold. Had dress parade.

3. In camp. Very cold. Had dress parade.

4. In camp. Very cold. Had dress parade. Snowing.

5. In camp. Very cold. Had dress parade. Snowing. Sergeant Geo. G. Earl, of "A" company, mustered as 2d lieutenant of "A" company.

6. Up at 3 P. M. Ordered foraging. Started at daylight, on Lebanon pike, to Stone river. Not being able to cross, turned to the left and marched two miles to a field. Pickets were stationed while the teams were being loaded. Marched back to camp, arriving at 4 P. M.

7. In camp. Ordered to be ready to march with three days' rations at 5:30 P. M. Cannonading is heard in the distance. Second Lieutenant Wm. S. Cardell, "C" company, promoted 1st lieutenant "C" company. Sergeant Edwin M. Byrkit mustered as 2d lieutenant of "C" company. Sergeant Isaac W. Stubbs, of "F" company, promoted 1st lieutenant of "F" company and mustered. Captain Manker, of "B" company, mustered in as surgeon of the regiment.

8. Up at 4 P. M. A detachment of the regiment marched to Murfreesboro. Got in wagons and started for Nashville. Marched to the court-house. Got supper there and slept in a very large room. Richard E. Perrott, of "F" company, appointed and mustered as 2d lieutenant of "F" company.

9. Detachment in Nashville while the teams were being loaded.

10. Up at 3 A. M. Detachment started for Murfreesboro with teams. The roads very bad. The teams strung out along the pike. Very muddy and badly cut up. Halted at Lavergne for the night.

11. Detachment up at daylight. Marched a short distance. Halted a long time, waiting for pontoon bridges. Waited until dark. Being out of rations, the colonel ordered the adjutant to draw rations of sugar, coffee, pork and crackers. Bivouacked.

12. In marching order at 2 A. M. Started to march at 4 A. M. Marched at quick time to the river. Crossed on a flat boat. Got to camp at 12 M.

13. In camp resting. Routine duties. No drills.

14. Regiment on picket. Raining. A forage train is attacked by the rebels, who are repulsed.

15. Relieved from picket. In camp. Called up at 10 P. M. and formed in line. Ordered to quarters and slept on arms.

16. Ordered to get ready for inspection. Raining.

17. Up at daylight. Had dress parade in the evening. Raining.

18. Regiment on picket. Marched three miles to the picket line. The line was moved out. Ordered to have no fires. Movement of rebels expected.

19. Relieved at 11 A. M. Marched to camp. Drew eight days' rations. Dress parade.

20. Policed quarters. Ordered to get ready for inspection. Dress parade in the evening.

21. Ordered on picket.

22. Relieved from picket. Marched to camp. Dress parade in the afternoon. Salute is fired, being Washington's birthday.

23. In camp. Drilled. Dress parade. Ordered to be ready to go foraging at 6 A. M.

24. Up at 5. Ready to march at 6 A. M. Marched at 7 A. M. to Stone river; down the river seven miles to a large corn field. Loaded up. Marched back to camp. Very muddy and hard marching.

25. In camp. Rain all day. No drills or dress parade. All in quarters.

26. In camp. Rain until nearly 5 P. M. Dress parade. Orders read. Reveille every morning at 5 A. M. In line of battle at 5:15 A. M. Roll called and stand to arms until daylight. Until further orders, details to be made for picket from each company.

27. Reveille 5 A. M. In line until daylight. Company drills.

28. Reveille 5 A. M. In line until daylight. Company drills.

MARCH, 1863.

1. Reveille at 5 A. M. In line. Inspection. George

Harris, "D" company, appointed 2d lieutenant "D" company, mustered in this day.

2. Reveille at 5 A. M. In line. Drilled.

3. Reveille at 5 A. M. In line. Drilled. Freezing.

4. Reveille at 5 A. M. In line. Drilled. Had dress parade. By general orders rolls are called five times each day.

5. Reveille at 5 A. M. In line. The regiment was mustered for pay.

6. Reveille at 5 A. M. In line. Rain.

7. Reveille at 5 A. M. In line. Drill and dress parade. Rain and hail in the night.

8. Reveille at 5 A. M. In line. At 1 P. M. the battalion is formed for divine services. Dress parade.

9. Reveille at 5 A. M. In line. Ordered to strike tents. Ready to march. Formed line and marched after dinner, on the Lebanon pike, to Stone river. Halted there to guard pontoon bridges. Bivouacked on a hill called Pebble Hill. Raining.

10. In bivouac at Pebble Hill. Cleared off.

11. In bivouac at Pebble Hill. Clear.

12. In camp at Pebble Hill. Ordered to put up tents.

13. In camp at Pebble Hill. The regiment received two months' pay. Drilled.

14. In camp at Pebble Hill. Drilled morning and afternoon.

15. In camp at Pebble Hill. Drilled morning and afternoon.

16. In camp at Pebble Hill. Moved camp about two hundred yards.

17. In camp at Pebble Hill. Ordered to be ready for general inspection at 2 P. M.

18. In camp at Pebble Hill. Raining.

19. In camp at Pebble Hill. Ordered to strike tents

ready to move. Marched back to Murfreesboro and camped. Colonel Kneffer in command of brigade during General Beatty's absence.

20. Camp at Murfreesboro. Ditching and fixing up camp.

21. Camp at Murfreesboro. Ordered to make ready for inspection. Dress parade.

22. Camp at Murfreesboro. Inspection. Divine services. Dress parade.

23. Camp at Murfreesboro. General inspection. Dress parade.

24. Camp at Murfreesboro. Drilled morning. Rain in the afternoon. William P. Mount mustered in as 1st lieutenant of "H" company.

25. Camp at Murfreesboro. Raining. Routine duties.

26. Camp at Murfreesboro. Drills and dress parade.

27. Camp at Murfreesboro. Rain and storm.

28. Reveille 4 A. M. Raining, cold and windy.

29. Reveille 4 A. M. Company inspections. Rain and wind. Shelter tents issued to regiment and the brigade.

30. Reveille 4 A. M. Drill and routine duties during forenoon. Dress parade. Rain and snow.

31. Reveille 4 A. M. Drill and routine duties during forenoon. Dress parade.

APRIL, 1863.

1. Reveille 4 A. M. Drill and routine duties during forenoon. Dress parade.

2. Reveille 4 A. M. Drill and routine duties during forenoon. Dress parade.

3. Reveille 4 A. M. Drill and routine duties during forenoon. Dress parade.

4. Reveille 4 A. M. Drill and routine duties during forenoon. Dress parade.
5. Reveille 4 A. M. Company inspections. Dress parade.
6. Reveille 4 A. M. Drill. Dress parade.
7. Reveille 4 A. M. Drill. Dress parade.
8. Reveille 4 A. M. Drill. Dress parade.
9. Reveille 4 A. M. Drill. Dress parade.
10. Reveille 4 A. M. Drill. Dress parade.
11. Reveille 4 A. M. Drill. Dress parade. Rain.
12. Reveille 4 A. M. General inspection of regiment. Drill and dress parade, witnessed by General Beatty and ladies.
13. Reveille 4 A. M. Drill and dress parade.
14. Reveille 4 A. M. Drill and dress parade.
15. Reveille 4 A. M. Rain.
16. Reveille 4 A. M. Brigade ordered on reconnaissance.
17. On reconnaissance.
18. Regiment returned in the evening to camp.
19. Reveille 4 A. M. Company inspection. Drew two months' pay. Ordered to be ready to march at moment's notice. Order to march countermanded.
20. Reveille 4 A. M. Company and skirmish drills, battalion drill and dress parade.
21. Reveille 4 A. M. Drill. Rain in afternoon.
22. Reveille 4 A. M. Drill. Dress parade.
23. Reveille 4 A. M. Company and skirmish drills in forenoon. Battalion drill. Dress parade. Regimental Quartermaster Wm. C. Shortridge resigned.
24. Reveille 4 A. M. Battalion drill. Dress parade.
25. Reveille 4 A. M. Battalion drill. Dress parade.
26. Reveille 4 A. M. Sunday. Had company inspection and dress parade. Order published private in Company "A" sentenced to carry a 24-pound ball

and chain 10 days for leaving post while on camp guard and getting drunk.

27. Reveille 4 A. M. Company skirmish and battalion drill. Dress parade.

28. Reveille at 4 A. M. Ordered to strike large tents and pitch the shelter tents. Order countermanded. Company skirmish and battalion drills. Dress parade.

29. Reveille at 4 A. M. Ordered to strike large tents and pitch shelter tents; shelter tents put up three times before it was approved. Quartermaster-Sergeant Jacob H. Colclazer mustered as 1st lieutenant and quartermaster of regiment.

30. Reveille 4 A. M. Regiment set out cedars in the company streets. Inspection and muster at 2 P. M. Dress parade.

MAY, 1863.

1. Reveille 4 A. M. Company skirmish, battalion drill and dress parade.

2. Reveille 4 A. M. Company skirmish, battalion drills and dress parade.

3. Sunday. Reveille 4 A. M. Regimental inspection. Dress parade.

4. Reveille 4 A. M. Dress parade.

5. Reveille 4 A. M. Rain. Dress parade.

6. Reveille 4 A. M. Rain. Dress parade.

7. Reveille 4 A. M. Rain.

8. Reveille 4 A. M. Rain. Dress parade.

9. Reveille 4 A. M. Company skirmish, battalion drill and dress parade.

10. Sunday. Reveille 4 A. M. Company inspection and dress parade. Order is read reducing William F. McIlvain, Company "F," to the ranks, for absenting himself from camp without leave.

11. Reveille 4 A. M. Put out more cedars in streets. Dress parade.

12. Reveille, 4 A. M. General inspection, 3 P. M. Brigade drill.

13. Reveille, 4 A. M. Fixed up streets in the morning. Battalion and brigade drills afternoon.

14. Reveille, 4 A. M. Routine same as yesterday.

15. Reveille, 4 A. M. Policed quarters and company drills in the forenoon. Brigade drill and dress parade afternoon.

16. Reveille, 4 A. M. Battalion drill from 5 to 6 A. M. Put up new cedar trees. Dress parade.

17. Sunday. Reveille, 4 A. M. Company inspection. Dress parade.

18. Reveille, 4 A. M. Battalion drill from 5 to 6 A. M.

19. Reveille, 4 A. M. Company and brigade drill and dress parade.

20. Reveille, 4 A. M. Company and brigade drill and dress parade.

21. Reveille, 4 A. M. Battalion drill from 5 to 6 A. M. Company drills. Dress parade.

22. Reveille, 4 A. M. Battalion drill from 5 to 6 A. M. Ordered to be ready for general review. No review. Battalion drill and dress parade.

23. Reveille, 4 A. M. Company and battalion drills. Dress parade.

24. Reveille, 4 A. M. Company inspection. Divine services. Dress parade.

25. Reveille at 4 A. M. Battalion drill from 5 to 6 A. M. Formed in line at 9 A. M. to receive orders. Three cheers for General Grant for good news of advance on Vicksburg. Dress parade and drilled until sundown.

26. Reveille at 4 A. M. Routine as yesterday, except as to orders.

27. Reveille at 4 A. M. General inspection. Dress parade at 5 P. M. Battalion drill until the moon shone.

28. Reveille as usual. Roll call and inspection before breakfast. Ordered to be ready for regimental inspection at 5 P. M.

29. Reveille. Regimental review. Dress parade. Battalion drill until dark.

30. Reveille at 4 A. M. Company and battalion drill. Dress parade.

31. Sunday. Reveille at 4 A. M. Regimental inspection. Afternoon, rain.

JUNE, 1863.

1. Reveille. Battalion drill between 5 and 6 A. M. Company drill. Dress parade at 5 P. M. and battalion drill until dark.

2. Reveille at 4 A. M., same as yesterday. A negro servant is accidentally killed.

3. Reveille at 4 A. M. Rain. Dress parade. Order read that Major Wallace was discharged from the service. Ordered six days' rations to be carried in haversacks and knapsacks.

4. Reveille at 4 A. M. Battalion drill from 5 to 6 A. M. Company drill. Dress parade. Battalion drill until dark. Cannonading is heard in the distance.

5. Reveille at 4 A. M. Ordered to prepare for general review at 5 P. M. It rained. Dress parade.

6. Reveille at 4 A. M. Rain. Dress parade at 5 P. M.

7. Reveille at 4 A. M. Drills and dress parade. General inspection.

8. Reveille at 4 A. M. Ordered to march at 1 P. M. to report at division headquarters to attend execution

of a deserter. Order countermanded. Dress parade at 5 p. m. Battalion drill until dark.

9. Reveille at 4 a. m. Battalion drill from 5 to 6 a. m. Company drill in the morning. Drew Enfield rifles in the afternoon. Dress parade and battalion drill.

10. Reveille at 4 a. m. Rain in forenoon. Dress parade and battalion drill.

11. Reveille at 4 a. m. Rain in the morning. marched to fort to turn over Vincennes rifles drawn at Louisville in September, 1862. Dress parade at 5 p. m. Surgeon Lewis Manker resigned. John L. Hanna mustered as captain of "H" company.

12. Reveille at 4 a. m. General inspection in forenoon. Dress parade. Battalion drill. First Assistant Surgeon William G. McFadden appointed surgeon of the regiment.

13. Reveille at 4 a. m. Battalion drill from 5 to 6. William Jacobs, of Company "C," accidentally shot while going on picket. Dress parade at 5 p. m., and battalion drill until dark.

14. Sunday. Reveille at 4 a. m. Company inspection. Dress parade.

15. Reveille at 4 a. m. Battalion drill from 5 to 6 a. m. Company drill in forenoon. Dress parade and battalion drill after. Ordered to be ready to march at 8 a. m. to attend execution of a deserter.

16. Reveille as usual. Battalion formed. Marched about one and one-half miles from Murfreesboro. Halted on the left side of the Lebanon pike in a cloverfield. Took position in the brigade. The division was formed in the shape of a three-sided square. The soldier was a member of the 9th Kentucky, and had deserted several times, and was apprehended each time. The last time he was sentenced to be shot. A

detail was made of a certain number of men from the division. These men were given guns, some loaded and some not. The man was blindfolded and seated on his coffin. At the command given, "Fire!" he fell over backward dead, and, as he lay in this position, the whole division marched past the body and were given an opportunity to see what was the doom of the deserter. Drilled. Non-commission drill. Dress parade. Battalion drill.

17. Reveille at 4 A. M. Battalion drill from 5 to 6 A. M. Company drill. Dress parade and battalion drill during day.

18. Routine same as yesterday.

19. Routine same as yesterday.

20. Routine same as yesterday.

21. Sunday. Reveille as usual. Company inspection. Dress parade. Sergeant Simeon J. Thompson appointed second lieutenant "B" company, but not mustered.

22. Reveille at 4 A. M. Battalion drill from 5 to 6 A. M. Company drill. Dress parade and battalion drill during day.

23. Routine same as yesterday.

24. Reveille at 4 A. M. Battalion drill from 5 to 6 A. M.; 9 A. M. ordered to prepare to march. Cannonading is heard in front. Struck tents at 1 P. M. Started at 2 P. M. and marched to the depot, and to the fortifications, and at 4 P. M. stacked arms in the mud and put up our tents near Lunette Davis. Raining.

25. Reveille at 4 A. M. Raining. Very muddy. Cannonading heard in front.

26. Reveille at 4 A. M. Raining hard. Wounded men brought to the rear.

27. Reveille at 4 A. M. Ordered to be prepared to

march at a moment's notice, with seven days' rations. Still raining.

28. Sunday. Reveille at 4 A. M. Marched at 3 P. M. to the Manchester pike in the center of a train. At 8 P. M. halted for the night. Still raining.

29. Reveille at 4:30 A. M. and marched at 5:30, and passed Hoover's Gap. Halted on the north fork of Duck river at 4 P. M. Twenty-one miles from Murfreesboro. Still raining.

30. Reveille. Fell in at 2 P. M. and marched back to the place where the regiment halted and bivouacked the night before. Put up tents at 9 P. M. A detail of twenty-four men from each company was detailed to load ammunition.

JULY, 1863.

1. Reveille 4:30 A. M. Started at 7 A. M. Marched in the rear of a train. Ordered to assist wagons out of the mud; passed through the Gap and reached Manchester at 8 P. M.; crossed the East fork of Duck river on a pontoon; camped, having marched nine miles.

2. Reveille at 5 A. M. Cavalry corps passed here, moving to the front. At 9 A. M. regiment started to hunt a camp, but could do no better, so came back to old position; put up tents in regular order; established pickets.

3. Reveille 4 A. M. Made detail for brigade guard. Remained in camp.

4. Reveille at 4 A. M. National salute fired by artillery. Raining. Heavy cannonading in front.

5. Reveille at 4 A. M. In camp. Raining still.

6. Reveille at 4 A. M. In camp.

7. Reveille at 4 A. M. Company and battalion drills.

8. Reveille at 4 A. M. Raining. A salute fired in

honor of General Grant's capture of Vicksburg and news of battle of Gettysburg.

9. Reveille 4 A. M. Six A. M. general sounded strike tent. Prepared to march and marched toward McMinnville. Halted 7 P. M. to camp, having marched nine and one-half miles.

10. Reveille at 4 A. M. Started at 5 A. M. Marched to the river; waded across, as both the railroad and wagon bridges were burned. Camped near the fair ground in the edge of the town of McMinnville, twenty-two miles from Manchester.

11. Reveille 4 A. M. Pitched tents. Company drills. Dress parade.

12. Reveille. Regiment formed for company inspection. Company inspection. Dress parade.

13. Reveille 4 A. M. Raining. Cleared off place for drill ground. Drew rations. Dress parade.

14. Reveille 4 A. M. Ordered to be ready for general inspection at 10 A. M. After inspection company drill. Dress parade at 5:30 P. M. Ordered to have 10 days' rations.

15. Reveille 4 A. M. Struck tents at 7 A. M. Ready to move. Marched 8 P. M. Marched one mile and bivouacked.

16. Reveille at 4 A. M. Battalion drill. Dress parade. Capt. Wm. B. Ellis of "I" company resigned.

17. Reveille 4 A. M. In camp.

18. Reveille 4 A. M. Detail ordered five men from each company for scout, Capt. Parker commanding. Dress parade.

19. Sunday. Company inspection 9 A. M. Scouts returned this evening. Dress parade.

20. Reveille. Company drill. Dress parade at 5. Battalion drill after.

21. Same as yesterday.

22. Same as yesterday.

23. Reveille. Formed the battalion, had roll-call. Company drill. Graded camp streets. Dress parade and battalion drill.

24. Same as yesterday.

25. Reveille 4 A. M. Regiment paid for 4 months. Colonel formed the regiment in square to give instructions how to send money home.

26. Sunday. Reveille. Captain Ellis started for home at 4 A. M. Company inspection 9 A. M. Dress parade in the afternoon.

27. Reveille. Company drills. Dress parade in the afternoon and battalion drill after.

28. Reveille. Formed line and had inspection. A detail of three men ordered from each company for foraging. Dress parade.

29. Reveille. Company drill in morning. Dress parade and battalion drill.

30. Same as yesterday.

31. Reveille. Ordered to prepare streets and quarters for inspection at 11 A. M. General inspection. Rain. Sergeant Wheatley, of Company "I," died in hospital. Dress parade. Battalion drill.

August, 1863.

1. Reveille. First Lieutenant D. W. Howe mustered captain company "I," vice W. B. Ellis, resigned. First Sergeant Batchelor promoted first lieutenant of "I" company, vice D. W. Howe, promoted captain of "I" company. Captain James A. Harris, of "A" company, resigned. Dress parade.

2. Sunday. Company inspection. Dress parade in the afternoon.

3. Reveille. Company drills in the morning. Dress parade and battalion drill after.

4. Reveille. Company drills in the morning at 4 P. M. Ordered on reconnaissance. At 5:30 P. M. marched out on Sparta road, waded the river. Marched over hills and mountains and at 12 M. halted at Collins river, near Rocky Island, about fifteen miles from McMinnville. Came on to the rebel cavalry pickets and captured them. Formed line of battle. Slept on arms after posting pickets.

5. Up at day. Marched back to camp at McMinnville by another road. Marched a few miles and rested until 12 M. Crossed over the mountains, having cattle, hogs and sheep for the division. Waded the river. Got to camp at 4:30, having marched thirty or thirty-five miles.

6. By order of President, Thanksgiving day, for victories at Vicksburg and Gettysburg. No duty. Dress parade.

7. Reveille. Rain all day.

8. Reveille. Company inspection at 10 A. M. Dress parade in the evening.

9. Sunday. Regimental inspection, 5:30 A. M. Dress parade, 6:30 P. M.

10. Reveille. Company drills in the morning. Dress parade. Battalion drill until 8 P. M.

11. Same as yesterday.

12. General inspection at 12 M. Dress parade. Battalion drill.

13. Reveille. Rain. Dress parade and battalion drill until 8 P. M.

14. Reveille at 4 A. M. Rain. Companies "A" and "F" are very noisy and the colonel ordered the two companies formed. Roll called and remain under arms all night.

15. Reveille at 4 A. M. Several members of companies "A" and "F" punished and some of the non-

commissioned officers reduced to ranks for suffering disorderly, drunken conduct in quarters. Inspection. 4 P. M. Dress parade, 6 P. M. Ordered to be ready to move at 6 A. M. to-morrow.

16. Sunday. Reveille at 4 A. M. General sounded. Struck tent. Ready to move. Marched at 12 M. Marched on road to Pikeville. Waded Baron fork of Collins river. It began to rain. At 3 P. M. waded Collins river and camped six miles from McMinnville.

17. Reveille at 2:30 A. M. Ready to march. A corn-cob battle took place and got very hot until stopped by the colonel. This bivouac was a great place for snakes of the black and copperhead species. Assembly sounded, marched at 10 A. M. Arrived at the foot of Cumberland Mountains at 12 M. Assisted teams getting up. Roads are very rough. Reached the top at 6 P. M. and had a beautiful view of the valley and country for miles around. The roll called and started again, the boys yelling. Result of a raid on sutler wagon. Many baskets of champagne found in them. Marched. When arrived at the hill descending to Stony branch, halted for teams to come up and park. Orders to bivouac before lying down to rest. Orders came to march to brigade headquarters some distance off. Marched and crossed the branch. Bivouacked eleven miles from McMinnville.

18. Reveille 5 A. M. Detail of six men from each company to help the teams along. Marched at 10:20 A. M. Found plenty of good springs on the mountain. Crossed Brushy branch at 1 P. M. Crossed Rock Creek at 3 P. M. Found good road at 7 P. M. Went down quite a hill and halted to bivouac. Marched thirteen and one-half miles.

19. Reveille at 4 A. M. Marched at 5:15 A. M. Brigade in front. Four men from each company with

teams. Roads very bad and rocky. Rocks twenty inches and two feet perpendicular in the road, making it very hard for teams to keep up. Worked the roads. Marching at 9 A. M. Got to a point on the mountain where the Sequatchee Valley could be seen, a beautiful sight. Began to descend the mountain road two miles to the valley below. Marching down old negro John entertained the regiment with his songs, that could be heard on the next range of mountains, the boys joining in the chorus and cheering him. At 10:10 got to the valley and halted for rest. Marched up the valley, our flags flying to the breeze, and passed through Pikeville. Camped at 2:30 P. M. Marched thirteen miles.

20. Reveille at 4 A. M. Green corn issued as rations. Put up tents.

21. Reveille at 4 A. M. Raining. Fixed up camp.

22. Reveille at 4 A. M. Raining. Fixed up camp.

23. Sunday. Reveille at 4 A. M. Company inspection at 9 A. M. Very hot.

24. Reveille at 4 A. M. Dress parade.

25. Reveille at 4 A. M. Rain nearly all day.

26. Reveille at 4 A. M. Cleared off and colder.

27. Reveille at 4 A. M. Nothing important.

28. Reveille at 4 A. M. Ordered to be ready for general inspection to-morrow at 10 A. M. Dress parade at 5 P. M.

29. Reveille as usual. General inspection at 10 A. M. Dress parade at 5:30 P. M. Ordered to be ready to go with supply train to McMinnville in the morning. The colonel ordered the men to stand in line for yelling.

30. Reveille at 4 A. M. The regiment in line at 6 A. M. Five companies start with train to McMinnville.

31. Ordered to prepare to march in the morning.

SEPTEMBER, 1863.

1. Reveille at 3:30 A. M. Struck tents, packed up everything, loaded wagons, marched at 6:10 A. M. toward Dunlap. Stopped to camp at 1:40 P. M., having marched fifteen miles.

2. Reveille at 3 A. M. Marched at 6 A. M. Arrived at Dunlap at 9 A. M. Passed through and marched toward Jasper. Bivouacked at 4 P. M. Marched nineteen miles. Second Lieutenant Richard E. Perrott resigned.

3. Reveille at 4:30. Marched at 6 A. M. Brigade in front. Very foggy. Arrived at Jasper at 1:15 P. M. Stacked arms. Bivouacked, having marched thirteen miles. Rations of beef and other rations issued. Cartridges also issued.

4. Reveille at 3:30 A. M. Started at 5 A. M. with the teams, so as to meet the other part of the regiment. Marched toward Bridgeport. A detail of forty is made as advance guard. Marched five miles and came to the Tennessee river. Marched down the river and crossed Battle creek near where it empties into the Tennessee river. Marched to Bridgeport, arriving at 2:45 P. M. Could not cross the river. Marched down about one mile and bivouacked for the night.

5. Reveille at 5 A. M. Marched at 6 A. M. to the bridge across the Tennessee river, where the other part of the regiment was waiting. Crossed the river at 9:45 A. M. to an island, and at 10:20 A. M. crossed from the island. The pontoon bridge is 1,500 feet long, the first section to the island being 1,000 feet; the other section 500 feet. Marched a few miles, and halted to allow the teams to close up. Marched again and camped about six miles from Bridgeport. Drew

three days' rations. Ordered to join the brigade. Marched very fast and caught up with the brigade. Marched very slow and unsteady by the side of a mountain for miles, where the road was only wide enough for two wagons to pass between the river and the mountain. Some of the teams rolled in the river. The railroad was up higher on the side of the mountain. Turned to the right among the hills and mountains over some very rocky road, making it unsteady marching, causing men to stagger as if drunk, it being dark. Halted in a corn field, in a hollow, between two mountains, about fourteen miles from Bridgeport. Bivouacked at 12:30 A. M. Marched half the night.

6. Reveille at 5:30 A. M. Marched at 8 A. M. Brigade in front of the division. Marched in a gap, and the road very bad. At 10 A. M. halted and stacked arms to rest. The ammunition train passed; also a large drove of beef cattle. The wagons kept passing in the night. Bivouacked for the night, having only marched two miles.

7. Reveille at 5 A. M. Rations of beef and bacon issued. Cannonading heard as if on top of the mountain. Halted all day waiting orders.

8. Reveille at 3 A. M. Regiment in the rear of division. Started at 5:45 A. M. and marched three miles. Stopped very often. Men who had no guns were ordered to carry stretchers and report to surgeons. Moved down about 100 yards further, and camped for the night.

9. At 1:20 A. M. the regiment was aroused without sound of bugle. Twenty rounds of cartridges were issued, to be carried in pockets, cartridge box being full. Ordered to march as quietly as possibly. The 79th Regiment in front of the brigade. Marched

through fields and hollows, over hills and down, waded creeks and streams. Toward morning got to the foot of Lookout Mountain. Started up the mountain by a path known as the Nicka Jack Trace. Companies "C" and "G" deployed in advance as skirmishers. Reached the crest without opposition. The skirmishers advanced toward the point. Halted and stacked arms at 7 A. M. The rebels had left a few minutes before. A signal station was established. On the mountain while waiting orders the regiment put in the time viewing magnificent scenery all around as far as the eye could reach. Filled canteens from Lula Lake, a body of water on top of the mountain. At 12:30 P. M. orders came to march to Chattanooga, which was reported to have been evacuated by the rebel army. Started and reached the point of Lookout at 3:30 P. M. The sight that here met the eyes was one never to be forgotten. Far down in the valley below was Bragg's whole rebel army marching on the roads out of Chattanooga leading south, raising clouds of dust, concealing them almost from view. The plateau of Lookout is so high (2,410 feet above the Tennessee river) that an army wagon in the valley below looks no bigger than an umbrella. The Allegheny and Cumberland mountains and Missionary Ridge are in plain sight. It is said that seven different States can be seen from the top of Lookout Mountain. When the whole division had assembled on the plateau, it was marched ten miles to the point, from the point five miles down to the town of Chattanooga by a fair road cut out of the side of the mountain. After resting the whole division marched down. When Chattanooga was reached the division turned to the right in the direction of where the rebels had been seen. When three miles beyond the town the regiment bivouacked for the night, having marched twenty-four or twenty-five miles. The dust on the road out of Chattanooga was shoe-top deep, the whole of the rebel army having marched over the roads.

10. Reveille, 4:30 A. M. Marched, at 8 A. M., a short distance and halted. Marched again soon, and at 2 P. M. formed in line of battle in rear of the artillery, waiting for train to come up, as the troops were out of rations. Heavy skirmishing in front, where rebel cavalry in strong force made its appearance. About twelve miles from Chattanooga bivouacked for the night.

11. Reveille, 5 A. M. Marched, 6:30 A. M., toward Ringgold, skirmishing all the way with rebel cavalry. The artillery shelled the rebel cavalry at 9 A. M., and, retiring, they set the railroad bridges in front on fire as they retreated. Marched into Ringgold at 10 A. M., having marched six miles to-day; formed in line of battle, then by the right of company to the front, and marched about one-half mile through the woods along the railroad in a gap and halted to let Wilder's brigade of mounted infantry pass to take the front. Wilder shelled the rebels for two hours, and, it was reported, killed and wounded many of the rebel cavalry. Marched three miles beyond Ringgold, wading the creeks where the bridges were burned. In camp at 3:45 P. M. Pickets exchanged shots with the rebels all night.

12. Reveille, 4 A. M. Marched, 5 P. M., back to Ringgold, and, after resting, the division marched toward Chattanooga, about eight miles distant. Marched on another road about four miles, and camped about twelve miles from Chattanooga.

13. Aroused 4 A.M. Formed in line of battle to await developments. At 9 A. M. marched about one mile and came in sight of the enemy's skirmish line in

front. The brigade formed in line of battle. Colonel Kneffer ordered to command skirmish line of division on both sides of the road. The skirmishers advanced, and, arriving on top of a ridge of hills bordering an open field, the enemy opened with artillery, about 11 A. M. The first shot struck just in front of the colors, passing under a fence behind which part of the regiment was in line, covering the men with dirt. The same shot or shell passed under the adjutant's and lieutenant-colonel's horses. The rebels had two pieces in the road, and had a good aim at the line. After the first shot, Captain Drury, of the 2d Wisconsin, ordered his battery in position by blowing a whistle. The battery came into position, and soon silenced the rebels with a few well aimed shots. When the battery came up Captain Drury was severely wounded and would have fallen off his horse, had not one of his lieutenants assisted him. The skirmishers pressed back the enemy for more than three miles, but their artillery fired very lively as they retreated. At 12:30 P. M. the line was halted, the object of the reconnaissance had been accomplished. At 3:30 P. M. marched back in the direction of the old camp. Crossed the river. Marched about one mile beyond and bivouacked.

14. Reveille 3 A. M. Marched at 8 A. M. toward the river, turned west instead of crossing, and marched toward Lookout Mountain about three miles. Halted and stacked arms in the shade. The men suffered much for water; none could be had. At 6:15 P. M. the bugle sounded. Marched around between hills in a gap about four miles. Halted and bivouacked at 7:45 P. M. ten miles from Chattanooga, a short distance from the foot of Lookout Mountain.

15. Reveille 4:30. Marched at 11 A. M., the same road marched over the night before. Marched five

miles, then turned south toward Lafayette, Ga. Marched one mile and the whole brigade formed in line of battle on the left of the road and went in camp at 2 p. m., about one-half mile from Crawfish Springs.

16. Reveille at 5 a. m. Issue of rations, shoes and clothing. General Rosecrans' headquarters at Crawfish Springs. The water comes out of a hill in a stream three feet deep and twelve feet wide, forming a river called Chickamauga.

17. Reveille at 3 a. m. In line until 4 a. m. Cannonading heard. Remained in this camp all day.

18. Reveille sounded at 5 a. m. A detail for picket was made at 8 a. m. Heavy cannonading on the right and left. The rebel artillery in position at short distance in sight of the picket line. The pickets ordered, if attacked, to fall back. The regiment marched to Lee and Gordon's mill, and about one mile down the river, and formed line of battle in a field overlooking the Chickamauga river or creek. Not allowed to have any fires, and it was very cold during the night. Heavy railroad trains heard moving all night in the enemy's lines.

Battle of Chickamauga.

19. Reveille 4 a. m. Formed line of battle expecting an attack by the enemy. 5 a. m. the rebel sharpshooters had a range on the line and the regiment fell back to Lee and Gordon's mill. Ordered to eat breakfast. 8 a. m. the artillery on the line near our regiment opened on the rebels and rapid musketry followed. Rebel shells exploded uncomfortably close to our line. Heavy musketry is heard on right some distance away. 10 a. m. the artillery on our immediate right opened a heavy cannonading and continued

a half hour or more. The firing ceased for a short time, then renewed more vigorously than before. Very heavy musketry is heard on the right, indicating hard fighting. 12 M. artillery opened on rebel cavalry and scattered them. 1 P. M. heavy musketry and loud yelling is heard, indicating severe fighting. It is rumored that the rebels are driving the Union troops. Ordered to fall in promptly. Marched at double-quick time to the left, fixing bayonets while marching. 1:30 P. M. marched by the flank, in the woods. Our regiment charged a rebel battery and captured it. Its guns were loaded to the muzzle ready to be fired. The battery was taken to the rear by a detail from each company. A line was formed and a continuous fire was kept on the rebels. Soon the troops on our right gave way and exposed the right flank. The rebel balls coming lengthwise of the line, our line fell back in the rear of the 17th Kentucky, who began firing at the approaching rebel column, who came in such force that our lines could not stop them and fell back. At this time reinforcements came, and for the time the enemy was checked. Our line held its position for a while, but soon it became apparent that the rebels had again flanked our line as the balls came thick and fast from the right. Fell back in the rear of the artillery, which kept up a tremendous fire on the advancing rebel column and for a time checked their advance. The detail that had taken the captured battery to the rear reported to the regiment here and the line was reformed. The firing ceased on the left at 4:30 P. M. 5 P. M. a line of field works was built of rails on the hill where the regiment had taken position, which was about the same as occupied by our troops in the morning. The fighting continued severely until dark. It was nearly 7 P. M. before the firing ceased, only an occasional shot was heard. Both sides rested till next morning.

20. Sunday. Awakened at 4 A. M. Cold and frosty. Nothing to eat but crackers. Ammunition issued. Fell in at 6 A. M. Marched into a hollow, where rations were issued. Heavy musketry is heard on the left, and is becoming heavier. At 9 A. M. marched in the direction from whence the firing was heard. Passed Generals Rosecrans and Van Cleve. Their looks were not very reassuring to the men. The regiment was formed at double column at half distance. Thus formed, marched to the front, balls and shells flying over our heads and among the men. The wounded were being carried to the rear. Ordered to lie down. In this position exposed to the missiles of the enemy. The regiment remained in this position until the line to our right was driven back in confusion. Then we fell back a short distance. Formed in support of a battery. The advancing column of rebels soon appeared, charged and captured the battery. A charge was ordered. The 79th Indiana, with the troops, charged and recaptured the battery from the rebels. This position could not be held very long. The troops fell back to a hill, formed a line connecting with other troops and held this position against the repeated charges of the enemy, who charged in column four deep, to be repulsed by the well-directed fire of our line. The regiment was engaged almost continuously until 2:30 P. M., when reinforcements came to the right, and the firing was again renewed. It soon ceased, however, and other troops occupied the place of the 79th Indiana. Vigorous firing was again heard on the right and extended along the entire line. The rebels fired shells and grape and cannister, but their aim was bad. They fired too high. Charge after

charge was made by the enemy on the temporary line of field works built on that hill, but General George H. Thomas's men (for it was he who was in command of the Federal troops on this hill), repulsed them as often as they came. The rebels were determined to capture the hill, as some of them were killed inside of our works, where a hand-to-hand conflict was had, with the result in favor of the Federal arms. The fighting continued until after dark, with our troops in possession of the hill called Snodgrass. Ammunition was given to the men during the afternoon. The cartridge boxes of the dead heroes were often emptied by the men who were out and could not get it elsewhere. It was expected the rebels would renew the attack after dark. They came not. Thus ended one of the hardest days in the experience of the 79th Indiana. The fragments of the regiment fell back down the hill in a hollow, the only way out. Marched quietly, gathering our men as we passed. The moon was shining brightly. Marched about six miles and camped for the night, almost exhausted for want of water.

21. Up at 5 A. M. After eating a bite and drinking a cup of coffee, started at 6:15 A. M., and soon came to where Van Cleve's division headquarters had been established. Heard the division had marched back to Chattanooga. Started for that place, arriving there at 12 M. Soon found the scattered men of the regiment and went into camp.

22. Up at 5 A. M. After breakfast the men were put to work fortifying, as it was expected the rebels would attack this place in the evening. Cannonading could be heard very plainly east of here. Worked very hard on the fortifications at 5 P. M.

22. The rebels shelled the pickets and were in sight

all evening, coming around on the left on a big hill, forming on the side of the mountain, with the intention to attack in the morning. Cannonading could be heard on the right all day. Burned the houses and brush that were in the way of a clear range for the firing line. The teams were sent across the river as fast as possible. A brigade was sent out to where the pickets were being shelled, where the firing of the rebel artillery could be seen. By sun-down the rebels were firing on our men between the river and the road. Firing was kept up until dark by the skirmishers. Worked on the breastworks after dark until they were in safe condition for protection; at 8 P. M. ordered out on picket. Went out half a mile and deployed the regiment on post, half of a company to each relief, and at 10 P. M. the rebels fired on the division pickets in front. Formed a new line and set the sentinels about ten steps apart and to stay on four hours. Watched for them all night, and were determined to give them a warm reception if attacked.

23. Relieved from picket at 10 A. M., and went back to the breastworks. Some other regiment had been working on them while the regiment was on picket, and got them in good condition, but worked and made them stronger. At 1:30 P. M. General Rosecrans rode along the lines, talking to the boys and cheering them up. Fell in line and gave him three cheers. Cannonading could be heard occasionally, and could see the rebel lines two or three miles off, passing along the side of the mountain. Each regiment had its flag planted on the breastworks in its front. At 2 P. M. were ordered to dig on a new line of works inside the other to shelter the reserve. Went to work, and never in the history of our regiment did the dirt fly so fast. We got the inside line done, and

lay down to sleep at 8 P. M. At 12:30 A. M. we were awakened to work on breastworks. Built an entanglement in front of the works to stop them, in case the enemy made a charge. Built fires when the moon went down, so as to make it smoky and foggy, so they could not see anything for a long time in the morning. Stopped working at 3 A. M. and stood in line of battle until daylight, another relief working in place. At 5 A. M. the artillery opened on the enemy, and kept firing for some time. General Rosecrans and other generals rode along the lines in the night to inspect the works, and their opinion was that we could hold the works against the rebels, and we thought so ourselves.

24. At 7:30 could hear musketry very plainly in different directions, but it ceased. At 9 A. M. blankets were brought to regiment. Had only rubber blankets. It was cold without woolen blankets. The sutler came up and brought a good many things the boys needed. Still worked on the breastworks in the fort. At 2 P. M. the artillery fired several times on the right at the rebels. At 3:30 P. M. the guns in the fort fired at a battery that the rebels were getting in position to fire. At 4:15 P. M. the artillery on the right was firing again. Drew rations of beef. At 4:30 P. M. the cannons in the fort and on the right began firing at different points at the rebels. Could hear musketry also. Stopped working in the fort at night and went to sleep at 7 P. M., not knowing how soon we might be called up. At 10:15 P. M. awakened and fell in line inside the breastworks. Heavy musketry could be heard on the right. At 10:30 P. M. the artillery opened on the enemy. Fires were built in front of the breastworks, and a wire had been stretched about one foot off the ground to trip the rebels in the event

they charged the works. The firing ceased at 12 M., except a few occasional shots. We lay down to rest.

25. Up at 6 A. M. Ordered to police the ground inside of the works, and to put up tents.

26. Up at daylight. Heard considerable firing on the picket line in front. Knapsacks came up at 8 A. M. Ordered to work on the fort, and at 11 : 30 P. M. the work was completed. The ditch in front was eight feet wide and four feet deep. The fortification was fifteen feet through at the bottom, sloping to about ten feet on top. It is considered secure against any ordinary artillery. Beef issued, but the amount was very small.

27. Sunday. Reveille, 5 A. M. Few shots are heard along the lines. At 9 : 45 P. M. there was sharp firing on the right for half an hour. Ordered to form line, expecting an attack. Firing ceased. Ordered to retire.

28. Reveille. Ordered to prepare camp and pitch tents. In line at 7 A. M. Details of six men ordered from each company to make another row of entanglements in front.

29. Reveille. Issue wormy crackers, unfit to eat. Rations are beginning to be scarce. Ordered to exercise caution and not throw them away. The enemy sent in a flag of truce to take off our wounded. It is reported five hundred ambulances and medical attendants sent out with ten days' rations for the wounded. George W. Clark, first lieutenant "G" company, died of wound received September 13, 1863.

30. Reveille 5 A. M. Nothing important.

OCTOBER, 1863.

1. Raining. Reveille 5 A. M. Thirty-pound Parrott guns mounted in the work in front of lines.

2. Reveille 5 A. M. Camp routine. Rebels can be seen on drill and dress parade on Missionary Ridge. Their drums and bugles are plainly heard, and the calls could be distinguished.

3. Reveille 5 A. M. Policed quarters. Our pickets are exchanging papers with the rebels every day.

4. Sunday. Reveille 5 A. M. Two days' rations issued ordered to last three days. Supplies becoming shorter every day. Company inspections at 4 P. M.

5. Reveille 5 A. M. Heavy cannonading all day on both sides. Some of the rebel shells explode over the fort in front, long range.

6. Reveille 5 A. M. Company inspection and stacked arms. Dug out a rebel shell that failed to explode, it proved to be a 42-pounder. Fort in front has been named "Fort Wood." Position of regiment to the left of the fort. Light cannonading during the day. Rain at dark.

7. Reveille 5 A. M. The guns in the fort opened on some rebels who are supposed to be planting a siege gun in front. Rations are getting more scarce.

8. Reveille 5 A. M. Regiment reserve of the picket line. Brisk cannonading on the right. The rebels opened on the pickets with their artillery at 4 P. M., the shells lighting close to the picket line. Guns in Fort Wood responded. Some of the shells exploded over Missionary Ridge three miles distant. Rebel cannon could not reach fort. Pickets ordered not to fire unless the enemy advanced or manifested disposition to advance, when fire is to be opened; reserve to reinforce line of sentinels; if hard pressed by the enemy, firing line to be supported by grand reserve of regiment, and in case of necessity to call out brigade, and report situation to headquarters of division. Firing ceased at dark. On account of proximity of

enemy utmost vigilance and caution enjoined upon all, while on outpost duty.

9. Relieved at 9 A. M. Rations growing scarcer.

10. Reveille 5 A. M. Cannonading on the right. Drew five days' rations. Strictest economy with rations impressed upon all.

11. Sunday. Reveille. General inspection at 4:30 P. M.

12. Reveille. Pickets ordered on to the line at 6:15 A. M. Company drill, 9 to 11 A. M. Detail from regiment ordered for fatigue duty, to work on Fort Wood.

13. Raining and cold.

14. Raining.

15. Raining. Report that Ohio had elected Brough governor was received with great enthusiasm in all the camps. Issue of rations for five days. Ceased raining before dark.

16. Reveille. Marched on picket before daylight.

17. Pickets ordered not to trade papers or communicate with the enemy under any circumstances.

18. Sunday. Relieved from outpost duty at 7 A. M. Inspection at 2 P. M. Dress parade at 5 P. M., ground too wet for parade. The regiment formed and orders read by the adjutant; rations of beef issued.

19. Reveille at 5 A. M. Routine duties of camp.

20. Reveille at 5 A. M. Orders to move camp at 8 A. M. Moved one-half mile to the left, about 400 yards from the river and 200 yards in the rear of the front line of works. Camp pitched and tents up by noon. Rations issued in much decreased quantities. Desiccated potatoes and vegetables issued; are not liked. No directions how to use supplies of that character.

21. Reveille at 5 A. M. Weather stormy.

22. Reveille at 5 A. M. Policed quarters. Several

shots are fired in the evening from the fort. Firing kept up nearly all night.

23. Reveille. Camp routine. Raining all day.

24. Reveille. Camp routine. Raining all day.

25. Reveille at 5 A. M. Ordered for general inspection at 10 A. M. Issue of one pound of crackers to each officer and soldier for three days. Salt beef, a little salt, short rations of coffee and sugar. Hereafter ordered to do picket by whole regiments, one regiment to cover brigade front. Cannonading on the right during the night. It was ordered that outposts be relieved before daylight, in order that changes should not be observed by the enemy.

26. Reveille at 4 A. M. Marched out on to the picket line at 5:30, relieving the 19th Ohio Volunteers.

27. Relieved from picket at 6:15 A. M. In quarters.

28. Reveille at 5 A. M. Put camp in order. Dress parade at 5 P. M. Orders published on parade that General Rosecrans relieved from command of the Army of the Cumberland, and ordered to report at Cincinnati, Ohio, and that Major General George H. Thomas has been appointed and assumed command of the Army of the Cumberland. Heavy firing of musketry and artillery at 12:30 A. M. It sounded as if it was in the valley at the foot of Lookout Mountain. At 2:30 P. M. the guns in Fort Wood also opened fire. Dress parade at 5 P. M. Firing not so brisk. After 2 A. M. firing almost ceased.

29. Reveille at 5 A. M. Heavy cannonading and musketry on the right continue all day. Dress parade 4:30 P. M. Order read that officers can get one-half rations on credit. Crackers issued during the night.

30. Reveille 5 A. M. Raining. Cannonading on the right all day. Raining very hard. The rain beats through tents.

31. Reveille at 5 P. M. Ordered to remain in camp to be mustered for pay. Two crackers issued to each officer and soldier. We mustered for pay at 4:30 P. M.

NOVEMBER, 1863.

1. Sunday. Up at day. Got ready for company inspection at 10 A. M. At 3 we assembled in front of the colonel's tent for divine services. We had dress parade at 5 P. M. We drew two-thirds of a cracker to a man, and ate it before we lay down. First Lieutenant William A. Abbett mustered in as captain of "A" company.

2. Reveille at 5 A. M. Our cannons began firing at 10:30 A. M. We drew beef at noon and ate it without anything else. It was all we had to eat. The rebs continued shelling all day. We drew a few crackers at night and got ready to lie down for the night, and the general assembly sounded and we fell in line in a hurry. We marched out to the works and stood one hour, and then went back to camp to lie down with our accoutrements and be ready to fall in in a moment's notice. Some cannonading on the right.

3. Reveille at 4:30 A. M. We drew a cracker for each man and got ready to go on picket at 5:45 A. M. The regiment went out. There was considerable cannonading on both sides all day. Four deserters came into our lines after dark. Second Lieutenant James I. Robinson, "E" company, resigned.

4. Relieved from picket at 6:30, and marched to camp. A few crackers issued. Dress parade at 4:30 P. M. In the reorganization of the Army of the Cumberland, regiment assigned to the 3d Brigade, 3d Division, 4th Corps, with 19th Ohio, 9th Kentucky,

17th Kentucky, 13th Ohio, 59th Ohio, 86th Indiana, and 6th Ohio Battery.

5. Reveille at 5 A. M. Few rations. Ordered roll-call four times a day.

6. Reveille 4 A. M. Brigade detail to work on Fort Wood until 9 A. M. Drew some molasses and vinegar. Back to the fort. Relieved, 3 P. M. Dress parade, 5 P. M.

7. Reveille 5 A. M. Drew small rations of very poor beef. Dress parade at 4 P. M. The whole army very hungry.

8. Sunday. Reveille. Nothing to eat. Inspection, 10 A. M. Dress parade at 4:30 P. M. At 11 A. M. issue of three-fourths rations—crackers, beef, sugar and coffee. Very cold. Scant fires. Wood very scarce.

9. Reveille 5 A. M. Dress parade at 5 P. M. Ordered to be mustered for pay, paymaster having arrived in Chattanooga.

10. Reveille 5 A. M. Marched out on picket at 6 A. M., relieving the 19th Ohio Volunteer Infantry. Cannonading on the right. Two rebels came into lines at night; of Allison's squadron of conscripts from middle Tennessee. Cold and frosty.

11. Relieved from picket at 7 A. M. Cannonading on the right at 9 A. M. Rations issued at 4 P. M. Dress parade at 4:30. Brigade band turned out with regiment.

12. Reveille 5 A. M. Frosty. Considerable cannonading in direction of Lookout Mountain. Signed the pay-rolls. Twenty-seven rebel deserters came in last night at the picket line at one place. Dress parade at 5 P. M. Orders received for orderly sergeants to go home on recruiting service; to start in the morning of the 14th.

13. Reveille 5 A. M. Wood was issued to each

company, brought from across the river. Dress parade at 5 P. M.

14. Reveille 5 A. M. The orderly sergeants ordered on recruiting started, but returned to camp until next day. Cannonading on the right. Dress parade, 5 P. M.

15. Sunday. Reveille 5 A. M. The orderly sergeants on recruiting service started. Ordered to be ready for inspection at 10 A. M. After inspection the chaplain preached a sermon. Dress parade 5 P. M.

16. Reveille 4:30 A. M. A few rations and some wood issued. Dress parade at 5 P. M.

17. Reveille 5 A. M. On picket 6:30 A. M. Heavy cannonading on the left. Thirty pieces engaged for twenty or thirty minutes. A detail ordered to go outside of the picket line to build a bridge across Citico creek to extend lines to the front. Issue of a loaf of bread to a man. Six deserters came into lines telling hard tales of hardships.

18. On picket. Advanced the line of outposts across Citico creek. Relieved 7:30 A. M. Paid at 4 P. M. for four months. The picket line was moved out still a little farther. Several shots were fired. Drew a few rations. Some deserters came in.

19. Reveille 5 A. M. One spoonful of beans issued to the man. Dress parade 5 P. M.

20. Reveille 5 A. M. Raining. One hundred rounds of cartridges to the man. Two days' rations. Regimental inspection 5 P. M. to see that every man has the cartridges. No rations issued this day. Orders issued as to conduct in action. Ordered to stand firm and aim low. Not a man to leave rank to care for the wounded. If any man left rank to be considered a deserter in front of the enemy and treated as such. When moving to the front one man to remain in camp

from each company to take care of property. At 8 P. M. ordered to turn over old cartridges. Fresh ammunition issued to all. The order to march in the morning countermanded. Rained all night. Captain George W. Parker, of "G" company, commissioned as major of the regiment.

21. Raining. Ordered to be ready for brigade inspection at 10 A. M. next day, Sunday. Dress parade at 5 P. M.

22. Sunday. Reveille. Inspection postponed until 1 P. M. The rebels can be seen moving along the side of Missionary Ridge with a train. Batteries opened fire on them. Inspection by Colonel Kneffler at 1 P. M. Every gun carefully examined. Dress parade at 5 P. M. Orders were read for every man to be supplied with 100 rounds of cartridges, ready to move to the front in the morning with two days' rations, one man to remain in camp from each company to guard the property left in quarters. Forty axes, twenty spades and ten picks to each brigade. Two days' rations of bacon and three-fourths day's ration of coffee, sugar and crackers issued per man.

BATTLE OF MISSIONARY RIDGE.

23. Reveille at daylight. Detail made for fatigue duty, to report at 7:15 A. M. The river very high. Cannonading on the right from our batteries and firing from Fort Wood. Four more men detailed for fatigue duty during the forenoon. Everything in perfect readiness to move to the front. Ordered to fall in at 2 P. M. Marched outside of the breastworks and formed on left of division by battalions en masse. At 2:30 P. M. the pickets advanced and began firing. At 2:35 P. M. the guns in Fort Wood opened fire. Heavy

firing of artillery on the right and brisk skirmishing could be heard all along the lines. At 3 P. M. deployed in line of battle and marched forward a short distance and halted. At 3:10 P. M. musketry is heard in front of the brigade, but on the right the skirmishing was lively. Shells passed over our lines while the brigade was in the thick woods of scrub oaks and underbrush, making it difficult to advance. Railway cars can be heard on the other side of Missionary Ridge. Rebel wagon trains can be seen moving up the mountain, crossing over to the other side. The guns in Fort Wood ceased firing for a few minutes. About 3:30 the 1st and 2d Brigades reached the top of the knoll a few yards to our right. The men hauled the 6th Illinois Battery to the top of the knoll, and the battery shelled the rebels. The rebel batteries were on top of Missionary Ridge and fired very fast, the shells exploding in front and all around the men. Ordered to lie down. There was heavy skirmishing all along the lines. Lay in line until dark, when the cannonading ceased on both sides. Cloudy and cool and sprinkling rain. At 8 P. M. bivouacked and large fires were kindled. Company " I " detailed to work in the rifle pits, the axes, picks and shovels having been brought up. Men of other commands had been at work on a line of rifle pits. Soon as the knoll had been taken a signal station was established on it. There was a reserve line of pits built in the rear. Lay down to sleep. Awakened at 4 o'clock next morning. Marched to the rifle pits and lay down again. The men were still working on the pits. It was very cold and windy.

24. At daylight the pickets began firing to our left and front. It was raining slightly. At 11 A. M. the guns on the knoll began firing. At 8 A. M. there was

cannonading on the right. It sounded as if it came from Lookout Mountain. Ordered to make small fires and make coffee. The line established was about a mile to the front of Fort Wood and as far forward as the rebel's outside line of rifle pits. These were captured, with a number of prisoners. When our pickets advanced the rebels could be seen on the ridge, marching to their left, in column. At 8:45 A. M. the guns in Fort Wood shelled them. At 10 A. M. the rebels shelled our pickets as they were relieving each other. There was more or less cannonading on our right all morning, and from the sound large guns were in action. Occasional cannon firing was heard on our left. At 12 M. the cannonading on our right began very heavy, and rapid musketry was heard also. The fighting continued very hard until about 1 P. M. The yelling of a charge was heard. Smoky and drizzling rain prevented the men from seeing very far. At 3:30 P. M. three guns, about one-half mile on our right, opened a brisk fire on the rebels. Heavy firing continued in the direction of Lookout Mountain, indicating hard fighting. It continued to rain, making it very disagreeable in the fresh dug rifle pits in which the men had to stand. At 4 P. M. the firing in the direction of Lookout seemed to be getting heavier. A staff officer brought the news that General Hooker had captured seven guns and was driving the rebels; also got word that General Sherman had crossed the Tennessee River, and had joined General Howard's lines on the left. Rations were sent to the front at 7 P. M. and issued. At 9 P. M. bivouacked. Too cold to sleep much.

25. Got up early and breakfasted before daylight to be ready to attack if the order came. The 86th Indiana Regiment was ordered to report to Colonel Knefler

to be consolidated with the 79th Regiment, and, under his command, the 86th Indiana was ordered in line on the left, the colors of the two regiments in the center. The 86th Regiment, for the time being, and, in fact, until evening, after the storming of the ridge, was a part of the 79th Indiana, under command of Colonel Kneffler. Heard firing at a distance on the left. At 7 A. M. the guns on the knoll to the right began shelling the rebels, who could be seen marching to the left on the ridge. It was reported that the troops of General Hooker were clear up on the side of Lookout Mountain, and had captured a battery of large guns and two thousand prisoners. Light cannonading can be heard some distance on the left occasionally. At 8:45 A. M. the pickets in our front began a brisk firing and kept it up. Could hear firing to the left and front. Soon yelling could be heard, indicating a charge. The cannonading continued on the left. The rebels have been marching to the left for hours. They can be seen from our lines. The guns from the knoll and Fort Wood are shelling them. There was cannonading on the right. It seemed to be on Lookout Mountain or in Chattanooga valley. The sky was clear, except a few thin clouds. The wind was cool. At 9 A. M. the rebels began firing their cannons at our lines in the valley, and soon increased considerably. At 10:30 A. M. our picket line moved forward toward the rebels and brisk skirmishing began along the lines. The cheering was loud and long, on the left, without much musketry, but on the right the musketry was heavy and the yelling loud, and heavy cannonading on both sides. Distant cannonading on the left. The musketry in our immediate front almost ceased at 11:30 A. M. Shells were flying all around, and many fell uncomfortably close to our line. Before 12 A. M. the rebels had almost ceased cannonading in front—only an occasional shell coming over. The cannonading on the left, at a distance, was incessant and regular. General Baird's Division, 14th Army Corps, in our rear, has been marching to the left for an hour or more to report to General Sherman. At 12 M. there was not a cloud to be seen—the sky was blue and wind brisk from the west. Nearly all our generals are on the knoll to our right. General Grant, General Thomas, General Meigs and others were there. It was the best place to see the army and command its movements. This was Orchard Knob. At 12:45 P. M. the rebels got range on our line of pits and sent a shell parallel with the works, just over our heads, cutting a large limb off a tree, hurting no one. Several others passed uncomfortably close to us. The heavy cannonading on the left indicates, from the sound, that General Sherman is certainly gaining ground on the rebels' right, and it will not be long before we, too, will have to advance on the enemy's works in front. The regiment fell in at 2:30 and formed in "double column at half distance," stacked arms and awaited orders. A steamboat whistle is heard at the landing, indicating that our troops hold Lookout Mountain and the river is open. Heavy musketry is heard far on our left. At 3 P. M. fell in and deployed in line of battle —marched out and formed line outside of the line of rifle pits. At 3:45 P. M. the signal to advance is fired from Orchard Knob. At this signal we advanced at double-quick for a short distance through thickets and bushes. Soon the skirmishers began a brisk firing in our immediate front, and as we emerged from the bushes the regiment was in plain sight of the rebels in their works at the foot of Missionary Ridge. The 79th Regiment advanced rapidly under the enemy's fire and soon was in possession of the enemy's second line of rifle pits, capturing many prisoners. The rebels fled up the ridge when they saw us coming, abandoning their rifle pits. On the crest of the ridge was a solid line of artillery, belching their deadly missiles as the regiment advanced. On the right and left of the regiment, up and down the valleys, solid lines of Union troops could be seen advancing rapidly toward the ridge, the top of which looked like a solid mass of fire and smoke. Our artillery responded promptly from our rear and kept a continuous fire at the ridge. On the regiment advanced double-quick, and soon had taken the rebels' strong line of works at the foot of the ridge. The line halted a few minutes only. Some of the men were nearly exhausted. Soon Colonel Knefler gave the command "Forward!" and the regiment advanced rapidly for the top of the ridge, yelling and cheering, under a perfect shower of shell, grape and cannister from the rebel artillery on the top of the ridge. There was a high projecting point on the ridge in front of our line and our regiment advanced on the run for that point under a very heavy fire from the batteries of the enemy. They had a cross-fire on the regiment from two points. The ridge in front of the regiment was very steep and rocky with a few scrub oaks growing on its sides. Our regiment was so far in advance of other troops that it was made a target for the batteries, the shells exploding right and left among the men and ploughing up the ground near the line, killing and wounding many of the men, though many shells went over us. The regiment advanced until within a few feet of the main line of works on the crest of the ridge, halted, lay down for a rest, the men being nearly exhausted, but kept up a continuous fire as they lay there. While in this position, looking to the rear of the line, columns of troops could be seen coming from the right and left to our support. The men of our regiment and the 86th regiment arose and jumped into the rebel works and a hand-to-hand struggle took place. The colors of the 79th Indiana and that of the rebels touched during the struggle, which ended in victory for the Union arms. The rebels fled down the eastern slope of the ridge in disorder. Their own artillery was turned on them and fired at them as they retreated. Some of the men of our regiment were killed on the top of the works on the ridge. On the right and left could be seen Union troops charging to the very mouth of the rebel cannons. They were determined to dislodge the enemy and were successful in driving him from his almost impregnable stronghold. His center having been broken made their task easier in the assault. Our regiment captured many prisoners and flags. Some officers were among the prisoners captured. The 79th captured two pieces of artillery, in addition to the pieces captured on the ridge. These two pieces were being taken to the rear by the rebels; the pieces were 12-pound brass cannons. When the regiment reached the summit of the ridge, brisk musketry was heard to the left about four hundred yards. It soon quieted down. The enemy was driven off the ridge and could be seen running in all directions in disorder. Our troops were in possession of the ridge from one end to the other with all the enemy's artillery and many prisoners. A big smoke could be seen in the distance to the left. The rebels are burning their train on their retreat. The men were ordered to make fire and make coffee. Some of the men went over the battlefield to the starting place of the regiment and wondered how our men had been so successful, taking the roughness of the ground gone over and the advantage the enemy had of the position into consideration. There was a great number of killed and wounded scattered over the field. The wounded were taken to the field hospital. The regiment bivouacked on top of the ridge. The men enjoyed a most needed rest.

26. Up at 5 A. M. Some of the men went down the ridge on the ground the regiment charged over at double quick. The hill is very steep and is 500 feet high. An occasional cannon shot could be heard on the right and some musketry. The 86th Indiana, which was consolidated with our regiment, had its flag pierced by a shell and eighty-eight balls. Our own flag was badly riddled with shots, but could not count the holes, it having been pierced before. At 9 A. M. a detail of three men from each company was made to go over the battlefield and gather up guns and accoutrements. At 9:45 A. M. cannonading is heard on the left and front, our men are following the retreating rebels. It was a little foggy in the morning, but at 10 A. M. the fog rose and troops could be seen moving about in the valley as far as the eye could reach. Chickamauga Station could be seen and many buildings burning. Our artillery could be seen shelling the retreating rebels. The men could imagine what a grand sight the rebels had of our army maneuvering during the battle. At 11:40 A. M. thirty-six shots were fired from Fort Wood. It is a salute in honor of the victory achieved by Wood's division and the whole army. At 2 P. M. the brigade band was playing on the ridge, and the men cheered. Our wagon trains can be seen going out with rations for the men at Chickamauga Station. At 6 P. M. ordered to lie down and rest. Soon awakened and rations issued. Ordered to be ready to march to camp. The

regiment was soon in line and cheer after cheer went up, and from right to left the whole army was a continuous cheer. Marched toward camp, passing over rebel works. Reached camp at 9 P. M. Built fires and rations were issued. Plenty to eat now. The men retired and enjoyed rest.

27. Up at daylight. Breakfast is eaten. Considerable cannonading is heard in the direction of Ringgold at 9 A. M. Soon ceased. At 1 P. M. orders are received to be ready to march at 6 A. M. to-morrow. At 5 P. M. dress parade an order is read from General Woods, expressing his thanks and gratitude to the troops for gallantry and intrepidity on the 25th, charging and occupying the enemy's works on Missionary Ridge. By its daring act of bravery our regiment had covered itself with glory. It is credited in the official report with being the first regiment to reach the top and plant its banners on Missionary Ridge.

28. Reveille at 4 A. M. Raining. Breakfast before daylight. Orders to carry forty rounds of cartridges. Formed line at 2 P. M. Stack arms, waiting to fall in place in the brigade. At 4 P. M. moved out of quarters and marched along the Knoxville railroad to the five-mile stone and bivouacked by the side of road. Turned very cold.

29. Sunday. Reveille at 5 A. M. Breakfasted and moved forward at 7 A. M., our regiment in front. Moved a short distance and halted on account of a train of wagons in front. Began to snow at 10 A. M. Crossed a swamp several hundred yards wide. Timber had been cut to cross on. At 12 M. passed the place where General Sherman crossed the Tennessee river to reach the north end of Missionary Ridge the day before the battle. The bridge upon which he

crossed was still there; also the rifle pits built after he crossed, and the position from where he charged the rebels. At 1:30 P. M. crossed the Chickamauga seven miles above Chattanooga, where it empties in the Tennessee river, on a pontoon bridge. Halted to camp at 7 P. M. near a little town called Harrison. Cold and freezing. Marched about twelve miles. Orders to be ready to start at 5 A. M. to-morrow.

30. Reveille at 4 A. M. Started on march at 5 A. M. Ground frozen hard; covered lightly with snow. Marched very fast. At 11 A. M. halted for dinner. Passed a large spring, the water boiling up out of the ground, forming a stream that runs a mill. At 12:45 P. M. arrived at Georgetown. Marched five miles beyond Georgetown and bivouacked by the side of the road in the woods.

DECEMBER, 1863.

1. Reveille 5 A. M. Rations issued at 2 P. M. At 6:30 P. M. detail made of three men from each company to assist ferrying troops over. Marched one mile to Hiawassee river; halted at 10 P. M. The regiment crossed the river on the steamer Dunbar. On landing moved forward a mile and bivouacked at 11 P. M. Very cold, fuel very scarce and some distance from camp. Suffering from cold.

2. Reveille 5 A. M. Marched at 7:30 A. M., the ground frozen hard. Very cold. Passed through some very hilly and rough country. Halted at 12 M. for dinner. Marched at 12:45 P. M. Passed through a little town called Decatur. Marched until 4:45 and bivouacked. Marched twenty miles.

3. Reveille 5 A. M. Marched at 7:15 A. M. Crossed Sewey creek. Halted for dinner at 1 P. M. Moved again before 2 P. M. Turned off on the Philadelphia

road, six miles before the town was reached. Arrived at Sweet Water at 4 P. M. Rebel cavalry appeared in front to contest advance, and driven off. Marched one mile beyond Sweet Water and bivouacked, having marched twenty miles. The rebels fired at a detail of the brigade engaged in securing forage. A whole regiment ordered on picket against rebel cavalry hovering about in large numbers.

4. Reveille 5 A. M. A detail of two men ordered from each company foraging for the brigade. Marched at 7:30 A. M. on Morgantown road. Halted 12 M. for dinner. Moved forward after 1 P. M. Marched twelve or fourteen miles. Went in bivouac at 2:30 P. M., four miles from Morgantown. The foragers returned, bringing one hundred head of sheep, a lot of hogs and beeves, flour, meal, potatoes, salt, bacon, etc. The surrounding country seems full of provisions.

5. Reveille 5 A. M. A detail for foragers was made. Marched at 8 A. M. Marched to the Little Tennessee river, arriving there at 9:30 A. M., three miles from starting point. Halted considerable time for troops in front to cross on a ferryboat. The bridge was rapidly repaired, and the troops passed on the bridge also. Marched through Morgantown and bivouacked, having marched sixteen or eighteen miles. Nothing to eat but meat.

6. Reveille 6 A. M. Marched at 6:15 A. M. Regiment in front of division. Marched through Maryville, crossed Little River and bivouacked. The regiment ordered on picket. Three quarts of meal issued to the company, a few small potatoes and little meat. Rations are very scarce.

7. Ordered to relieve the pickets at 7:30 A. M. Marched to the station. Weather foggy and frosty Marched at 9:30 A. M. Regiment in the rear. We

crossed the Little River at noon at Rockford. Shows where our men had a skirmish with the rebel cavalry a few days ago. Bivouacked at sundown two miles from Knoxville.

8. Reveille 5:30. Cloudy and cool. Some of the men had nothing to eat. It began raining at 2 P. M. A little salt and pork issued, and had little bread for supper.

9. Reveille at 5 A. M. A mutton issued to the company; one and one-half pint of meal per man. Another sheep issued to each company in the evening, and some more meal; also some salt, tobacco and three loaves of bread to the company.

10. Reveille at 5:30 A. M. Four men from each company are permitted to go into Knoxville.

11. Reveille 5:30 A. M. Some meal issued. Camp ordered to be pitched in regular order.

12. Reveille 5:30 A. M. Rations of salt, flour and mutton issued. Raining.

13. Sunday. Reveille 5:30. Ordered on picket at 8 A. M. Raining.

14. On picket. Relieved at 9 A. M. Issue of beef and flour; rations scarce.

15. Reveille 5:30 A. M. Issue of some meal, meat and molasses, and one mutton to the company. 1 P. M. the general sounded; a few crackers issued; 2 P. M. marched out to the road and stacked arms; ordered back to old camp. Ordered to have 60 rounds of cartridges per man. Ordered to keep crackers for march. At 8 P. M. flour and coffee issued.

16. Reveille 4:30 A.M. Moved at daybreak. Marched toward town—crossed the river at sun-up on pontoon bridge. Marched through Knoxville on the main street in column of companies. General Burnside reviewed column in front of his headquarters. Marched out on

8

the Strawberry Plains road; 4 miles beyond town the rebels chopped down trees across the road. Halted for dinner at 12 M. Moved again at 1 P. M. Met some troops coming back with a train; they reported fighting in front. Halted to bivouac at 3 P. M. fourteen miles from Knoxville. One-half cracker issued to the men. Raining at 10 P. M.

17. Reveille 4 A. M. Raining. Fresh pork, a little flour and meal issued. Cold and windy.

18. Reveille 4:30. Very cold, windy and cloudy. General Wilder's mounted infantry passed to the front. Some mutton issued.

19. Reveille 5:30 A. M. Very cold. A little mutton. Socks, shoes, pants, shirts and blankets issued. Ordered on picket.

20. Sunday. Very cold. Relieved from outposts at 4. P. M. Marched back to camp. Rations of mutton, crackers, coffee, sugar and salt issued.

21. Reveille at daylight. Very cold. Mutton issued. Roll call ordered four times a day.

22. Reveille 5:30 A. M. Company "I" detailed to go to Strawberry Plains as train guard.

23. Reveille 5:30 A. M. Moved camp about one-quarter of a mile. Half rations issued of bread, coffee, etc. Very cold.

24. Reveille 5:30 A. M.

25. Reveille at 5:30 A. M. Christmas. Routine duties. At 7 P. M. the regiment was ordered to form and stand in line, because some one fired his gun, and for promiscuous yelling. In line one hour.

26. Reveille 6 A. M. Rations of flour and beef issued. Ordered on picket at 3 P. M. Raining.

27. Sunday. Relieved from picket at 4 P. M. March to camp in the rain. Beef issued.

28. Reveille 6 A. M. One-half rations of beef, coffee, sugar and salt issued.

29. Reveille 5:30 A. M. Rations of meal and shorts and one-half loaf of bread to the man issued.

30. Reveille 5:30 A. M.

31. Reveille 5:30 A. M. During the forenoon considerable cannonading is heard in the direction of Knoxville. Raining. One-half rations of coffee, sugar, salt, meal and crackers issued.

JANUARY, 1864.

1. Up late. Very cold and disagreeable. Ordered on picket at 3 P. M. Much suffering from cold on account of insufficient clothing.

2. Relieved from picket at 4 P. M. Back to camp. Rations of beef issued. Very cold and much suffering.

3. Sunday. Very cold, windy and altogether very disagreeable.

4. Reveille at 5:30 A. M. Raining. Two and one-half days' rations issued for four days. Aroused at 3 A. M., ready to march at a moment's notice.

5. Reveille 5:30 A. M. Rained all night. Ready to march. Waiting orders.

6. Reveille 5:30 A. M. Cold and snowing. Cartridges ordered returned. Much suffering from cold and smoke. Very windy.

7. Reveille 5:30 A. M. Ordered on picket at 3 P. M. Sleet, turning to snow.

8. On picket. No rations. Hungry. Relieved at 3 P. M. Back to camp. Issue of flour, crackers, etc. Clear and cold.

9. Reveille 5:30 A. M. Issue of rations of beef.

10. Sunday. Reveille 5:30 A. M. Cold and cloudy.

11. Reveille 5:30 A. M. Rations very scarce. Little

prospect for increase. The roads over which supplies must be hauled in almost impassable condition.

12. Reveille 5:30 A. M. Issue of a few rations. Raining.

13. Reveille 5:30 A. M. Issue of some mutton. Five companies go out on picket. General Wood gone home on leave. General Willich in command of the division. Ordered to be ready to march at 7 A. M. Issue of one-half rations at night. Food supply very unsatisfactory.

14. Reveille 5 A. M. Marched 7 A. M. to Strawberry Plains. Crossed the Holston river on railroad bridge. Marched on the Dandridge road over the little hills. The ground is frozen hard, thawing a little in the afternoon. Camped at 3:45 P. M., about ten miles from Strawberry Plains. Marched thirteen miles. Ordered to be up at 5 A. M. and ready to march at 7.

15. Reveille 4 A. M. Drizzling rain and sleeting. Marched, 7 A. M., about two miles. Company "E" detailed to guard a mill and grind grain. The balance of the regiment marched two hours and forty-five minutes without halting. Arrived near Dandridge, turned to the right and camped at 11:30 A. M., having marched eight miles. In camp five miles from the Smoky Range Mountains, which are in plain view. Cavalry to the front, skirmishing. Orders to be in readiness to march at a moment's notice to support cavalry.

16. Up early, ready to march. Ordered to form and stacked arms. The order to march is countermanded. Cannonading heard on the left, getting closer and heavier. Ordered to fall in, ready to march. Issued beef and flour. Did not march.

17. Sunday. Up early. In line of battle at 6 A. M. At 10 A. M. ordered to be ready for picket. Drew

clothing. Formed line at 12 M. Cannonading heard at a distance. Troops are moving out at 4 P. M. Musketry can be heard about two miles distant. Marched nearly to town, halted, stacked arms and remained until 8 P. M. Returned to camp. The firing ceased. Ordered to be ready to march at a moment's notice.

18. Marched early to the bridge at Strawberry Plains and camped in a grove. The rebel cavalry attacked wagon trains, capturing a few wagons. Rebels driven off by cavalry.

19. Up early. Cold and cloudy. Snowed during the night. Everything covered with snow. 12 M. marched to the bridge to cross. Waited and crossed at 2 P. M. Recrossed and marched on the railroad within thirteen and one-half miles of Knoxville and camped. A few rations issued. Five companies ordered on picket.

20. Drew clothing and a few rations issued at 4 P. M. Ready to march. The pickets relieved, join the regiment. Started at sundown. Marched five miles and camped. Issue of a little meal.

21. Reveille 4:30 A. M. Marched at daylight in direction of Knoxville. Halted one mile from Knoxville for dinner. Colonel Knefler gone home on leave. Lieutenant-Colonel Oyler in command of regiment. At 1:30 P. M. marched through Knoxville. Crossed the Holston river. Marched two miles on the Severe road. Went in camp 3 P. M. Nothing but bread for supper. Many had nothing; everything very scarce.

22. Up early. Ordered on foraging trip, returning at sundown. Issue of coffee, sugar, salt, flour, etc.

23. Up early, ready to march. Drew clothing. At daylight marched toward old camp two miles in column closed *en masse*. Ordered not to straggle.

Rebel cavalry hovering about. Marched out on the Maryville road. Reached Rockford and crossed the Little river at 2 P. M. on a slab in single file. Some of the boys fell into the water. In camp at 3 P. M. Brigade in the advance. Marched fourteen miles during the day.

24. Sunday. Up very early. Marched at daylight toward Maryville. Halted and formed *en masse*. General Willich, commanding the division, ordered that two brigades should remain in this town. The 9th Kentucky ordered to do provost duty. He gave very strict orders every one would be punished if brought before him for violation of orders. Exposed to rebel cavalry scouting around the place. Orders that no one leave camp. Camp laid off and tents pitched, put up in line. Prepared for winter quarters. Rations very scarce.

25. Reveille 5:30 A. M. 9 A. M. five companies ordered on picket. Issue of coffee, sugar, soap and pepper. 3 P. M. detail from regiment was called for nine men and a non-commissioned officer for picket.

26. Detail relieved from picket. Some beef and meal issued.

27. Reveille 5:30 A. M. Ordered not to burn rails. One man of each mess to go to town market. Plenty of meal and beef but no salt. Policed quarters.

28. Reveille 5:30 A. M. Policed quarters. A beautiful day; just like April in the North.

29. Reveille 5:30 A. M. Guard mounting at 9 A. M. and inspection. Cavalry came in and reported having had a fight with the enemy and repulsed them.

30. Reveille 5 A. M. Stand in line until daylight. Some meal and beef issued. Raining. Company "I" ordered to the Little Tennessee to guard the ferry.

31. In camp; routine duties. Company "I" on

guard at ferry. The citizens of Maryville are found to be rebels.

FEBRUARY, 1864.

1. The 79th Indiana and 17th Kentucky ordered on reconnaissance with the 1st East Tennessee and 4th Indiana cavalry on the Sevierville road. Marched fifteen miles and to within five miles from the rebel camp.

2. Colonel Brownlow reconnoitered the camp of the enemy, found to be about 10,000. Reconnaissance returned. Recrossed Little river behind the cavalry. On return to camp each man was ordered to be searched by Colonel Oyler for stolen property. None discovered.

3. Earnest arrested and taken to provost marshal's office charged with straggling and theft of a coffee bucket.

4. Men were allowed to go to Maryville to buy molasses and corn bread of citizens. Citizens of vicinity bringing produce to town to sell to the soldiers.

5. Refugees and deserters come in to Maryville every day from the rebel army; some of them look in a very distressing and ragged condition. Captain James M. Buchanan honorably discharged—wounds and disability.

6. Routine duties.

7. Reveille. Routine duties. Sermon preached by Rev. Ashmore, chaplain of an Illinois regiment.

8. Reveille. Routine duties.

9. Reveille. Routine duties.

10. Reveille. Routine duties. The 9th Kentucky are provost guards in the town, and keep order. They halt no one for a pass.

11. Reveille. Routine duties.

12. Reveille. Routine duties. Kingsley and Stow, recruits, arrived. Assigned to Company "A."

13. Reveille. Routine duties. General Beatty's headquarters is in town. The refugee camp is south of town.

14. Sunday. Reveille late. Began raining at 8 A. M. Ordered to be ready to march at 6 A. M. next morning with one day's rations in haversacks.

15. Reveille 4 A. M. It is raining. Marched at 7 A. M. to Little river at Rockford without resting. Halted at 9:30 A. M. Very muddy marching. Four companies are detailed to go and escort a drove of cattle. At 2 P. M. the cattle arrived. Started to camp, arriving before dark. Rations of sugar, coffee, salt, meal, etc., issued at 8 P. M. Ordered to strike tents and be ready to march. Marched at 2 A. M. in direction of Knoxville. Surgeon McFadden rejoined the regiment, having been a prisoner, captured at Chickamauga.

16. Reveille. Marching very slowly. Halting often. Cold. Arrived at Little river at Rockford at 12 M. Marched seven miles. Marched at 4 P. M., after all the teams had crossed, to within one mile of Knoxville by 8 P. M., and bivouacked on a hill. Very cold, and the ground frozen hard.

17. Reveille after sun-up. Very cold and freezing. Rations of beef; some crackers; also some flour issued.

18. Reveille early. Cold and cloudy. At 7 A. M. it began snowing. At 1 P. M. regiment marched into city and stacked arms. Marched to the depot. Closed column *en masse* and stacked arms. Marched about a mile from Fort Sanders, and formed in line of battle and bivouacked. Four companies detailed for picket.

19. Reveille. The four companies on picket were relieved. Came to camp nearly frozen. Pitched tents. Rations of meat issued.

20. Reveille early. Ordered to be ready for general review and inspection. At 2 P. M. the brigade was formed; passed in review and was inspected; returned to camp. Rations of pork, sugar, coffee, salt, molasses, crackers, etc., issued.

21. Sunday. Reveille at 5:30 A. M. Not so cold. Began snowing. Signed pay-rolls. Drew clothing and camp equipage.

22. Nothing important. First Lieutenant Edgar I. Foster, of "K" company, resigned. Disability from wounds.

23. Reveille very early. Policed quarters, and the whole camp ordered to move at daylight.

24. Reveille 3:30 A. M. Some rations issued. Marched at 7:30 A. M. Eighty rounds of cartridges issued to every man. Marched to city. Then in the direction of Strawberry plains by another road. Regiment in front of division. Halted at the Holston river ford two miles below Strawberry plains. 4 P. M. came in sight of the position occupied by the enemy the day before. Bivouacked for the night.

25. Reveille very early. Skirmishing can be heard across the river. At 11 A. M. heard the cars, indicating that the railroad is all right. Some beef issued.

26. Reveille 5 A. M. Some rations issued. Regiment paid for three months.

27. Reveille 5:30 A. M. Ordered to march at 10 A. M. Marched at 11 A. M. along the railroad to the bridge. Halted and stacked arms. Crossed the river in little pontoons and pulled them across with ropes. Marched one mile northeast of the plains. Stacked arms at 3:30 P. M. Rations issued at 4:30 P. M. for nine days. Ordered to leave everything not required on the march under guard.

28. Sunday. Reveille early, ready to march.

Marched at 12 M. to the bridge and on the New Market road to Van's station, then on to New Market. Into bivouac one-half mile northeast of town at 4 P. M.

29. Reveille 4 A. M. Ordered to be ready to march at 5 A. M. Raining. Marched through Mossy Creek station. Halted at 12 M. for dinner. Marched again at 1:45 P. M. and at 3:45 P. M. halted and bivouacked in the rebel camp at Morristown. Marched eighteen miles. Raining still.

MARCH, 1864.

1. Reveille at daylight. Raining hard. Some of the men who had been detailed on recruiting service came up to the regiment. Rations of beef, coffee, sugar, bacon, etc., issued. Ordered to be ready to march in the morning. First Lieutenant John T. Newland mustered as captain of "D" company.

2. Reveille 4 A. M. Marched at 5 A. M. back in the direction of Knoxville. Halted 11:45 A. M. at Mossy Creek station for dinner. Marched at 12:30 P. M. on the railroad. Arrived at New Market in one hour and five minutes. Marched a mile southeast of town and bivouacked. Beef and three days' rations issued. Ordered to be ready to march at moment's notice.

3. Reveille 3:30 A. M. Ready to march. Beef unfit to eat issued. Remained in bivouac.

4. Reveille 5 A. M. Some beef issued. At 7 P. M. Companies "I" and "C" are detailed to guard a train loaded with rations.

5. Reveille 5 A. M. Some rations issued. Companies "I" and "C" returned to regiment. Cool and clear. Drew clothing.

6. Sunday. Reveille 5 A. M. Ordered to be ready to march at a moment's notice.

7. Reveille 5 A. M. Policed camp. Began raining at 3 P. M. and continued during the day.

8. Reveille 5 A. M. Property left behind at the plains was brought up to-day. Some beef and crackers issued.

9. Reveille 5 A. M. Rations issued in the morning and again at night. Rained in the night.

10. Reveille 5 A. M. One day's ration of ham issued at 2 P. M. Camp pitched. Put up tents in line.

11. Reveille 5 A. M. Raining. Drew clothing. Ordered to be ready for picket at 3 P. M. Marched out to the line.

12. Relieved from picket 5:45 A. M. Rations issued. Marched to the depot and stacked arms. Marched at 8:30 A. M. in the rear of supply train. Arrived at Panther Springs at 2 P. M., twelve miles from New Market. Bivouacked; all very tired and hungry. Reveille ordered at 4 A. M.

13. Sunday. Reveille 4 A. M. Marched at 6 A. M. Arrived at Morristown at 8:15 A. M. and bivouacked near old camp.

14. Reveille 4 A. M. In line of battle until 5 A. M. Considerable musketry is heard at noon in front. Three days' rations issued.

15. Reveille at 4:30 A. M. In line of battle one hour. Some beef issued. Major Blankenship, ex-major, paid the regiment a visit. Five companies ordered on picket.

16. Reveille 4:30 A. M. In line of battle until sunrise. The wind is blowing very cold. The five companies relieved from picket. Five days' rations issued. The coldest weather since the regiment arrived in this vicinity.

17. Reveille 4 A. M. Ordered to have breakfast and be ready to march in one hour. Marched at 5:15 A. M.

through town and about one mile east of town and pitched regular camp. Beef, crackers, etc., issued. One and one-half potato and one onion to the man. Ordered to be ready for general inspection at 1 P. M. to-morrow.

18. Reveille 3:30 A. M. Ordered ready to march in one hour. Marched at 5 A. M. Orders to call the roll when the regiment halts. Marched two miles and halted. Marched in direction of Knoxville. Marched very fast. Arrived at New Market at 1:30 P. M. Marched eighteen miles. Some rations issued. Ordered to be ready to march at 5 A. M.

19. Reveille 4:30 A. M. Marched at 5:30 A. M. toward Strawberry plains, two miles. Crossed Holton river on pontoon bridge at 9:30 A. M. Marched about one mile up the river and bivouacked. Ordered on picket at 3 P. M.

20. Sunday. Reveille 5:30 A. M. Marched at 11:30 A. M. Regiment in the rear of the brigade. Marched to the crossroads. Marched on the Rutledge road eight miles. Halted in bivouack at 4:45 P. M.

21. Reveille 4:30 A. M. Ordered to have breakfast and to be in line ready to march 6 A. M. Marched at 6:30 A. M., 3d brigade in front. Marched two miles and halted. Bridges' battery ordered to the center of the brigade. Skirmishers deployed to the front at 12:15 P. M. Marched into Rutledge. Turned to the right and went into bivouac near the town at 12:30 P. M. Marched ten miles. Orders not to leave camp. Roll call ordered at 4 P. M. Beef and other rations issued. Ordered to have reveille at 4:30 A. M. and stand in line of battle.

22. Reveille 4:30 A. M. Stood in line of battle until after 6 A. M. Cold and cloudy. Began snowing at 8 A. M. Detail of foragers ordered. Stopped snow-

ing at dark. Rations issued. Colonel Knefler returned to the regiment and assumed command.

23. Reveille 4:30 A. M. Stood in line of battle until 6 A. M. Cleared off. Cold. Ordered on picket at 10 A. M. Marched to the picket line in front of town in the valley.

24. Aroused at 4 A. M. In line of battle on picket. Relieved from picket at 10:30 A. M. Marched to camp. Ordered to be ready to march immediately. One day's rations issued. Marched at 1 P. M. toward the plains, Colonel Knefler in command of the regiment. Marched ten miles from Rutledge and bivouacked at 5:30 P. M.

25. Reveille 4 A. M. Snow during the night. Stand in line of battle. A detail of six companies ordered from the regiment to go on a scout. The order is countermanded. The six companies marched out on a scout at 2 A. M.

26. Reveille 5:30 A. M. Stand in line of battle. The six companies came in from scout, not having discovered the rebels. At 11:30 A. M. the regiment is ordered to be ready to go on a scout with three days' rations in haversacks. Rations issued. At 1 P. M. three companies of the regiment marched on a scout with two brigades. They marched in direction of Rutledge, two and one-half miles, up the Richland valley, and turned to the left. Marched through a gap between the Poorland knobs and turned down the Poorland valley. Marched along the side of the Clinch Mountains to Powder Spring Gap, five miles, then into Flat Creek valley, northeast up the valley five miles, and went in bivouac at 6 P. M.

27. Reveille 4:30 A. M. Marched at 6:25 A. M., marching very fast. When five miles out our cavalry came up with a rebel home-guard. He was called to

halt; started to ride off and was shot dead. After marching nine miles formed in line of battle for dinner. Marched at 12:45 P. M. back toward the place marched from. At 5 P. M. bivouacked.

28. Reveille 5:30 A. M. At 7 A. M. a squad is detailed to go upon the mountain in search of rebels. None are found. The squad returned to camp at 12 M. Two days' rations issued.

29. Reveille 6 A. M. Rained all night. Rations of beef issued. Captain Ellis, sutler, is reported with goods at Knoxville.

30. Reveille 5 A. M. Snowing. Rations of beef issued. Ordered to have reveille at 4 A. M. and stand in line of battle until sun-rise.

31. Reveille 4 A. M. In line of battle until sun-rise. Marched on picket at 10 A. M. A few rations issued.

April, 1864.

1. Relieved from picket at 11 A. M. Marched to camp. The four companies returned to camp.

2. Reveille 4 A. M. Very cold. Beef issued.

3. Sunday. Reveille 4 A. M. Three days' rations issued. Colonel Kneffer presented the men of the regiment with tin buckets with bales which he had specially manufactured in Indianapolis while on leave of absence.

4. Reveille 5 A. M. In line of battle. Ordered on picket at 10 A. M. Marched to the picket line.

5. Reveille. Stood in line of battle. Relieved from picket at 11 A. M. Marched to camp. Rations issued. Ordered ready to march at 6 A. M. Colonel Kneffer presented to the first sergeants a coffee mill for use of their respective companies.

6. Reveille 4 A. M. Marched at 6 A. M., regiment in front of the division. Marched through fields and

woods to within one and one-half miles of Strawberry
plains. Camped at 12:45 P. M. Three days' rations
issued. Reveille ordered at 4 A. M. To march at 5 to
Knoxville.

7. Reveille at 4 A. M. Marched at 6 A. M., cheering
and yelling, to the railroad. At 11:45 halted for dinner.
Marched again after noon to within two and one-half
miles of city; ordered to dress up lines, fixed bayonets and marched through city in platoon column,
at right shoulder shift. Marched three and one-half
miles from city on Louden road; bivouacked at 5
P. M. Marched twenty miles. Captain John N. Scott
honorably discharged on account of wound received
in battle of Stone River.

8. Reveille 5 A. M. Raining. Marched at 1:45 P. M.
seven miles, and into bivouac at 5 P. M. One day's
rations issued.

9. Reveille 4 A. M. Marched at 6:30 A. M. Halted
at 12:45 P. M. for dinner. Marched at 1:40 P. M. to
Lenoir Station and into bivouac at 3:10 P. M. Marched
fourteen miles. Rained. Ordered to have reveille at
4 A. M. March at 5 A. M. Drew potatoes.

10. Sunday. Reveille 4 A. M. Marched at 6 A. M.
Raining. Marched six miles and halted on the banks
of the river opposite Louden at 8:45 A. M. Marched
up the river one mile and bivouacked. A few rations
issued.

11. Reveille 5 A. M. Marched and crossed the river
on improvised ferry boats and marched two miles
down the river. Rations issued. Raining.

12. Reveille 5 A. M. Raining. One-half pint of
whisky for six men and rations issued; rations issued
to last until 17th. Ordered to have reveille 4 A. M.
and march at 5 A. M.

13. Reveille 3:30 A. M. Marched at 5:30 A. M.

Third brigade in front. Arrived at Philadelphia at 9 A. M. Marched through Sweetwater at 11:45 A. M. Into bivouac at 12:30 P. M. Marched 15 miles.

14. Reveille 3:30 A. M. Marched at 5:45 A. M. Third brigade in the rear. General O. O. Howard in command of 4th army corps since the 10th inst. Passed through Mouse Creek station at 9:30 A. M. and at 12:15 P. M. into bivouac one-half mile from Athens. Marched twelve miles.

15. Reveille 4 A. M. Marched at 6 A. M. through Athens and Riceville. Arrived at Calhoun at 1:40 P. M. Crossed the Hiawassee river. Marched into Charlestown, and into bivouac one-half mile from the town at 2:15 P. M. Marched fifteen miles.

16. Reveille 4 A. M. Marched at 5:30 A. M. Third brigade in front. Marched to near Cleveland and halted at 10:20 A. M. Marched again at 10:45 A. M. in column of companies. Marched, in reviewing order, past General Sherman, through the town, and halted on the other side. Raining. Marched toward Chattanooga about seven miles and halted at 2:15 P. M. In bivouac. Marched eighteen miles. Captain Newland and First Sergeants Eaton and Many returned to regiment from recruiting service.

17. Sunday. Reveille 5 A. M. Company inspections. Rations issued.

18. Reveille 5 A. M. Ordered to be ready for regimental inspection at 3 P. M. Ordered to move at 10 A. M. Colonel Kneffer in command of regiment, General Beatty having returned to his command of the brigade and relieved Colonel Kneffer. Marched at 12:45 P. M. Seven miles to McDaniel's Gap. Passed through the gap and the regiment halted 4:30 P. M., to relieve some troops, among them 21st Illinois, stationed here guarding the gap. Pitched camp.

19. Reveille 5 A. M. Pitched camp, put up tents in regular order. Country hilly and wild.

20. Reveille 4:30 A. M. Two days' rations issued. Marched at 9:15 A. M. to report to brigade, arriving near brigade at 12:45 P. M. Bivouacked in the woods and ordered to pitch camp again. Ordered not to cut any trees.

21. Reveille 5 A. M. Policed camp. Onions and potatoes in small quantities issued.

22. Reveille 5 A. M. Policed camp. Ditched tents, graded streets, etc. Ordered to be ready for general review by General Howard commanding 4th Army Corps, Army of the Cumberland, at 11 A. M. to-morrow. Ordered for picket at 6 A. M. in the morning.

23. Reveille at 5 A. M. Marched out on picket line at 6 A. M. General review postponed. It began raining at 10 A. M.

24. Sunday. Reveille 5 A. M. Raining. Relieved from picket and marched to camp. Drew clothing. Ordered to be ready for dress parade at 6:30 P. M. Received very strict camp orders and rules for the government of the camp.

25. Reveille at 4:30 A. M. All orders again by bugle call. Battalion drill.

26. Reveille 4:30 A. M. Brigade guards stationed around the camp. Ordered to practice target shooting.

27. Reveille at 4:30 A. M. Regiment practiced target shooting. Each man firing three times. Ordered to have pay-rolls made out for month's pay. Officers are ordered to pack all surplus baggage, to be forwarded to Chattanooga for storage.

28. Reveille 4:30 A. M. Cannonading is heard in the direction of Ringgold. Two days' rations issued. Ordered to be ready for brigade camp guard in the morning at 5:45.

9

29. Reveille at 4:30 a. m. Raining. A heavy detail is made for camp guard and picket. Strict orders are issued governing the men while on duty. General grand review by General Howard, of the 4th Army Corps. The regiment on picket line.

30. Reveille 4:30 a. m. Ordered for muster by 11 a. m. Mustered. Five days' rations issued. Dress parade. Brigade band beat off in front of regiment. Chaplain L. H. Jameson resigned.

MAY, 1864.

1. Reveille 5 a. m. Rained all night. At 8 a. m. company inspection. Some potatoes issued. Officers notified to have their things packed and at the station by Monday. Dress parade. Order read allowing but one wagon to the regiment.

2. Reveille 5 a. m. Beautiful morning. Packed up all extra camp equipage and overcoats for storage. Two men are detailed from each company as pioneers. Practiced target firing. Raining at 10 a. m. Cleared off after dinner. Company drills. Drew some clothing.

3. Reveille 5 a. m. Heavy frost. Some potatoes issued. Ordered to be ready to march 12 m. Marched 12:30 p. m., brigade in front, toward Ringgold. Marched eight miles. Bivouacked at 4:15 p. m.

4. Reveille 4:30 p. m. In line 5:30 a. m. Waiting on the other two brigades to pass. Marched at 6:15 a. m., marching very slowly. Halted at Catoosa Springs at 12 m. There are fifty-two different kinds of water. It has been a pleasure and health resort. Marched beyond the springs half mile. Bivouacked at 12:15 p. m. three miles from Ringgold, having marched eight miles. Ordered to have reveille at

4 A. M., form line and remain in line till daylight. Nearing the enemy.

5. Reveille 4 A. M. Stand in line until breakfast time. Shots heard on the picket line. Went on picket at 12:15 P. M. Ordered to advance picket line three-quarters of a mile. A line of skirmishers sent forward. Ordered to advance. The regiment supported the skirmishers. The new advanced picket line was established. Were ordered in extension of the line with other troops.

6. Called into line at 3 A. M. Relieved from picket by the 9th Kentucky at 8 A. M. Returned to camp. Warm. Rations issued. Orders to put guns in perfect shooting order. All signs point to great activity.

7. Reveille 3 A. M. Ordered to march at 5 A. M. Very foggy morning. Brigade marched at 6 A. M. Regiment in rear of brigade. Marched toward Tunnel Hill. Marched very slowly. Skirmishing heard to the right at some distance. The road is littered with knapsacks, overcoats, woolen blankets, etc., thrown away by soldiers who do not want to carry them. At 8:45 A. M. artillery firing some distance to the right and front. The rebels cut trees in the road to impede advance. At 10:30 A. M. formed in line of battle and ordered to form double column at half distance. Artillery takes position on knolls in front. Rebels can be seen moving out. Their signal corps visible. Very warm. At 12 M. deployed columns and marched. Some cannonading is heard. Arrived at the tunnel at 1:15 P. M. Marched up on a hill and halted. Marched six miles. The rebels can be seen destroying the railroad. Our batteries are shelling them.

8. Sunday. Reveille 4 A. M. The regiment formed at 5 A. M. We are ordered to leave all things behind, to go on a reconnaissance in light marching order;

8 A. M. formed double column at half distance; at 8:45 signal was fired by a cannon shot to move forward; marched forward and skirmishers were engaged immediately as the advance was made. The rebels can be seen to the left on top of Rocky Face ridge. Halted at a little branch in the bottom. Some beautiful red fish, with spots on their backs. Mountain trout in the water. Light skirmishing in front at 12 M. Rebels running to the left, firing at our men. Fell back, a little distance. Stacked arms. At 2 P. M. marched down the valley. At 2:45 P. M. two companies of the regiment are deployed as skirmishers. The skirmishers advanced to near the gap, left extending up the side of the ridge or mountain. At 4:10 P. M. the artillery opened on the rebels in the gap. Heavy skirmishing on the right of the gap. At 4:45 P. M. the regiment advanced a considerable distance. Fired a few shots. At 6 P. M. the rebel artillery opened on the Union lines, the first cannonading heard to-day. The rebels yell at our men from the top of the high bluff. The skirmishers were ordered to return, and the regiment joined the brigade. Details were sent after things left behind on line of march, and returned at 11 P. M.

9. Reveille 4 A. M. Very foggy. The rebel sharpshooters are shooting into Union lines from top of the ridge and talking. At 6 A. M. brisk skirmishing on the left and rear. Artillery firing shells in that direction. The rebels are seen marching to the left. At 8 A. M. fell in and reformed line. There was brisk skirmishing in front next to the ridge. At 8:30 A. M. ordered to pile knapsacks. At 8:45 the front line of the 3d Brigade began heavy firing. It extended to Willich's 1st Brigade on the left. Marched forward and halted at the foot of Rocky Face Mountain. Sixth

Ohio battery is firing over the regiment at the enemy. Musketry by volleys can be heard at some distance to the right. At 4 P. M. marched to the right toward the gap, about a mile, formed line and halted. The skirmishers keep up a brisk fire in our front, and the rebels are firing down and wounding some of our men. At 6 P. M. there is heavy musketry and artillery firing on the right near by. It sounds like Union troops are advancing, driving the rebs to the end of Rocky Face ridge. Ordered to move up near. A detail is sent for knapsacks left behind. The firing continued until 8 P. M., and gradually ceased. Brigade band came up and played a few tunes. Rations issued at 11 P. M. S. Walker, of "C" company, wounded.

10. Reveille 4 A. M. Sharp shooters are firing from the ridge. Sharp skirmishing begins at 6 A. M. Ordered to fill canteens. At 7 A. M. heavy cannonading on the left. The sharp shooters are sending balls among our men. Louis McFadden, of Company "E," is seriously wounded in the arm. At 7 P. M. regiment ordered on picket in front of the ridge. It is raining, thundering and lightening and the rebs yell and fire at the picket line.

11. The sharp shooters are firing down briskly, but overshoot the lines. Very cold and wet; the men are shivering. Rained all day. Regiment relieved at 8 P. M. by the 9th Kentucky. The rebels asked, "What regiment is that down there?" Our men answered, "The 9th Kentucky." "You lie," said the rebs, "the 9th Kentucky is up here." One 9th Kentucky asked the rebs, "Is Bill So-and-so, Jim So-and-so and Dick So-and-so up there?" "Yes," said the rebs. Then they, the rebs, asked about persons they knew also. The two regiments, 9th Kentucky Federal and 9th Confederate, had been raised in the same neighbor-

hood. The conversation was kept up by the two regiments. The 79th Regiment marched back to Tunnel Hill to bivouac. The first time out of range of rebel bullets since the 8th.

12. Up at daylight. Cold and windy. Rebels still firing at 1 P. M. Ordered into line in a hurry. Marched to the left. Stacked arms and ordered to put up a barricade of rails and logs against a cavalry attack. Rebel cavalry hovering about. Skirmishing in front and the rear. Union cavalry returned, reporting the enemy advancing in force. Unable to hold them. Looked for them; prepared to receive them, but they came not. Bivouacked in readiness for any emergencies.

13. Reveille 4 A. M. Cold and quiet. Marched at 6:45 toward Tunnel Hill, countermarched and marched in the rear of the 2d Division. Troops can be seen marching toward the gap known as Buzzard Roost. Marched around the base of Rocky Face ridge and marched down the valley back of the ridge facing rebels' advanced line of works, which are very strong. At 9 o'clock turned to the left before reaching the gap, passed through the enemy's advanced works and marched to the Knoxville and Dalton railroad, toward Dalton. At 12:30 P. M. struck Dalton, halted, captured some of the rebel knapsacks; very nice, made in England. They are better than ours. Started and marched very slow, as there were teams in front. Marched toward Resaca. Halted at 5:45 P. M. for supper. Started in a half hour. Skirmishing in front. The regiment is guarding an ammunition train. Halted at 9 P. M. Slept by the teams. Marched twelve miles.

14. Reveille 4 A. M. Three days' rations issued. At 10:30 A. M. started the regiment in rear of the

division as train guards. Distant cannonading. Marched very slowly. At 12 M. halted near some rebel breastworks, having marched about three miles. Pickets were sent out; the teams were parked. Heavy cannonading is heard on left and front; it is becoming closer, a perfect roar, and not very far. Heavy musketry is also heard. Ammunition is sent to the front. Cannonading very heavy at 2 P. M., accompanied by volleys of musketry. At 4 P. M. firing much decreased. At 7 P. M. cannonading began again on left and front in the direction where the division was in position. Heavy musketry. Received orders to be ready to march at moment's notice. The 20th Corps passing to the left. Started forward with the ammunition train. Marched about a mile to the front and halted. Bivouacked at 10 P. M.

15. Sunday. Reveille 4 A. M. Quiet until 5:15 A. M. Two cannon shots are heard. The regiment ordered to report to the brigade. Marched at 5:30 A. M.; 3d Brigade not engaged. Twenty rounds of cartridges issued to the man; heavy cannonding and musketry in front. At 11:30 A. M. called into line. Good news is read from the Eastern Army. At 1:10 heavy cannonading and musketry began on the left and front, and lasted ten minutes or more. At 5 P. M. General Willich, commander 1st Brigade, 3d Division, passed in ambulance, wounded in the breast. Bivouacked for the night. Adjutant Eli F. Ritter mustered in as captain of "C" company.

16. Reveille 4 A. M. Cannonading heard. At 7 A. M. marched past where the battle was fought the day before. Passed several of the killed. The enemy had many lines of formidable breastworks on all the hills and knolls everywhere, the ground was very hilly and rough and indicated a hard fought battle. Marks

of shell, solid shot and cannister could be seen all around; the ground in many places plowed up by them, trees ten and twelve inches cut in two, one pine tree twenty-two inches in diameter shot through in three different places. Marched about two miles and reached the main road and railroad crossing and halted. Marched at 3 p. m. through Resaca. Strong fortifications all around. Crossed the Ostenoola river on an old wagon bridge, which the rebels failed to burn. Halted at 3:45 p. m. just across the river. Marched again at 5 p. m. Heavy skirmish line on the flank. Marched down the railroad. Some cannonading at a distance in front. Halted, in bivouac, at 7:45 p. m., four miles from the river.

17. Reveille 3:15 a. m. Raining. Three days' rations issued. Musketry is heard far off. Marched at 7 a. m. Marched through Calhoun at 8 a. m., six miles from Resaca, skirmishing in front. The rebels are contesting every foot of ground. Marched along slow. At 3 p. m. the rebels fired on telegraphers' train. Soon put to flight. Heavy skirmishing on the left and right. Formed in line of battle at 4 p. m. The rebels could be seen firing at the advance a little to right of front. Are ordered to build a line of rail barricades. Heavy skirmishing begins on the right and front and the skirmishing on the left continued. Ceased raining at 5:20 p. m. Artillery opened on the rebels. Rebels can be seen passing to the rear occasionally. At 5:30 p. m. the rebel batteries opened to reply on the line in front, killing and wounding some of the troops. Regiment moved off the knoll to allow the artillery to take position there. They opened on the rebs with heavy fire and soon silenced them. There is still heavy firing to the left and front. The batteries ceased firing at dark and regiment was ordered out on the

picket line. Heavy skirmishing continued until after 9 P. M. Marched about eight miles to-day.

18. Picket line relieved at 4 A. M. At 7 A. M. ordered in from the picket line. Marched past strong rebel breastworks toward Adairsville. Halted at 9 A. M. and formed a line of battle. Company "I" is detailed as flanker. Advanced a short distance and halted. There is skirmishing in front. General McPherson's Corps passed in rear to the left. Number of amputated arms and legs lying around unburied indicate the site of an abandoned rebel hospital. Saw quite a number of unburied dead rebels. At 1:15 P. M. marched, 3d Brigade in front. Turned to the right of the railroad, halted and formed in line of battle. Advanced and ordered back. Marched into very thick woods. Hard marching. Rebels can be seen to the left and front in the distance. After reaching the brow of a hill the skirmishers began to fire briskly, at 6 P. M., which continued until 7 P. M. Relieved from the front line and bivouacked.

19. Reveille 4:20 A. M. Marched at 5 A. M. to the road and halted until other troops passed. Followed at 8 A. M. and marched very fast. Very hot weather. At 10:15 A. M. the 3d Division marched into Kingston, Ga., fifty-nine miles from Atlanta and seventy-nine miles from Chattanooga. Marched through town and halted to rest. Sharp skirmishing in front. Marched again at 12 M. Marched only a short distance near where the 1st Division of the 4th Corps was engaged with the enemy. Formed line on their right. Skirmishing very brisk in front, and batteries were firing on the rebels very fast. Heavy cannonading on the left, supposed to be General Hooker's command, near Cassville. Advanced in double column, at half distance, about a mile, through very thick

woods, and halted. Ordered back a short distance and stacked arms. At 5 P. M. moved forward again. Brisk skirmishing in front. At 5:45 P. M. the artillery opened on the rebels by volleys. The earth fairly trembled. Advanced in line through the fields to a strip of woods. Skirmishers soon began hot firing. Artillery soon came up and took another position. Darkness prevented further action for the night. The right of the 3d Brigade joined the 14th Corps. The 17th Kentucky deployed to the front as skirmishers. The 86th Indiana and 59th Ohio Volunteer Infantry in front line. Seventy-ninth Indiana and 9th Kentucky in second line. All in line of battle supporting the skirmish line. The rebel bullets fell all around. Captain Hanna, of Company "H," wounded in the hand and thigh. Quite a number in the brigade wounded. Halted at dark. The skirmish fire ceased along the line at 9 P. M. Ordered to build barricades of rails, and bivouacked. Marched nine miles.

20. Roused at 3:30 A. M. Three days' rations issued. At 5:30 A. M. relieved the 86th Indiana on picket line. All quiet. Fresh beef issued. No advance or other movement during the day.

21. Reveille at 4:30 A. M. At 6:30 A. M. the assembly sounded. The regiment ordered into line on account of some one having fired off his gun against orders. Regimental inspection ordered to ascertain the guilty ones. Forty-three empty guns discovered. Non-commissioned officers reduced to ranks; privates fined one month's pay. Remained in bivouack during the day.

22. Sunday. Rations for five days issued. Ordered to send everything back to Bridgeport which the men do not want to carry. Everything to be prepared

and put in shape for a hard campaign and marching. Very hot. We remained in bivouack.

23. Reveille 4 A. M. Ordered to move at 12 M. Marched from near Cassville, and marched south. Captain Ritter relieved as adjutant. Took command of Company "C." Sergeant Major Dunn is appointed adjutant. Corporal Munhall, of Company "C," sergeant major. Colonel Knefler is commanding the brigade. The badge of 4th Corps is an equilateral triangle, blue for 3d Brigade. Marched through some well cultivated country. Crossed the Etowah river at 5:30 P. M. The rebels did not succeed in burning the bridge. Turned eastward more, and at 9 P. M. went into bivouack, having marched 9 miles.

24. Reveille 3:30 A. M. Marched at 6:15 A. M. a short distance, crossed a small stream and 3d Brigade halted for other troops to pass to the front. At 10:15 A. M. marched again; marched on cross-roads, through woods and fields. Very hot and dusty. Marched very slow and passed over some very hilly, rough country. At 12:45 P. M. artillery shots in front. At 1 P. M. halted for dinner. Marched again at 3 P. M. over the Raccoon hills in the Allatoona mountains through very rough defiles; bad place for an army to pass. Halted in bivouac at 5:30 P. M., having marched ten miles during the day.

25. Reveille 4 A. M. Troops and teams are passing to the front. Marched at 10 A. M. One man from each company detailed to wait until the wagons come up to bring up shoes, which are very badly needed, and one man from each company detailed to report to Lieutenant Mount for forage guard. March southward. Weather very hot. Marched a short distance and halted. Marched again at 2 P. M.; very slow. Roads are bad; over hills, through hollows, through

a very poor country. Marched in the rear of two batteries and could not march fast. At 4:45 P. M. heavy cannonading in front, and at 6 P. M. considerable musketry. Reached Punkin Vine creek at dark; crossed on a bridge. At 7 P. M. it began raining very hard. Marched on about three miles. Met the wounded of General Hooker's corps going to the rear. At 10 P. M. were ordered to bivouac by the side of the road. Marched about ten miles during the day. Ordered to have reveille at 3 A. M. and form line at 4 A. M.

26. Reveille 3 A. M. Formed in line of battle. Roll-call orders. Many wounded of Hooker's corps going to the rear. Brisk skirmishing in front. Marched 6 A. M. about one and one-half miles, and formed in line of battle on the left of the skirmish line. At 7 A. M., as soon as the skirmishers advanced, they were fired upon by the rebels in a very thick wood and in matted underbrush. The rebels fired heavily, and brisk skirmishing was kept up until 11 A. M. The artillery opened fire on the rebels; advanced but a short distance to give the right and left time to complete the allignment. At 3:40 P. M. the rebel batteries began shelling our men, and the shells burst all around us. They were soon silenced. At 7 P. M. marched back a short distance and bivouacked for the night. Marched about three miles during the day. Three days' rations issued for five days. Shoes and socks issued.

27. Reveille 3:30 A. M. Two days' rations of beef issued. At 5:20 A. M. artillery opened on the enemy in front, and soon the whole line was engaged, rebel shells exploding all around; 9:45 A. M. marched to the left, Colonel Kneffer commanding 3d Brigade, Major Parker commanding regiment. The 3d Division formed in six lines preparatory to an attack upon the

enemy. For a mile the march was nearly due southward, through dense forests and the thickest jungles, over a country scarred by deep ravines and intersected by difficult ridges. Added to these difficulties, the hot rays of a tropical sun made it almost impossible to advance under such adverse circumstances. Moved a mile southward, then about a mile and a half to the west. 4:45 P. M. there was brisk skirmishing and some cannonading to the right and front. At 5 P. M., while the regiment was in line preparatory to the charge about to be made, a man of Company "A" was killed in his place in line by a rifle ball. Several others were wounded. The command "Forward!" was given, and the regiment advanced rapidly under a heavy fire of grape and cannister from the rebel batteries posted on the hills in front; advanced about one-fourth of a mile and found that the Federal troops who had occupied the front line had been forced to fall back, being out of ammunition. The 79th Indiana was the front line at the edge of a field sloping down to a rail fence at the edge of the woods. Under the heavy fire from the enemy the men of the 79th Indiana picked up the rails, and, advancing to the brow of the hill, made a temporary line of field works to protect them from the enfilading fire of the enemy. The regiment lay behind the rails and kept up a continuous fire at the rebels, and thus kept them in check until after dark, when a continuous flash of their guns could be seen not more than two hundred yards distant. At 10 P. M., being almost out of ammunition, the regiment was ordered to fall back quietly and in order, which was done under a heavy fire from the enemy. The rebels advanced their line in the darkness, and their bugle sounded the charge. The regiment fell back about half a mile, where a brigade of regulars had built a very strong line of fortifications, expecting the rebels to follow and attack. Marched to Picket's saw-mill under heavy fire of artillery; thence marched to the left in the woods a short distance; put up a temporary line of works of stones, stumps, etc. At 1 A. M. lay down to sleep, very much fatigued from the day's work. Marched about eight miles. The regiment lost severely in killed and wounded.

28. Awakened 4 A. M. by rebel shells exploding uncomfortably close. Ammunition issued. Ordered to build a line of works at once. The men have had nothing to eat since yesterday A. M. and are not allowed to build fires. Brisk firing in front and left and sounds nearer and nearer. Skirmishing and cannonading all along the lines. At 2 P. M. ordered to move back, change front and build strong works. Skirmishing was not so brisk. 5 P. M. artillery began shelling the rebels on the left and front. Two days' ration of beef issued. Ordered to have reveille at 3 A. M.

29. Sunday. A brisk firing on the skirmish line during the night. General alarm along the lines. Formed in line. Rested again until 3 A. M., when firing began again. Fell in and managed to eat breakfast during the excitement. There was brisk skirmishing all along the line. It is comparatively quiet in front of the 3d Brigade. Only an occasional shot is heard. At 2 P. M. the rebels shelled the Union lines, the shells exploding uncomfortably close. The regiment ordered on picket at 5 P. M. Was quiet until sometime after darkness set in when brisk firing began along the lines and in front. Skirmishing did not cease during the night.

30. On picket. Awakened at 3:30 A. M. by heavy cannonading on the right and left. Pioneers were at work on the left all night. It was a cool night. Re-

ceived orders, that if attacked to hold ground, as reinforcements would be pushed forward immediately. Relieved from outpost duty at 7 P. M. Marched to bivouac. Three days' rations issued. Ordered to be ready to march at 9 A. M. Marched forward toward the picket line through very heavy woods, to take place in line with the brigade. Lost the way in the darkness. Did not find proper position until after midnight. Built some strong barricades and lay down to rest behind them.

31. Considerable skirmishing all night. At 8 A. M. ordered to move, not being in the right place in line. Just formed our new line when the rebels charged the picket line, without any serious result. Men were reinforced by a regiment, repulsing the rebels. Worked very hard on the breastworks, gathering logs, rocks and rails to make them as strong as possible. Could not work steadily, having to form line whenever heavy musketry firing was heard. Worked between volleys and by 10:30 A. M. the line was good and strong. The lines were strong and secure against any attack the enemy might make. Very hot day. The men very much fatigued, having lost much sleep and having worked so hard. The rebel skirmishers sent bullets over the works all day. Some beef was issued and the regiment lay down to take much needed rest. Awakened during the night by brisk firing in front. Skirmishing did not cease all night.

JUNE, 1864.

1. Awakened at 4 A. M. Skirmishers still firing. Some beef issued. Other rations scarce.

2. Up at 3:30 A. M. Very hot. Raining at noon. Some beef issued at night.

3. Alarmed during the night by brisk skirmishing,

lasting, however, but a few minutes. Up at 4 A. M. Cloudy and raining. At 9 A. M. ordered to strike tents, pack knapsacks and move close to the works. At 12 M. ordered to put up tents again. Three days' rations issued.

4. Reveille 3 A. M. Raining. At 8:30 A. M. tents are struck. Marched to the right and took the place of one division of the 14th Corps that had been ordered to the left. Pitched tents. Orders to police our quarters. The rebel bullets fell all around. At 2 P. M. the rebels began to cannonade, the shells flying in all directions. No casualties. Ordered to strengthen the works. At 4 P. M. the rebels made a charge on the right and were quickly repulsed. Ordered on picket after 8 P. M. At 9 P. M. the order was countermanded.

5. Sunday. Up at 3 A. M. Ordered to strengthen the works. Still raining. At 8 A. M. pickets saw the rebel pickets hastily withdrawing from their works. Our men followed and found the works evacuated. Some of the boys went to the battlefield of Pickett's Mills, where the 3d Division was engaged on the 27th of May. They reported they saw where our men had fired with a great deal of accuracy at the rebel works, and the trees and everything around showed evidence of hard fighting that was done on that day by the 3d Division.

6. Reveille 3 A. M. Ordered to be ready to march at sunrise. Marched at 5 A. M. Roads very muddy. Marched eastward through the bad grounds, woods and fields. Halted at 10 A. M. to rest. An order is read from General Sherman that no one must leave the ranks to look after the wounded. Any one violating the order would be arrested by patrols and severely punished. Musicians are detailed to look after the wounded. Officers will be treated the same as enlisted

men. Very hot and sultry and hard marching. Cannonading on the right and front at a considerable distance. Halted at 1 P. M., pitched tents, marched about eight miles. Rations of beef issued.

7. Reveille 4 A. M. Ordered to be ready for inspection at 3 P. M. Three days' rations issued. It rained.

8. Reveille 4 A. M. One day's rations issued and some clothing and shoes.

9. Reveille 3:30 A. M. About three miles southeast of Ackworth. One day's rations issued. Very warm.

10. Reveille 3:30 A. M. Ready to march at 8 A. M. Marched at 12:15 P. M. Raining hard. Marched very slow. Cannonading in front. Halted in camp near the 70th Indiana, many of whom visit friends in the Seventy-ninth. Marched two miles during the day. Beef issued.

11. Reveille 4 A. M. Raining very hard. Marched, at 12:30 P. M., one mile to the left and halted. A rebel battery began firing at 1:30 P. M. to right and front. Pitched tents. Beef issued at 4 P. M. Artillery opened fire on the rebels and kept it up until night. The enemy could plainly be seen. Skirmishing.

12. Sunday. Reveille 4 A. M. Rained all night. Some beef issued. We have no crackers. Raining hard. First Lieutenant Luman Jones, "E" company, promoted and mustered as captain of "E" company.

13. Reveille 4 A. M. Rained all night. Skirmishing all night. At 7 A. M. heard the whistle of a locomotive. Three days' rations issued.

14. Reveille 4 A. M. Marched at 12 M. to the left and front. Considerable skirmishing in front. Marched about a mile and formed in line of battle. Some other

10

troops in front. Marched back a short distance. At 3:30 P. M. a feeble charge was made in front. At 5:45 P. M. the 6th Ohio Battery began firing at the rebs from the knoll where the regiment was in line. Beef issued and pitched tents.

15. Reveille 4 A. M. skirmishing and cannonading all night. Rifle balls pass over. Three days' rations issued and some cartridges. Marched at 2:30 P. M. to the front. Halted *en masse* in an open field. The skirmishing very brisk in front at times. At 5:30 A. M. skirmishing renewed with vigor, and some of the batteries got in position on the ridge to the right and began shelling the rebels. At 6:15 P. M. skirmishing increased, and at 6:30 P. M. marched forward to the front a little distance. Ordered back to camp. Countermarched again and went forward toward the skirmish line. Halted at 8 P. M. on the side of a high knoll. Ordered to make coffee. A battery near by is shelling the rebels. Some rations issued.

16. Reveille 4 A. M. Skirmishing in front. Very brisk all night. At 5 P. M. the batteries on the right and left opened on the rebels. Advanced the skirmish line in front, and there are now two lines of works in front. Batteries are shelling the rebel trains and works. The batteries and works can be seen from the knoll. At 4 P. M. the rebel batteries opened fire, but the Union batteries soon silenced them.

17. Reveille 4 A. M. Skirmishing is still heard, but farther off. Deployed and marched at 7:30 P. M. a short distance and halted. Marched again and marched through the line of works where the timber was badly scarred by shot and shell and musket balls. Marched over the rebel works, which were very strong. At 10:30 A. M. relieved the 1st Division of 4th Corps.

Formed line of battle and loaded. There was skirmishing in front, the 79th Regiment in the front line, the 19th Ohio Volunteer Infantry on the right, 9th Kentucky on the left. Skirmishers kept up brisk firing. The artillery got in position, but could not hold it on account of the enfilading fire of the enemy. At 3 P. M. the 19th Ohio Volunteer Infantry and the 17th Kentucky went on the skirmish line. At 4:30 P. M. the 79th Regiment marched to the front, close to the skirmish line. The rebel bullets came very thick. Put up a barricade of rails for protection. At 6:15 P. M. the batteries got into position a few rods on each side of the line, firing as fast as they could and made the earth fairly tremble, and the rebel fire decreased rapidly in intensity at 7:15 P. M. The rebels continued shelling the lines and our men advanced the skirmish line. The firing along the line very hot. At 8:15 P. M. we moved out and built a line of field works and lay down to rest. At 11 P. M. aroused by brisk skirmishing. It proved a false alarm and lay down again.

18. Aroused at 1 A. M. by brisk firing on the picket line. It was supposed the rebels were attacking the picket line. Ordered to be ready to move at 4 A. M. Began raining at 3 A. M. Marched at 4 A. M. without breakfast. Marched to the front to support the 9th Kentucky, which was deployed as skirmishers in front. It was raining very hard. Advancing, the skirmishers began brisk firing and advanced the whole line. The left and right also advanced, gaining the top of a small hill, the skirmishers in the bottom in front. Halted. The rebels shelled the line very hard. Still raining very hard. The shells and balls flying thick and fast all around. At 11 A. M. the regiment deployed as skirmishers and began continuous firing

until relieved. Returned to camp and saw where several of our brigade had been killed by the rebel fire. The rebels made one of the batteries fall back, having perfect range on it. Three days' rations and one-half gill of whisky issued per man. Loss to the regiment during the day, three men killed and several wounded. Musketry fire kept up all night.

19. Sunday. After daylight firing ceased. At 1:30 A. M. ordered to march, and marched at 8 A. M. At 8:30 A. M. halted. Artillery opened on the enemy in front. Cannonading all along the line on the left. The enemy retired. Marched at 10 A. M. Passed through the rebel works a short distance from where the heavy skirmishing occurred yesterday in the woods. Cannonading on the right and left at some distance, and also in the immediate front. At 11:30 P. M. the rain began pouring down. At 1 P. M. halted for dinner. Marched again at 3:15 P. M. Marched a short distance and formed line of battle, fronting toward Marietta, the big knoll or mountain called Kenesaw Mountain, to the left, not very far off. At 4:15 P. M. the artillery on the left and front seemed to fight a duel, firing fierce and furious. A continuous roar. The rebels finally ceased firing, and rapidly retreated. It is raining. Drew cartridges. At 6:15 P. M. marched into the woods and bivouacked, having marched only one and one-half miles during the day. Ordered ready to march at 4 A. M.

20. Awakened at 3 A. M. Skirmish firing all night, but little cannonading. At 11:15 A. M. the artillery on the right began firing. Marched at 1:30 P. M. to the right, and halted in a field and stacked arms. Began raining at 2 P. M. At 2:30 P. M. big guns (twenty pounders) opened on the mountain. At 4:15 P. M. a charge was made in front. It was very lively from

the noise and yells. The rebel artillery opened on the line with shell and solid shot. Shells exploded among the line. A solid shot went through a stump, and jarred some of the men who were near by badly. Marched to the right and relieved some of the 20th Corps. It rained very hard. Very heavy cannonading is heard to the left, and fierce fighting is going on in various places. Marched to the right some distance. At 9 P. M. into bivouac.

21. Awakened at 3 A. M. Ordered to be ready to march at 4 A. M. At 4:30 A. M. the artillery near by on the left opened fire on the enemy. Raining. Heavy skirmishing on the left and at 12 M. charge after charge was made along the line. Yelling and cheering are continuously heard. The artillery in front shelled the rebels out of their rifle pits and our skirmishers advanced and occupied them. At 2:15 P. M. the 17th Kentucky sent to the front to support the skirmish line. At 3:15 P. M. marched out in a field, and ordered to put up works of rails and anything that could be got. Skirmishing very heavy in front. Some of the men were wounded by stray balls coming over. William Haggard, of Company "C," was wounded here. Three days' rations issued, also desiccated potatoes and vegetables. Skirmishing was kept up all along the line during the night.

22. Up at daylight. Ordered to be ready to march at 6 A. M. Skirmishing. Still brisk cannonading on the right. At 9 A. M. the rebel artillery on Pine Tar Mountain opened fire upon the line, in position in an open field. At 12 M. ordered to march. At 2 P. M. brisk firing on the left and front. At 4 P. M. ordered to fortify. At 5 P. M. skirmishers are advanced and brisk skirmishing is kept up. Several of the skirmishers are brought to the rear wounded. The rebels opened

on our artillery and the shells and shot passed over us and frequently struck in the works. Everything in readiness for advance of the enemy as their artillery ceased firing suddenly. Two companies ordered to reinforce the picket line of the brigade. The skirmishers advanced close to the rebel works, but had to fall back on account of a heavy cross-fire from the rebel lines. Several killed and many wounded out of the brigade. Reinforcements are marching to the right to the relief of the 20th Corps. Rations issued and bivouacked.

23. Aroused at 3:15 A. M. Ordered to be ready to go on skirmish line at 4 A. M. Relieved the 19th Ohio Volunteer Infantry. Two companies going on the outpost line, the rest of the regiment in reserve. The balls are passing over thick and fast. There is a battery in the rear in support. Clear day. Considerable cannonading on the left. The skirmish line was reinforced at 11 A. M. The rebels fired at the skirmishers from behind their works and have a cross-fire. The only shelter is such trees and thick bushes as the men get behind. The rebels began cannonading from the top of Kenesaw. At 3 P. M. the regiment deployed and came out on the skirmish line within two hundred yards of the main line of the rebel works and advanced, rifle pits covering approach all along the front. At 4 P. M. a signal cannon shot fired in the rear. At the same time heavy cannonading is going on from the top of Kenesaw. Our men are charging along the mountain. The artillery in the rear fired a certain number of times and the artillery all along the line opened on the enemy. The solid shot and shells passed over the regiment from all directions, cutting off limbs and large branches of trees. Then the artillery ceased firing and the line ordered "forward," and,

yelling, started forward charging the enemy's advanced works, going from tree to tree, firing rapidly. The right drove the rebels out of their rifle pits into their main line. Then the rebels charged our men in strong force and drove them back a little distance, firing volley after volley, as the skirmish line retreated, dodging behind trees, falling back in fair order. The rebels followed as far as they could, nearly in the rear and right. The left was compelled to fall back also. Exposed to a cross-fire, our men on the left of our regiment could see the rebs trying to get around to flank us. The left poured a volley into them checking their advance some. We were out of ammunition. The major, the commissioned officers and the color-bearer kept the regiment supplied. The guns, after the rapid firing, became so hot that they could hardly be handled, and the barrels expanded so that the cartridge slipped down the barrel without ramming. Some of the men fired two hundred or more rounds of ammunition during the day and were nearly exhausted with the toilsome struggle. The heavy cannonading almost ceased at sundown, only an occasional shot being heard. Heavy musketry on the right and left continued until 8 P. M. when the regiment was relieved by the 9th Kentucky. The loss of the regiment was four killed and seventeen wounded. Marched back to the works and bivouacked. The skirmishers kept up light firing during the night.

24. Aroused at daylight. Skirmishing is still heard in the front. It is warm and clear. Drew very necessary clothing. Lieutenant W. S. Cardell in command of Company "I" in place of Captain D. W. Howe, wounded the day before. Rations issued.

25. Aroused at daylight. Little skirmishing in front and along the line. Ordered to pitch tents and to police quarters. Clear and very hot. At 10 A. M.

brisk cannonading by the enemy on Kenesaw. Our batteries replied strongly. At 4 p. m. the artillery exploded a caisson on top of Kenesaw. The explosion was caused by one of the shells fired by the Union batteries. Beef issued. Balls are passing over the Union lines very fast. It is not safe to be away from the breastworks.

26. Sunday. Aroused at daylight. Warm and clear. Drew clothing. At 12 m. a battery to the left opened on the enemy, which was replied to very promptly. The cannonading lasted for some time. Heavy cannonading some distance on the right. The 11th Indiana Battery took position to the right and front. Pioneers having built a small epaulment for it, the 11th Indiana Battery armed the epaulment with four twenty-pound Parrotts and two twenty-four-pound Howitzers. Entanglements have been placed in front of the work.

27. Aroused at daylight. Ordered to pack up everything, but not strike tents, and be ready to move. The battery on the left opened on the rebels, and they replied promptly. Marched at 7:30 a. m. to the right. The whole line is moving to the right. The cannonading to the left was very heavy. At 9:15 a. m. Union troops began advancing all along the line. Brisk firing. The whole division in reserve, ordered to lie down under shelter of rise in front, and wounded men rapidly coming to the rear. At 10 a. m. balls passed over us as we lay waiting for orders. Cheering is heard in front, with brisk musketry. The division ordered to advance a short distance and support General Newton's 2d Division. Wounded men increasing on the firing line, coming to the rear. At 10:45 a. m. ordered back a short distance, and brisk musketry on the left. Heavy cannonading on both

sides all along the lines. At 11:30 A. M. the whole division ordered back to quarters. Very hot day. Three days' rations issued in the evening.

28. Aroused at daylight. Ordered to put up tents in line. Very warm. Cannonading heard on the right. Beef issued. Ordered to be ready to move on short notice.

29. Awakened at 3:30 A. M. Ordered on picket or skirmish line. The regiment has but 190 men for duty, a great many being sick from the constant exposure and severe hardships of the last few days of the campaign, and ordered to the hospital. Marched on picket at 7 P. M. But little firing is done by the pickets. At 2 A. M. very brisk firing is heard by volleys on the right, and expecting an attack in front. Men are cautioned to keep cool, and reserve their fire until the enemy come close within short range. The firing on the right is very heavy, a perfect roar, and continued for some time. Relieved at daybreak, having been in the rifle pits all night without sleep, and on the alert all of the time.

30. The regiment was allowed to rest and sleep in the rear of the reserve. The men are talking with the rebels, and permitted trading coffee for tobacco; the rebels having a large supply of tobacco, are very willing to exchange. The division sent a detail under a flag of truce to bury the dead killed on the 23d. It rained to-day. Some rations issued.

JULY, 1864.

1. Heavy firing on the picket line during the night and ordered into line. The artillery on the right opened on the rebels at 6:45 P. M. In front and on the left at 7:30 P. M.

2. Awakened by heavy cannonading all along the

line. No reply from the rebels. Skirmishers yelled some in the morning. By noon all still. Ordered to be ready to move and not strike tents. At 7:30 P. M. ordered to strike tents. Marched to the left, about one mile. Raining and thundering. Third division took the place of one of the divisions of the 14th Corps, in the line of breastworks in the front line. Sent out skirmishers. The rebels fired close all along the line; could be heard talking. The breastworks were very hard to get into, more especially in the dark. Muddy and wet.

3. Sunday. Awakened at daylight and discovered the enemy evacuated his position in front. The lines of breastworks are only about seventy-five or eighty yards apart. From all appearance of the surroundings there was fierce fighting at this part of the line. The dead bodies of many rebels only partly covered over by earth thrown out of the Union works indicating that the rebels attempted a charge and were killed on the top of the works. These bodies were in a bad state of decomposition; the smell was horrible. The dead bodies of a few Union soldiers were also unburied and badly decomposed. Ordered to be ready to march. Marched at 7:30 A. M. Marched back to the right to the position left the night before. At 10 A. M. heavy cannonading in front. Marched through some of the strong and almost impregnable works abandoned by the enemy. Stopped at noon for dinner. Marched past the brick college near Marietta. The regiment ordered to report to Colonel Cram, of the 9th Kentucky. Major Parker in command of the regiment. Ordered to escort the corps train. Crossed the railroad, and passed several lines of rebel breastworks just built, with head logs and abatis in front.

Heavy cannonading in front. Stopped in bivouac at 8 P. M.

4. Reveille 4 A. M. Ordered to be ready to march in one-half hour. Heavy cannonading all night and this morning in front and on the left. Three days' rations issued. Very warm. Some musketry can be heard. Marched at 2:15 P. M. to the left about a mile, and Herman Frauer, of Company "A," was seriously wounded in the leg. The rebels' rifle pits can be seen in a field in the distance. Formed line and ordered to put up line of breastworks. The rebel bullets were flying all around, but no one hurt, while putting up the works. After dark pitched tents and covered them up with brush. A battery in position in the rear.

5. Awakened at 3 A. M. The rebels disappeared from the front. Saw some prisoners going to the rear. Marched at 7:30 A. M. to the railroad, passing through some of the rebel lines of works. Marched on the railroad some distance and halted. Brisk skirmishing in front. Artillery opened on the enemy at 10 A. M. The railroad destroyed by the enemy. The batteries cannonaded the rebels. Brisk skirmishing in front and on the left. Rifle balls coming over thick and fast. Our men charged them, drove them in and they retreated. Marched to the left of the railroad a short distance. Batteries began shelling the rebels across the Chattahoochee river. Very hot. Skirmishing continued until dark. In bivouac at Vining's Ferry, on the bank of the Chattahoochee.

6. Got up early. Batteries opened on the rebels across the river. At 3:15 A. M. ordered to pitch tents. Three days' rations issued. Rebel bullets pass over. Are aroused in the night by locomotive whistles.

7. Up late. Very warm. Skirmishing in front. Rations of beef issued. Marched at 1 P. M. about one

mile to the right and halted in the woods. Pitched tents. Fell in at 8 p. m., and ordered to build a line of breastworks. We began the work and the battery on the left opened on the enemy across the river at 8:30 p. m. At 10 p. m. ordered to go to sleep and finish the line of works in the morning.

8. Up very early. Finished the line of works. Regimental inspection. Ordered on picket at 6 p. m. One of the men was hit by a ball while at the reserve.

9. Relieved from picket at 7 a. m. Marched to camp. The battery on the right opened fire on the rebels on the other bank of the river at 8 a. m. Some musketry on the right. Three days' rations issued. Several rebel shells fell close to the regiment.

10. Sunday. Up late. Marched at 10 a. m. to the left up the river, over bluffs and hills. Very hot marching. A thunder shower. Halted near the river about six miles from late camp. Bivouacked near the river bank. There are two pontoon bridges across the river.

11. Up late. Cloudy and foggy. Routine duties.

12. Up early. At 8 a. m. ordered to get ready to march. Marched at 11:45 a. m. Marched down the river about one mile to the pontoon bridge, and crossed the Chattahoochee river at 3 p. m. Very hot. The 3d Brigade formed line on the left of the 4th Corps, the 23d Corps joining on to 4th Corps. Pitched tents at 8 p. m. Ordered to carry rails to build breastworks. In the morning the rails ready for covering with earth.

13. Up late. Three days' rations issued. Marched at 11 a. m. about a mile to the right and halted. Pitched tents. Built a strong line of field works. Drew some clothing. Ordered to be up at 3 a. m. Ready to march at 5 a. m.

14. Up at 3 a. m. Ready to march at 5 a. m. Made

works stronger, and built some entanglements in front. Drew more clothing. Wind and rain storm.

15. Up early. Policed quarters three days. Rations issued.

16. Up late. A detail made for picket ordered to be ready to go on reconnaissance in the morning. Captain Joseph W. Jordan, Company "K," discharged.

17. Sunday. Reveille sounded at 3 A. M. Ordered to march at 4:30 A. M. Marched at 6:30 A. M. down the river. Marched very slow. Skirmishing in front. Came to the river. The 9th Kentucky and a detail from 79th Regiment were ordered to the left on picket to protect flank. In the woods in front the rebel cavalry are seen. Ordered to assist to put a pontoon bridge across the river. Deployed on the skirmish line. At 5 P. M. marched back to the river, waited for a division to pass, and marched back to camp by 7 P. M. Two days' rations issued at 12 midnight.

18. Reveille 3 A. M. Relieved from picket at 8 A. M. Cannonading in front and left. We halted at noon, and marched again at 1:30 P. M. Very hot and dusty. Crossed Nance's creek over a bridge the enemy tried to burn, and failing in that, tried to cut it down, but were driven off at 4:30 P. M. Halted, having marched six miles, and bivouacked.

Peach Tree.

19. Reveille 4:30 A. M. Marched at 5 A. M. The 3d Brigade marched on a reconnaissance in force at 5:30 A. M. Part of the 86th Indiana and 59th Ohio Volunteer Infantry formed the line of skirmishers in front of the brigade. Heavy musketry in front. Marched very slowly. Artillery opened on the enemy. Volunteer skirmishers were called for from each company. More than enough responded. These

volunteer skirmishers marched to the right. The regiment marched to the west of the road and formed in line of battle. Advanced to a bluff near a small stream called Peach Tree creek and ordered to put up a line of field works. The rebel rifle pits and the rebels moving about can be seen across the creek. While the regiment was lying behind the line of works the rebel artillery from their position across the creek opened on the line with four guns. Their aim being bad, not much damage was done. Very warm. At 3 P. M. ordered to cross the creek. A detail is made from the regiment to reinforce the skirmish line, the 79th Indiana to support the line. Marched down to the creek loaded with rails, the pioneers following the regiment, bringing poles, etc., to build a bridge, the creek being too deep to wade. Advanced across the creek and formed line. Here Major Parker, commanding the regiment, was seriously wounded in the leg. Captain John G. Dunbar, ranking captain, was in command of skirmishers, and Captain Eli F. Ritter was ordered to take command of the regiment. Advanced rapidly through a corn field under heavy fire from the enemy to a bluff and into thick woods. Charged the enemy's works, driving his skirmishers from their pits. Followed the enemy for some distance to a road. The rebel artillery opened on the regiment. Ordered to build a line of field works, which order was obeyed with promptness, and soon the works were completed. The artillery soon came up and silenced the rebel artillery. A lieutenant-colonel, a captain, a lieutenant and twenty-three men surrendered to Captain Ritter, commanding our regiment, and were sent to the rear. More rebels came in during the night. Relieved at 9 P. M. by the 2d Brigade. Marched to camp. Arrived at camp at

10:30 p. m. Marched six or eight miles. Captain Dunbar returned and took command of the regiment. The men were much fatigued from the day's work.

20. Reveille 4 a. m. Marched at 6:30 a. m., Captain Dunbar commanding the regiment. Marched to the left. Crossed Peach Tree creek above the original crossing the day before. Occupied a line of breastworks built by the 1st Division, the 1st Division having moved to the front. The 3d Division to follow them. Marched slowly. Heavy cannonading all along the lines. At 1:30 p. m. the batteries in front began firing, and at 1:45 p. m. heavy musketry is heard to the front and right. The skirmishing is very brisk. Marched to the left, and marched direct toward Atlanta. Advanced to the front line, shells and bullets falling all around. Marched some distance to the right in rear of the front lines. Marched about six miles. Halted four miles north of Atlanta on Buckhead road. 3d Brigade took position in front line on the right of the 2d Division, the 79th Regiment in the second line. Ordered to remain in position for the night. Cannonading and musketry all night along the lines.

21. Up late. Sergeant Hanes, of Company "E," wounded. Rations issued. Marched at 9 a. m. a short distance to the right and front of the works. A detail ordered to reinforce the picket line. Pioneers cut timber to build works. Began to carry the logs to the top of the hill in front in full view of the rebel works. Some of the men were wounded working on the works. Very hot. Worked very hard and completed the works. Companies "A," "F" and "E" each had one man wounded, and Company "C," John Warner, killed. Adjutant Dunn was slightly wounded. At 6 p. m. received orders to march. It began to rain.

Marched one mile to the right along the line, and bivouacked, the rebel balls flying all around. The enemy vigorously contested the advance all along the lines.

22. Ordered up at 3 A. M. Everything very quiet. At 7 A. M. marched to the left, where works had been built. Marched to the front, passing over abandoned rebel line of works. Heavy skirmishing and cannonading all along the lines. At 11 A. M. formed line of battle on a ridge about two miles from Atlanta, and last line of works occupied. Began on a new line of fortifications, the rebel skirmishers about five hundred yards in front. Heavy cannonading on the left. A good line of works was built rapidly in the timber hidden from the enemy. Shelled by the enemy at 2 P. M., the shells exploding all around. The Union artillery rapidly replied, and the cannonading became hot on both sides. At 4 P. M. heavy cannonading on the left of the 1st Division. Very heavy musketry. The dull sound of the artillery fire indicated that grape and cannister were being used. The rebels yelled much. Firing very lively in front, but no attack.

23. Awakened at 3 A. M. A great deal of skirmishing all along the lines and considerable of cannonading. Three days' rations issued. At 3 P. M. brisk skirmishing began on the right, but did not last long. The rebels shelled all day, musket balls passing through the tents. Some of the men wounded in the tents.

24. Sunday. Awakened at 3 A. M. Skirmishing and cannonading all along the line. The brigade is occupying the best line of works since the beginning of the campaign. A solid shot passed clear through a tree two feet in diameter. Traverses are ordered for protection against the enfilading fire of the enemy. Ordered to have roll-call at 3 A. M.

25. Up at 3 A. M. Brisk skirmishing all night. Beef issued. Policed camp. Ordered to build entanglement or abatis of sharp stakes put in the ground close together in front of the works. Very hot. Drew some clothing.

26. Up late. Skirmishing continues in front and cannonading on both sides. Three days' rations issued. Inspection at 4 P. M. Clouding up.

27. Raining. At 5 A. M. heavy cannonading on the left. Very brisk at times. At 7 A. M. brisk skirmishing commenced in front. The rebel shots hit close all around the pickets. Ordered to keep up a continuous fire, and if the rebels abandoned their rifle pits to take possession of them. At 6 P. M. the pickets were ordered to keep up heavy firing. At 7 P. M. a big blaze is seen in the direction of Atlanta. The rebel balls strike very close.

28. Quiet in front until 4 P. M. Brisk skirmishing began on the left and some yelling. It started in the front and spread along the lines. Ordered to fall in and move forward. Marched forward to support the skirmish line. At 5 P. M. the skirmishers dashed out and captured the rebel rifle pits. The rebels retreated to their next line. The pioneers built some works for the men. Charged the rebel rifle pits. Back to camp at 8 P. M.

29. Reveille 3 A. M. Skirmishing continued all night. The rebels shelled the lines with sixty-four-pound shells. Pieces of the shells passed through some of the tents. A man in the 9th Kentucky on the left was killed by a piece of a shell. Three days' rations issued.

30. Reveille 3 A. M. and roll-call. After 4 A. M. heavy skirmishing on right, with some cannonading and part of the 3d Brigade skirmish line was advanced

and rifle pits dug. Ordered to be ready for inspection at 9 A. M. next day. General Wood and Colonel Knefler inspected our works to-day and pronounced them very formidable.

31. Sunday. Reveille 3 A. M. and roll-call. Inspection 9 A. M. Heavy cannonading.

August, 1864.

1. Reveille 3 A. M. Roll-call between 4 and 5 A. M. Brisk skirmishing began on the right at a distance. Great deal of cannonading is heard. Three days' rations issued. At 3:40 P. M. ordered into the rifle pits. The artillery opened on the rebel works, and the cannonade continued until night.

2. Reveille 3 A. M. Raining. Skirmishing kept up all night. Cannonading and skirmishing all day along the line. Munhall and Many of Company C and John Hoop of Company A made a lookout of a large poplar tree just outside of the breastworks, from the top of which the rebels can be seen maneuvering in and around Atlanta.

3. Reveille 3 A. M. Skirmishing and cannonading continues. Heavy cannonading at a distance. Ordered in line to be ready to move out. Rebel regiments can be seen moving out as if for an attack on the Union works. At 3 P. M. the Union artillery opened out all along the lines. The rebels did not reply. A rain storm came up and the artillery ceased firing. Some of the rebels could be seen leaving their rifle pits. But little skirmishing. At 4:50 P. M. Hazen's Brigade skirmishers on the right, advanced on the rebel rifle pits and captured them. The 3d Brigade skirmishers also advanced and captured the pits in their front. The brigade to the left advanced also. At 5 P. M. the rebel artillery opened on the Union lines

in front, and brisk musketry is also opened. The pioneers attacked the rebel skirmish line in front, the rebels in return charged with a strong line of battle, driving the pioneers to the place of starting. The rebels did a great deal of cannonading. Their solid shot and shells flew over the works and exploded in every direction. The works sheltered the troops. The casualties were light.

4. Reveille 3 A. M. The large guns in position on the right fired all night. Three days' rations issued. The artillery on the left opened a brisk cannonade on the rebels at 6:30.

5. Reveille 3 A. M. Roll called. Cannonading and skirmishing all along the line. Policed a piece of ground in the rear of the regiment and in front of the works. Warm. At 2 P. M. the artillery on the left began brisk cannonading. There is some skirmishing in front. At 2:30 ordered to fall in in the entrenchments. The 2d Brigade marched to the front to support the skirmish line. Heavy skirmishing begins all along the line, and yelling and cheering are heard. The rebel artillery opened briskly. At 4:30 P. M. very heavy musketry and cannonading began at the right, and continued for some time, almost until night. Some smoke in Atlanta can be seen from the position on the lookout tree. It is off to the right. The cars came up to and crossed the Chattahoochee river to-day.

6. Reveille and roll-call 3 A. M. Skirmishing and cannonading all along the line. At 5 P. M. a brisk skirmishing and yelling begins on the right not far off. Ordered into line to be ready. Moved to the right in the place of the 19th Ohio Volunteer Infantry. Heavy skirmishing continued on the right. Returned to quarters at dark. Raining hard. Some skirmishing on the left.

7. Sunday. Reveille and roll-call 3 A. M. Company inspection at 9 A. M. Three days' rations issued. Skirmishing continued all day.

8. Reveille and roll-call 3 A. M. Raining. Policed quarters. Made a tunnel under the works to drain the water off. Skirmishing and cannonading all along the line. The brigade band played some pieces to-day.

9. Reveille and roll-call 3 A. M. At 10 A. M. our artillery on the right and left began cannonading the enemy's works. Drew some clothing.

10. Reveille 3 A. M., also roll-call. Still raining. Three days' rations issued. Cannonading and skirmishing along the line. At 4:40 P. M. the rebels opened on the front with artillery. Cannonading continued on the right until 8 P. M.

11. Reveille and roll-call 3 A. M. Brisk skirmishing on the right. Ordered to pitch the tents on a line. Some clothing was issued. Cannonading all night.

12. Roll-call and reveille 3 A. M. Brisk skirmishing and cannonading on the right. At 10 A. M. brisk musketry began on the right. Bugler ordered to the skirmish line to sound the calls. At 12 M. the signal to advance sounded and a heavy skirmish began. Yelling and cheering, some of the rebels left their rifle pits. The rebel artillery opened on the Union lines. Ammunition issued. The battery near the regiment began firing and cannonading is heard all along the line. At 3 P. M. the bugle sounded again. The men all being ready in their pits, brisk firing began all along the line and continued until dark and for some time after dark.

13. Reveille and roll-call 3 A. M. Inspection at 9 A. M. Three days' rations issued. Lieutenant Cardell was placed in command of Company "I." Skirmishing and cannonading all night.

14. Sunday. Reveille and roll-call 3 A. M. Inspection at 9 A. M. At 5 P. M. very heavy cannonading began on the right at a distance. It continued very heavy during the night.

15. Roll-call and reveille 3 A. M. Brisk firing on the right before reveille, it lasted until daylight. A very hot day. Ordered to be ready to go on a foraging expedition at 4 A. M. to-morrow morning. Second Lieutenant Augustin T. Stone, "K" company, resigned.

16. Reveille 3 A. M. Ready to start on foraging expedition. A great deal of skirmishing and cannonading all night. Started on foraging expedition at 5 A. M. on the Marietta road to Buckhead. Ordered to load guns 7 A. M. Front and rear guard and flankers left the Marietta road, turned to the right and marched about 10 miles from camp. Halted at 9 A. M. Formed line of battle across the road and pushed forward skirmishers. The teams were loaded with corn and the expedition returned to camp. Arrived at 3 P. M. Three ears of corn issued to the man. Three days' rations. Some whisky and some sanitary goods issued.

17. Reveille and roll-call 3 A. M. At 3:30 P. M. a very brisk skirmish began on the right and continued all along the line and in front. It continued some time. The regiment and a part of the 3d Brigade marched across an open space in full view of the enemy several times, as though moving or massing to the left. At 5 P. M. the skirmishing ceased to some extent. Cannonading along the line.

18. Awakened at 3 A. M. and roll-call. The artillery was kept moving all night. At 4 P. M. the bugle sounded for a demonstration to be made in the front and yelling and firing began. It was only a feint. All

along the line there was considerable cannonading on both sides. The 3d Brigade marched around the same place as before to make the rebels believe it is moving. Some of the men ordered to march to the left and build fires to attract the attention of the enemy. The regiment marched several times across the same place for the same purpose. At 11 A. M. there was a brisk fire in front. At 1:30 P. M. a very brisk firing and yelling began on the right. Very warm to-day. Cannonading all day.

19. Reveille and roll-call 3 A. M. At 3:30 brisk cannonading began on the right. The bugles sounded forward, the signal to commence firing; heavy firing is heard all along the line. It is about the heaviest of the campaign. Three days' rations issued; there was some demonstration all day. Locomotive whistles are heard. At 4:45 brisk firing commenced all along the line. At 5 P. M. ordered to get accoutrements on ready to move. Heavy skirmishing is kept up all along the line. One day's rations issued. At 5 P. M. the recall sounded; took off accoutrements; skirmishing and cannonading continued all night.

20. Reveille and roll-call 3 A. M. Lively skirmishing and cannonading is still going on on both sides. Ordered to get accoutrements on and be ready in half an hour. Marched across the same place as on the other day. Raining hard. Returned at 2:15 P. M.

21. Sunday. Reveille and roll-call 3 A. M. Inspection at 9 A. M. Rained part of the day. Skirmishing and cannonading all along the line.

22. Reveille and roll-call 3 A. M. Three days' rations issued. Ordered to have roll-call four times a day. Skirmishing and cannonading on the right.

23. Reveille and roll-call 3 A. M. The adjutant returned to the regiment from Chattanooga, where he

had been ordered after the necessary books and papers for the regiment. At 12 M. the rebels began shelling the lines. The Union artillery soon silenced them. The enemy had good range of the camp, and put the shells and balls all around. One-half ear of corn to the man and some beef issued.

24. Reveille and roll-call 3 A. M. Ordered to have sixty rounds of ammunition to the man. Cannonading on the right is heard all day. It is very warm. Lieutenant-Colonel S. P. Oyler resigned; disability. D. W. Hoadley mustered first lieutenant "K" company.

25. Reveille and roll-call 3 A. M. Three days' rations issued. It rained. Drew rations of whisky. After dark the camps were ordered to be struck very quietly and to make no fires. The bugles sounded tattoo and taps as usual and the bands played. At 10 o'clock P. M. marched to the rear, out of hearing of musketry and artillery. Marched a short distance and halted four miles from the seige lines and bivouacked for the night.

26. Up at sun-up and breakfast. Some skirmishing on the left. The rebel artillery in their lines shelled the marching columns, some of the shells going over and some very close to the column. At 7 A. M. ordered to put up works in front. Constant cannonading is heard on the right some distance. A hot day. At 10 A. M. marched in the rear of the 2d Division. The hottest and hardest marching of the campaign—to march fast with the heavy loads and very little sleep the night before. The whole army had moved to the right. Halted at noon an hour for dinner. It rained. Marched about ten miles to the right. Marched through many lines of entrench-

ments. Halted at 4:30 to bivouac in the rear of the 23d Army Corps.

27. Reveille at the usual hour. Raining very hard. Troops and teams have been passing for some time. Ordered to get ready to march at 8 A. M. Marched back a short distance, then marched out on the Sandtown road. Very warm day and muddy. Skirmishing on the left at 11 A. M. and halted. Cavalry to the left and front and two pieces of artillery in rear of the regiment. Moved further to the right and fronted, and took position on a hill on the right at 12 M., having marched five miles. Ordered to build line of works in a hurry. The rebels can be seen moving in front. Skirmishing and cannonading heard on the left. The works ordered were soon built. At 5 P. M. ordered on a reconnoissance. Marched to the front. The 79th regiment and 9th Kentucky in line with skirmishers in front. Advance nearly a mile and not a shot was fired in front, which was disappointing to us, as the enemy had left. Relieved by the 2d Division of the 4th Corps, and returned to the works at 8 P. M. A few shots on the left are heard.

28. Sunday. Reveille 4 A. M. Clear and a little cooler. Ordered to move at 7 A. M. Skirmishing and cannonading to the left. Waiting for orders. Marched at 6 P. M. back about a mile and halted until the train moved out, the brigade in rear of the corps, guarding the train. Started at 8 P. M. Marched over hills and hollows and muddy branches, halting every few steps. Came up with the 3d Brigade at 12 midnight. Marched about three miles.

29. Up at sunrise. Clear. Marched at 7 A. M. a short distance, and rations were issued in haste. Ordered to leave everything except gun and accoutrements and rubber blanket, and marched at 9 A. M.

Reached the Montgomery railroad. Troops tearing it up, burning ties and bending rails. Followed the railroad toward the junction of the Macon and Montgomery railroad at East Point. Brisk skirmishing in front. Halted at 12 M. Began to destroy the railroad by raising the track bodily and turning it over; loosen the ties from the rail and set them on fire to heat the rails and bend them around trees and telegraph poles. At 1 P. M. marched back to camp. Went in line in rear of the front line and halted in the woods at 3 P. M. Marched about five miles.

30. Up early and ordered to get breakfast ready to move. Marched at 7 A. M. Halted a short time to let other troops pass. At 8 A. M. marched out on the road to the Montgomery railroad, and turned toward East Point, marching but a little distance at a time. At 10 A. M. heard cannonading a considerable distance off to the right and front, 3d Brigade on the extreme left. Halted at 3:30 P. M., and formed in line of battle, having marched five miles. At 4:30 P. M. marched again, and marched to the right a mile. Formed line at 5:30 P. M., and halted for the night. Took position on a knoll. The rebels are reported to be advancing on the left flank. The bugle sounded at 7 P. M. Advanced to the front. Took position on a ridge and built a line of works. Bivouacked for the night. Sergeant John W. Gosney, of "F" company, mustered as first lieutenant of "E" company.

31. Reveille 3:30 A. M. Ordered to eat breakfast at once. Rebel cars and wagon trains can be heard moving, and rebel columns can be seen from the tops of trees. Skirmishing in front. At 7 A. M. the artillery began shelling the rebel trains on the right. Strengthened line of works and moved to the front a short distance. Formed in line of battle and built

another line of field works. The enemy can be seen running across an open field in front, the skirmishers driving them. The regiment was ordered on the skirmish line. The skirmishers advanced without firing very much, and soon reached the rebel line of works just abandoned. Halted at a mill for dinner. Started the mill and ground corn and wheat. Marched at 2 P. M. Heard brisk skirmishing and the locomotive whistles. The regiment had advanced a good distance deployed as skirmishers. Relieved and came back to the road. Moved on slowly, and at 4:45 P. M. the battery to the left fired several shots. Very brisk skirmishing began, and continued until the Macon railroad was reached. Halted at 5 P. M., having come about three miles. Some of the men were tearing up the railroad. Moved around and formed line. Put up a line of works, with wire stretched in front to trip the rebels should they attempt to attack. Ordered to lie with guns by the men's sides, ready to get up at a moment's notice, as an attack is expected.

SEPTEMBER, 1864.

1. Reveille 4 A. M. The 1st Division and pioneers are passing to tear up the railroad. Cannonading on the right all night, several miles off. After 3 A. M. it was very heavy, from the sound. They are using large guns. Strengthened the works; the cannonading on the right ceased at 7 A. M; ordered to stop working on the works and get ready to march immediately. Marched at 8:30 A. M. to the right. Company "I" detailed as flankers. Marched about two miles and halted near the 14th Corps. Marched again in the direction of the cannonading; halted at 12 M. Skirmishing and cannonading on the left and front and some on the right not far off. Ordered to make coffee.

At 1:30 P. M. heavy skirmishing and cannonading is heard on the line in front. Marched toward the Macon railroad; it is torn up and burning. March down the railroad to the right and turned the railroad upside down; loosed the ties from the rails and built cribs, burning the ties; heated the rails red-hot and twisted them in all kinds of shapes around trees and telegraph poles. Cannonading on the right at times very heavy. At 5 P. M. marched again. Heavy musketry and artillery is heard in front; hard fighting is in progress, judging from the cheers and yelling. At 6 P. M. we heard a great cheering and yelling at a distance. The firing ceased at sundown. Halted and stacked arms. Skirmishing begins again further off. At 6 P. M. very heavy firing began again, accompanied by artillery in the front and on the right. Shells and shots came right over the brigade. At 6:15 P. M. brisk skirmishing began on the left and front; the batteries opened on the rebels and other batteries are taking position. At 6:40 P. M. very heavy firing and yelling are heard and growing brisker. At 7 P. M. marched to the front and left, marching about six miles; halted in the rear of other troops and ate supper and were ordered to lie down and rest. Soon awakened and ordered to be ready to march in one-half hour. Soon ready, awaiting orders. After waiting some time the order to march is countermanded. Again lay down. About 11 P. M. the troops are awakened by a distant roaring and explosions, apparently in the direction of Atlanta. Great light was seen in the direction of the explosions; the heavens were all red from the flames; it was terrible and lasted a long time. Ordered to be ready to march in case of emergency. After 2 A. M. the noises and disturbances ceased, and ordered to lie down again.

2. Awakened at 3:30 A. M. by heavy skirmishing

in front. Marched to the left to picket on the flank. It rained. At daylight pickets and skirmishers commenced yelling and firing. The artillery opened on the rebels in front of the brigade. Heard the whistle of a locomotive and the continuous rumbling of large trains. The pickets that went out in the morning found themselves very near the enemy. Captain Dunbar, in posting the pickets, went too far to the front and was taken prisoner, and Captain Ritter was again ordered to take command of the regiment. Ordered to march to the rear a short distance. Rations issued and ate breakfast. The news circulated that the heavy cannonading of last night was caused by the rebels blowing up their ammunition trains which could not be saved, and burning the buildings and contents containing stores and ammunition before evacuating Atlanta. Marched again at 9 A. M. Captain Ritter placed in command of the regiment. Marched through a line of rebel works along the railroad, where the battle was fought yesterday. Several dead rebels are lying on the ground unburied. Arrived in front of Jonesboro and halted for rest. Marched in town at 10 A. M. Cannonading in front, and some in the direction of Atlanta. Very hot and dusty. Halted at 12 M. to eat a bite, and marched again at 1 P. M. Brisk skirmishing in front. A whistle from a locomotive is heard. The artillery pushed to the front, and soon opened on the rebels. Marched slowly on the railroad. Turned to the left in a field. The enemy was in view and opened heavy fire from a battery up the railroad track. A piece of shell struck Adjutant Dunn in the head, killing him instantly. At 3 P. M. formed line of battle some distance to the left of the railroad. Brisk cannonading at times. Marched further to the left and stacked arms. At 4:30 P. M.

a heavy skirmishing line was ordered to the front. The line advanced and the regiment followed in column of divisions, halting occasionally. Advanced thus about a mile. Then our skirmishers began a brisk firing. The column was deployed and changed front parallel to the skirmishers. Halted where the rebels had cut down the trees and bushes to impede our advance. Captain Miller, of General Kneffer's staff, was killed here, and Lieutenant Colclazier was wounded by the same ball. Colonel Kneffer's narrow escape. At 5:50 P. M. ordered to advance and charge the rebel works. Started with a yell, going hop, step and jump over the cut trees and bushes. Captured their skirmish pits, with some prisoners, and reached the edge of a corn field. The lines were dressed. The rebels' strong works, with head logs, just in our front about two hundred yards, could be seen. Captain Ritter, commanding the regiment, gave the command "Forward!" and the regiment advanced with a yell through the corn field, in full view of the rebels. Reached a small ridge in front of the rebel works a short distance, and the rebels fired a volley at the regiment. Their artillery shelled also. Lay down just this side of the ridge. Some of our men advanced to within a few yards of the rebel works. The regiment fired several times. The rebels kept up their deadly fire on the regiment, and our right gave back, and as our line had advanced nearer the works than any troops, could not hold our place. The regiment retreated. It fell back to the woods and put up a line of works. The mystery is that so few were hurt. It is thought the ridge protected the line from the rebels' fire. They overfired. Some of the men did not get back until after dark. Our loss was slight, considering the place we charged. Three severely wounded was our loss. General Wood, commanding division, was wounded in the foot, and General Kneffer assumed command of the division. Colonel Stout, of the 17th Kentucky, in command of the brigade when the line of works was completed, lay down with accoutrements on to be ready in the event an attack is made by the rebs during the night. Marched and fought eight miles to-day. Colonel C. D. Bailey, of the 9th Kentucky, and Charles F. Manderson, of the 19th Ohio Volunteer Infantry, were seriously wounded.

3. Awakened at 3 A. M. The rebels are firing very low at our works. Strengthened them some for better protection. Raining hard. Brisk skirmishing kept up in the front. The rebels had slipped up close to our works during the night. At 7:30 A. M. the rebels began shelling. Some of the rebel balls passed under the head log, demonstrating by close practice that they had a good range. The works were made nearly shell-proof by noon. Rained hard and put up tents. Other batteries to the left opened on the enemy. At 1 P. M. the rebels are in plain sight very near to the line, and are busily working on their works. At 3:30 P. M. the artillery on the right opened on the rebels, and kept up a brisk cannonading until night. Rations of beef issued. The pickets were ordered not to fire unless the rebs advanced. The rebels kept up a continuous fire all night, firing very low. It is raining. Sergeant-Major Munhall appointed adjutant, vice Dunn, killed in action.

4. Sunday. Up at daylight. The position is very dangerous. Men are wounded behind the works. It is not safe to move around. The rebels fire into the tents. It is the opinion that the rebels have sharpshooters out. They are not more than 150 yards from the line. The artillery on the right keeps up a con-

tinuous fire on the enemy, occasionally firing cannister. The rebels kept up a brisk firing, firing shells and kept yelling. It is believed they will attack in the night. Drew extra ammunition and are prepared. Received orders that in the event of an attack every man must be in his place in the breastworks without word of command or bugle signal.

5. Awakened at 3:30 A. M. The artillery is firing continuously on the enemy in the immediate front. Very hot. Every man is ordered to have sixty rounds on his person. Work has been stopped on the breastworks. Three days' rations issued. The rebels fired a few shells into the camp. Ordered to be ready to march at 8 P. M. Raining. Marched 8:30 P. M. with as little noise as possible. Lieutenant Burns acting adjutant. Marched through the woods. Mud ankle deep. Very dark. Marched through Jonesboro and halted at 5 A. M., having marched about eight miles of the worst marching ever known.

6. Lay down to sleep at 5:30 A. M. Awakened at 9:30 A. M. and ready to move at 11 A. M. Can hear some cannonading in our rear. The rebels may be following us up. Six thousand bales of cotton are burning along the railroad track. Formed in line and put up field works. Skirmishing and cannonding is heard. Ordered to be ready to march at daylight tomorrow. Raining hard. Bivouacked for the night.

7. Reville 3 A. M. Marched at 6:30 A. M. to the railroad. Marched fast. Turned to the right of the railroad at 10 A. M. Halted at 12 M. and formed line of battle and bivouacked, having marched about ten miles. Position seven miles from Atlanta. Ordered to put up tents the first time for four months without hearing a gun fired or being out of range of bullets. The men were feeling well and full of fun.

8. Reveille 5 A. M. Ordered to be ready to march at 7 A. M. Marched at 7:30 A. M. Marching slow. Every man ordered to remain in place. Began raining at 9 A. M. At 12 M. passed through the rebel line of works in the rear and south of Atlanta, in the opposite direction from where the Union lines were during the siege. Halted near town. Counted off in platoons of fourteen men front, and ordered to pass in reviewing order in a soldierly manner. Marched through Atlanta, the regiment in front of the division and the brigade band in front of the regiment. Saw where the rebels had burned cars loaded with ammunition, which made the light and the noise on the night of the 1st. It was a great sight to see. Passed through the rebel line of works at 1:30 P. M. and passed where General McPherson was killed on the left on the 22d of July. Halted. Formed in line at 2:30 P. M. About two miles from Atlanta, near Rough and Ready, having marched ten miles, camp was laid off and tents pitched.

9. Reveille 5:30 A. M. Policed quarters. A warm day. Three days' rations issued. Also, whitefish and pickled cabbage issued.

10. Reveille 5:30 A. M. Policed quarters. Drew whisky, vinegar, etc., also beef issued.

11. Sunday. Reveille 5:30 A. M. Policed quarters. Company inspection at 9 A. M. Attended divine services at 10:30 A. M. Drew some clothing.

12. Reveille 3:30 A. M. Ordered on picket at 9 A. M. Five days' rations. Some onions, potatoes, etc., issued.

13. Reveille 5:30 A. M. Pickets relieved at 9:30 A. M. Ordered to ditch the camp.

14. Reveille 5:30 A. M. Drew clothes and cooking utensils. Ordered to be ready for general inspection on the 16th at 10 A. M.

15. Reveille 5:30 A. M. Ordered to be ready for dress parade at 5:30 P. M. Dress parade. Order was read from President Lincoln on the fall of Atlanta, tendering thanks to the troops.

16. Reveille 5:30 A. M. Policed quarters. Inspection and dress parade at 5:30 P. M.

17. Reveille 5:30 A. M. Five men from each company detailed for picket. Five days' rations issued.

18. Reveille 5:30 A. M. It is raining. Routine duties.

19. Reveille 5:30 A. M. Drew some clothing. Ordered to have four roll-calls each day. Dress parade at 5:30 P. M.

20. Reveille 5:30 A. M. Battalion drill in the morning. Dress parade at 5:30 P. M.

21. Reveille 5:30 A. M. Rained during the night. Rations are getting scarce.

22. Reveille 5:30 A. M. Company drills. Ordered to be ready for general inspection by corps inspector. Five days' rations issued.

23. Reveille 5:30 A. M. Five men are detailed for picket from each company at 7:30 A. M. Inspection at 2 P. M. Lieutenant Burns, acting adjutant, started home on leave of absence. Lieutenant Cardell is acting adjutant.

24. Reveille 5:30 A. M. Rained all night. Rations of beef are issued. Complaints are made to Captain Ritter, commanding regiment, of the poor quality of the beef, which is unfit to eat. Ditched the quarters. Good news received from the Eastern army, and three cheers are given.

25. Sunday. Reveille 5:30 A. M. Company inspection at 9 A. M. Divine services by the chaplain at 3 P. M.

26. Reveille 5:30 A. M. Company drill from 9 to

10 A. M. Lieutenant W. S. Cardell is detailed to go to Bridgeport after the regimental baggage. Battalion drill from 2 to 3 P. M. Ordered to be ready for general inspection and review by General Stanley at 2 P. M. to-morrow.

27. Reveille 5:30 A. M. At 12 M. the battalion is formed for review, the companies being equalized and reduced to eight companies for the occasion. Marched out to a field that had been prepared for the occasion by the pioneers. It is a beautiful day for the review. 3d Brigade on the right of the division, the 9th Kentucky on the right of the brigade, the 79th Indiana next. Regiments formed in columns of division at 2 P. M. General Stanley and staff. General Wood came in a carriage on account of wound received at Lovejoy Station. "Attention'!" was sounded. A regiment marched to the front from the left of the division, headed by a band, to the center of the division, where a division flag was presented to it for the division headquarters. Then two companies of the 19th Ohio Volunteer Infantry, with band, marched to the center of the brigade and was presented a flag for the brigade headquarters. The 1st and 2d Brigades also received flags. The whole division presented arms. General Stanley and staff rode to the center of the division, and all presented arms. He rode along the front and rear of the division. He then returned to the front and the whole division passed in review. Each battalion was inspected, and at 5 P. M. marched back to camp. Rations issued.

28. Reveille 5:30 A. M. Six men from each company ordered for picket. Rained.

29. Reveille 5:30 A. M. Captain Dunbar returned to the regiment, having been exchanged. He was captured on the morning of the 2d of September while

placing the pickets on the line. Drill by companies. Dress parade. Some beef issued.

30. Reveille 5:30 A. M. Company drill from 9 to 10 A. M. Captain Dunbar assumed command of the regiment. Dress parade. Captain Dunbar related his experience while prisoner. It was very interesting and was enjoyed by all.

OCTOBER, 1864.

1. Reveille 5:30 A. M. Rained in the night. Some light bread issued. Dress parade at 5:30 P. M.

2. Sunday. Reveille 5:30 A. M. Company inspection at 8:30 A. M. Five days' rations issued. Dress parade. Ordered to have reveille at 2 A. M., have two days' rations and forty rounds of ammunition to the man. Ordered to be ready to march at 5 A. M.

3. Reveille at 2 A. M. Raining. Rations of whisky issued. Struck camp, marched at 6:30 A. M. through Atlanta toward Marietta. At 11:30 A. M. halted for dinner. At 12:30 P. M. crossed the Chattahoochee river on a pontoon bridge, the railroad bridge being washed away. Marched on the Marietta road to where the regiment camped July 4, and went into bivouac at 7 P. M. Marched sixteen miles. Beef issued.

4. Reveille 4:30 A. M. Rained. Marched at 11:30 A. M. into Marietta. At 2 P. M. marched out to the rebel line of works they evacuated on July 2 near the foot of Kenesaw mountain. Bivouacked for the night at 4 P. M., having marched eight miles. Eight men from each company detailed for picket. Two days' rations issued.

5. Up before day. Marched at 9 A. M. west, across works. Drew ammunition; halted for dinner at 2 P. M. Marched at 4 P. M. to near Pine Top Mountain and

bivouacked at 5 p. m. Marched about four miles. Built a line of light field works.

6. Up at daylight. Rained in the night. General Sherman is on the top of Pine Top Mountain, sending out orders.

7. Up at day. 1 p. m. heavy cannonading is heard in a westerly direction. Did not continue long. Three days' rations issued.

8. Up at day. Still on Pine Top Mountain. Marched at 3:30 p. m. toward Ackworth and went in bivouac at 6 p. m. Marched seven miles. There is a herd of about 12,000 head of cattle near by on the road toward Atlanta.

9. Up early. Whisky and beef issued. Ordered to lay off regular camp and pitch tents.

10. Reveille 5:30 a. m. Cold and frosty. Three days' rations issued. Marched at 3:30 p. m. through Ackworth. Passed Altoona Pass. Saw where the rebels attacked our troops under General Corse, and were repulsed. Crossed the Etowah river to near Cartersville. Bivouacked at 9 p. m., having marched eleven miles.

11. Reveille 4:30 a. m. Marched at 6:30 a. m., 3d Brigade in front. passed through Cartersville, marching very fast. Passed near Cassville and halted near Kingston for dinner at 11:00 a. m. Marched at 1:30 p. m. toward Rome. At 3:30 p. m. into bivouac, having marched thirteen miles. A vote was taken in the regiment, and resulted 222 votes for Morton and 6 for McDonald.

12. Reveille 5 a. m. Marched at 11 a. m. across the railroad in the direction of Rome. Cannonading at 12 m. Halted at 1:15 p. m. for dinner. Marched again at 3:30 p. m., marching through some hilly, very rough country. Raining. Halted in bivouac

at 10:45 P. M., near Rome, having marched about eighteen miles.

13. Up at sunrise. Cannonading is heard. Rations issued. General Sherman's order to waste no ammunition was read. Marched at 2:30 P. M. Company commanders are to be held accountable for stragglers of their command. Marched back on the same road. Marched about six miles, then marched northeast, leaving the road. Marched on to the right, strict orders issued against straggling. Bivouacked at 8:15 P. M. Marched about fourteen miles during the day.

14. Reveille 3 A. M. Marched at 5 A. M. through Calhoun. At 9 A. M. arrived at Resaca. Met four trains loaded with troops. Marched through Resaca at 11:30 A. M. Passed near where the rebels had destroyed the railroad, two miles beyond Resaca. Halted for dinner at 12:45 P. M. At 3:30 P. M. marched a mile and formed line of battle. Bivouacked for the night. Rations issued. Brisk skirmishing heard at 2 A. M., about two or three miles off.

15. Reveille 4 A. M. Marched at 9:15 A. M. Brisk skirmishing on the left in direction of Snake Creek Gap. Marched to the left and formed line of battle fronting north. Ordered to build a line of field works. At 4:30 P. M. ordered to have sixty rounds of cartridges to the man. Marched at 3 P. M. westward up a mountain, through woods, over the mountain into a very narrow gorge at dark. Started up a large mountain, very steep and rocky. Reached the top and saw our troops in bivouac, in the valley below. Marched down through Snake Creek Gap. Bivouacked in the woods at 7:30 P. M., having marched eight miles. Saw where the rebels had cut down timber to obstruct advance of Sherman's army.

16. Reveille 4 A. M. Rations of beef and other rations issued. Marched at 10 A. M. Troops and teams passed all night. Passed out of Snake Creek Gap. Marched westward about six miles and bivouacked. Snake Creek Gap is from twenty-five to one hundred yards wide, between the bases of two mountains, and several miles long.

17. Reveille 5 A. M. Ordered to turn over all extra guns and accoutrements to be sent to Chattanooga. Rations issued and some clothing drawn. Men were allowed foraging, but must take their guns with them for protection.

18. Reveille 2:45 A. M. Marched at 7 A. M. Crossed over Pigeon Mountain. Raining. Turned west down the valley and halted for dinner at 1:45 P. M. Marched again at 2:45 P. M. Turned to the left on another road and bivouacked at 6:45 P. M., having marched about twenty miles.

19. Reveille 4 A. M. One man was detailed from each company for foraging. Marched at 12 M. Order is read from Colonel Post temporarily commanding the division holding the company commanders accountable for the straggling of their men. Crossed Catoosa river and halted for dinner. Started at 2:15 P. M. to Summerville and beyond the town one mile and bivouacked at 4:15 P. M., having marched about six miles. Nine men from each company are detailed for picket duty.

20. Reveille 4 P. M. One man from each company is detailed for foraging. Marched at 7:15 A. M. No more rations to be issued in the immediate future, only such as can be procured by foraging, the railroad having been destroyed by rebel cavalry. The regiment is in front. One man is detailed at each house as guard, to remain until the 4th Army Corps

pass. Ordered to have company roll-call at each halting place. Halted at 12:45 P. M. for dinner. Marched again at 1:45 P. M. Crossed the Georgia and Alabama state line and marched into Alabama. Bivouacked at 4:30 P. M., having marched about eighteen miles.

21. Reveille 4 A. M. Drew shoes. Three days' rations of coffee, salt and crackers issued for five days. Beef issued. Remained in bivouac.

22. Reveille 5 A. M. Two men from each company detailed for foraging. Cold and frosty. Four additional men detailed for forage for the regiment. Drew shoes. The foragers returned with plenty of forage. Remained in bivouac.

23. Reveille 5 A. M. Cold and frosty. Two men from each company for forage duty. Ordered to police camp. Rations issued.

24. Reveille 4 A. M. A large train is passing, going to Rome with a heavy guard. Ordered to pitch camp and put up tents in regular order.

25. Reveille 5 A. M. Policed camp. Beef and vegetables are issued. Ditched the camp.

26. Reveille 5 A. M. Two men of each company for forage duty. This camp is near Gaylesville, in the Cherokee Valley, Cherokee county, Alabama, near the Coosa river.

27. Reveille 5 A. M. Raining. Ordered to get ready to march and marched at 8:30 A. M., the regiment in rear of the division, through a gap in the Shindig Mountains, into the valley. Marched from there into Lookout Valley and bivouacked at 3:10 P. M. Marched about fifteen miles. Raining. Beef issued.

28. Reveille 4 A. M. Marched at 6:30 A. M. through Alpine Valley. The 2d Division of the 4th Corps is camped here. Halted for dinner at 12 M. Two men from each company detailed for forage duty. Marched

again at 12:45 P. M. into Georgia and bivouacked near Lafayette at 4:10 P. M., having marched about twenty-two miles.

29. Reveille 3:30 A. M. Marched at 5:40 A. M. through Lafayette, the brigade in front. At 10 A. M. passed the place of the reconnoissance in force on Sunday before the Chickamauga battle. Passed near Lee and Gordon's mill. Marched along the road, where regiment double-quicked and turned to the right on September 19, 1863, and captured a battery. Saw many graves. The timber and bushes indicated that a hard battle had been fought here. Marched through the gap in Missionary Ridge through Rossville, and stopped to bivouac at 3 P. M. in front of Chattanooga fortifications, having marched about twenty-three miles. Locomotive whistles at Chattanooga are distinctly heard. Rations of beef issued.

30. Sunday. Reveille 4 A. M. Marched into Chattanooga. Stacked arms at the depot at 8:15, having marched five miles. There are any number of locomotives steamed up and trains ready to take the troops. Got aboard a train of box cars and started toward Bridgeport. Passed through a tunnel. Stopped at Whitesides. Passed through Shellmound at 12:20 P. M. Crossed the Tennessee river at Bridgeport. Arrived at Stevenson at 1:10 P. M. Changed engine and started at 3 P. M. Stopped at 4 P. M. for dinner. The railroad in our front, destroyed by rebel cavalry, is being repaired while the troops are eating. Started again at 10 P. M. The troops are so crowded in the cars that it is impossible to sleep. Passed through Huntsville, Ala., during the night, then took the Nashville railroad.

31. Arrived at Athens, Ala., at 6 A. M. Disembarked from the cars at 6:45 A. M. Ate breakfast.

Marched at 11:30 A. M. to a fort and rations issued. At 1:15 P. M. marched through town on the road toward Pulaski, and bivouacked at 6 P. M., having marched about ten miles.

NOVEMBER, 1864.

1. Reveille at 2:30 A. M. Marched at 4:15 A. M. The 3d Brigade in front. Crossed the Alabama line into Tennessee. Arrived at Elk river at 8 A. M. The boys undressed and waded across, waist deep. Marched through Elkton. Halted for dinner at 11:30 A. M. Started at 12:45 P. M., when it began sprinkling. Marched to Pulaski and halted. Marched through town and camped at 3:45 P. M., having marched twenty-five miles. Seven men from each company detailed for picket. Rations issued.

2. Reveille 5 A. M. Some rations and beef are issued. Raining. A. M. Colelazier, wounded at Lovejoy Station, returned to regiment.

3. Reveille at 5 A. M. General Wood issued a congratulatory order on the good order maintained and marching without straggling. The order was read to all the regiments in the division.

4. Reveille 6 A. M. Cold and snowing. Drew clothing. Rations issued.

5. Reveille 6 A. M. Very cold. Rations issued, and drew some clothing. Ordered to pitch camp and put tents in regular order.

6. Reveille 6 A. M. Four men from each company detailed for picket. Large detail ordered for fortifications on the surrounding hills.

7. Reveille 5 A. M. Rained all night. Four men from each company ordered for fatigue duty.

8. Reveille 5 A. M. The regiment is detailed to work on the fortifications.

9. Reveille 5 A. M. Rained all night. The regiment marched out to work on the fortifications. It was raining too hard to work. Ordered to march back to camp. Some rations issued.

10. Reveille 5:30 A. M. Three men of each company for forage and four for picket. At 12 M. the regiment marched out to work on the entrenchments. Ordered to make out pay-rolls.

11. Reveille 5:30 A. M. At 12 M. the regiment marched out to work on the fortifications. Good news of the Presidential election was received.

12. Reveille at 5:30 A. M. Signed the pay-rolls. Strengthened the works by building a line of entanglement in front and cheval-de-frise. Some rations issued. Ditched the camp.

13. Reveille 5:30 A. M. The regiment paid for eight months. Major Parker returned to the regiment. Mustered as lieutenant-colonel, and Captain John G. Dunbar, of "B" company, mustered as major of the regiment.

14. Reveille 5:30 A. M. Ordered to make requisitions for all kinds of clothing. Ordered to put camps in good order.

15. Reveille 5:30 A. M. Drew some clothing. It is raining. Rations issued. Routine duties.

16. Reveille 5:30 A. M. Raining. Four men of each company ordered for picket, and two men with the teams foraging.

17. Reveille at 5:30 A. M. Raining. Routine duties in camp.

18. Reveille 5:30 A. M. Raining. Two men of each company for forage train guards and two for lumber. Krout and onions issued.

19. Reveille 5:30 A. M. Raining. Flues are being built by the men in the tents, as it is growing cold.

20. Reveille 5:30 A. M. Two companies detailed as bridge guards. Rations issued.

21. Reveille 5:30 A. M. Companies "E" and "I" returned to camp. Almost surrounded by the approaching enemy—in danger of capture.

22. Reveille 5:30 A. M. Two days' rations issued. Began snowing. A detail is ordered for picket.

23. Reveille 5:30 A. M. Cold and clear. At 12 M. ordered to be ready to march in one hour. Colonel Knefler in command of the regiment. General Beatty assumed command of the brigade. Marched at 4:30 P. M. to Pulaski, and out on the Nashville pike, 3d Brigade in the rear. Rear guard did not leave town until fire was opened on the rebels. Marched very slowly. Passed crowds of negroes in large numbers. At 1:45 A. M. halted and bivouacked in the woods by the roadside, having marched twelve miles. The place of the bivouac is a graveyard. Prepared to lie down between the graves, but the bugle sounded the reveille and assembled again, the enemy's cavalry hovering around in large numbers to attack the wagon trains. General alarm along the lines.

24. Marched at 4:30 A. M., very fast. Halted for rest at 9 A. M. Cannonading in the distance to the front. At 11:30 ordered into position on the left flank. The regiment was not all present, many having fallen out from the hard marching. Those present marched into a corn field one hundred yards from the pike, and deployed, and advanced firing on the rebel cavalry dismounted and deployed, fighting as infantry, the horses in rear of them. Enemy retreated to the woods. Skirmished with them until relieved, and joined the whole regiment, all now together. Ate dinner. Cannonading is still heard to the left of the pike. Teams are passing very fast. At 3:30 P. M.

joined the brigade in camp near Columbia. At 4:45 P. M., having marched about twenty-one miles, ordered to lie down immediately and sleep.

25. Reveille 4:30 A. M. The whole division put up a line of works. Ammunition issued. At 12 M. skirmishing began in front, and cannonading is heard on the west. Occasionally heavy musketry is heard, and yelling. At 2 P. M. there is brisk skirmishing in the front. The rebel shells come over the lines. Three days' rations issued. At 6:45 P. M. ordered to get ready to march immediately. Marched a short distance to the left and into bivouac.

26. Reveille 3:30 A. M. Heavy skirmishing and yelling in front. Ordered to pack up everything and be ready to march. It is raining. Ate breakfast. Before 7 A. M. the artillery began firing on the right. Skirmishing and yelling is heard further to the right. At 9 A. M. a detail of seventy-five men ordered for picket. Rebel shells are flying all around. At 10 A. M. Fred. Barton, of Company "A," was wounded in the side. Cannonading ceased. Only an occasional shot is heard. It rained all day. Frank Jelleff, sutler, came up to the regiment after dark. Ordered to get ready to march. Did not march.

27. Up at 4 A. M. Scattering shots heard all night. The artillery pulled away from the line. At 9 A. M. a few cannon shots on the right. Relieved from picket at 7 A. M. Ordered to be ready to march at a moment's notice. At 4 P. M. it is reported that the rebels are advancing. At 6 P. M. marched quietly to town. Company "C" remains in the works waiting for the pickets to be relieved and covered the retreat. Marched through town and about three miles. Crossed Duck river on a pontoon bridge, near the railroad bridge.

Halted in the woods at 9:30 P. M. to bivouac, having marched about six miles.

28. Before 5 A. M. aroused by what appeared like heavy fighting across the river. Company "C" came up and reported that the heavy firing was the blowing up of the fort across the river. At 7:20 P. M. marched across Rutherford creek on the railroad bridge. There were several lines of battle in front, and heavy skirmishing was kept up. Reached the Nashville pike. A wagon train is blockading the road. Marched to the left of the whole line, fronting Columbia, forming line at 10 A. M., having marched six miles. Ordered to put up a line of works. Skirmishing in front. In position about one hundred yards from the river and the town plainly to be seen. At 11 A. M. moved a short distance and began on field works again. At this time the enemy opened fire very briskly. The Union batteries soon silenced them for a time. Reinforcements came to the brigade by addition of a Missouri regiment, eight hundred strong. The railroad bridge and pontoon bridge were destroyed before daybreak. Rations are issued, and bivouacked.

29. Reveille 4 A. M. Light skirmishing kept up all night. At 8:30 A. M. the general sounded. Troops are marching from the right toward the pike. At 9:35 A. M. the enemy opened fire with eight guns. The Union artillery promptly responded, and there was a duel which lasted some time, and finally the rebels ceased firing. At 10:30 A. M. the regiment deployed along the line of works, and the 3d Brigade marched to the rear. At 11:30 A. M. the rebels began firing again. The artillery answered very promptly. Brisk skirmishing in front and on the left. Ordered to carry sixty rounds of ammunition. The rebels attempted to drive the Union troops from the ford, but

did not succeed. At 4:10 P. M. the rebels are attacking, charging the lines in force. They again failed. Brisk firing was kept up until dark. At 5:15 P. M. marched to the pike, the 23d Corps also marching out. At 8 P. M. marched about two miles, very slowly. Roads very muddy. Crossed a creek at 11 P. M., and marched very fast. After midnight ordered to be very still and march very quietly. Marched in front of a rebel line of battle more than two miles long and only one-half mile from the pike. The column soon came in sight of a long line of camp fires to the right, and not more than one-half mile distant. A line of battle was seen advancing toward the pike. At first it was believed to be a rebel line of battle advancing, and the men began to be nervous, preparing to defend themselves. Soon the happy discovery was made that the advancing line of battle was a part of the 2d Division, placed there to protect the flank of the column between the pike and the rebel line of battle. Marched into Spring Hill, a small town on the pike, without further obstruction. Halted on the other side of town, facing to the northeast. At 3 A. M. marched about ten miles. Bivouacked in line of battle on arms in close proximity to the enemy.

30. Awakened after having slept one-half hour. Skirmishing heard to the right. Marched at 5:45 A. M. on the pike toward Franklin. There were three columns of troops marching side by side on the pike. The rebels are gone from the pike; some cannonading in front. Came to a place where the rebels had destroyed thirty or forty of our wagons the day before; they were still burning. Arrived within a mile of Franklin; halted at 9:15 A. M., having marched about eleven miles, resting but once. At 10:25 A. M. the artillery in rear opened on the rebels who were follow-

ing very closely. At 10:45 marched into Franklin. The troops were strongly entrenched; marched through the town, crossed the river and formed in line of battle, having marched about fifteen miles. Rations of beef issued. Ordered to be ready to move. Heavy cannonading and fighting to the left. Heavy cannonading all along the line. Shells could be seen exploding all along the line. At 4:30 P. M. moved to the left a mile to Fort Granger in reserve. Charge after charge is being made in front; the rebels are fighting hard, as little time elapses between the cheering. The flash of the guns could be seen from Fort Granger, where the brigade was in line. The fighting continued until 9 P. M., after the regiment had built a line of works. At 10 P. M. moved again to the fort on the bank of the creek near the railroad bridge. The troops in front abandoning the front line began crossing the river in retreat to Nashville. The brigade is ordered to hold the fort until the troops have all crossed. Bivouacked in line, expecting attack.

DECEMBER, 1864.

1. As soon as the troops retiring from the front crossed the river the railroad bridge was set on fire and is burning. At 3 A. M. marched, evacuating the fort. The cavalry deployed on the banks of the river. The rebels in pursuit appeared and began skirmishing. Their artillery soon came up and began shelling. The cavalry and artillery, in position on the north bank of the Harpeth river, responded vigorously. Cannonading very brisk for a half hour, when the position in and about Franklin was entirely abandoned. Marched about ten miles, halted and allowed to cook. Marched at 10:15 A. M. Heavy cannonading in the rear, the rear guard of cavalry engaged. Halted within three miles

of Nashville and formed line of battle at 12 M., having marched about sixteen miles. Troops very tired and footsore. Three days' rations issued. Marched again at 2:25 P. M. Moved two miles to the left and took position in the line of defense. At dark moved a mile to the right and bivouacked for the night.

Reveille 4 A. M. Detail made for picket. Heavy cannonading. At 2 P. M. in front of Nashville. Ordered to move. The line was changed. Stone fences were ordered to be utilized for breastworks. Lieutenant-Colonel Parker commands the regiment, Colonel Kneffer the brigade, General Beatty the division and General Wood the corps. Rain. The camp very muddy.

3. Reveille 4 A. M. Ordered to stand in line of battle at 5 A. M. At 8 A. M. moved a short distance and built a line of works of stone and dirt. Skirmishing in front. Three days' rations issued. At 2:15 P. M. the rebels began advancing along the front, taking position. Brisk skirmishing. The rebel line so close that rifle balls fall around. At 3 P. M. the artillery right and left opened on the rebels. Cannonading heard far into the night. On some parts of the line the rebels drove in the advance skirmish line and halted. Built two lines of brush entanglements in front of the works. Pitched tents. Cannonading ceased in front at dark. Firing of heavy guns in the forts on the right during the night.

4. Reveille 4 A. M. Stood in line of battle. The rebels built a line of works during the night where they halted the evening before, and their musket balls fall into camp continuously. The batteries along the lines began brisk shelling of the rebel works. The rebels did not fire artillery. Every one worked on the breast-

works. Drew clothing, and some sanitary goods are issued.

5. Reveille 4 A. M. Stood in line of battle. Very cold and frosty. Skirmishing all night. At 8 A. M. the artillery opened on the rebels and continued regular fire. The rebels do not reply.

6. Reveille 3:30 A. M. Detail made from the regiment for picket. Marched out to the line at 5 A. M. The rebels very near. Skirmished with them all day. The artillery fired at their rifle pits, and scattered them considerably on the right. Heavy cannonading by gunboats in the river.

7. Reveille 4 A. M. The pickets relieved and returned to camp. It was reported that the rebels would attack at daylight. No attack.

8. Reveille 4 A. M. Stood in line of battle. Cold and windy; the ground frozen hard. Some skirmishing on the extreme left. The rebels charged the skirmishers of the 1st Division and drove them in. The artillery opened on them, and the rebels were driven back. Captain Ellis and Frank Jelleff brought up some sutler goods and put up a tent.

9. Reveille 4 A. M. Stood in line of battle. Sleet and hail fell to a depth of several inches. Cold and disagreeable. Three days' rations and some whisky issued. Skirmishing all day all along the lines.

10. Reveille 4 A. M. Stood in line of battle. Very cold. Some beef issued. Brisk skirmishing all day along the front and cannonading.

11. Sunday. Reveille 3:30 A. M. Stood in line of battle. Seven men of each company detailed for picket. It is the coldest day the regiment experienced in the service, but plenty of fuel for fires. Some beef issued. The 17th Kentucky started for home, their time of service having expired. Drew some clothing.

12. Reveille 4 A. M. The pickets returned to camp nearly frozen. Three days' rations issued. Brisk skirmishing and cannonading all along the front. It is rumored that there is to be a general movement. Cold.

13. Reveille 4 A. M. Stood in line. Very cold; in the sun it is thawing a little. Rained in the night and turned warmer. All roads in very bad condition.

14. Reveille 4 A. M. In line of battle. Very muddy.

BATTLE OF NASHVILLE.

15. Reveille 3 A. M. Ready to march at 4 A. M. Four men from each company detailed for picket. Struck tents before daylight. It is very foggy. After 8 A. M. troops are moving and massing on the right. The 13th Ohio deployed in the brigade line of works. Brisk cannonading on the left. Garrison of Nashville making a demonstration on the left to attract the attention of the enemy while the right is taking position to attack. Heavy firing of artillery and gunboats on the right, where Wilson's cavalry is attacking the enemy's left. The 79th Indiana regiment moved a short distance to the right and massed behind a hill. Brisk skirmishing kept up all the time. At 11 A. M. very brisk skirmishing began in front. Yelling by the advancing skirmish line. The 4th Corps lines ordered to advance. The troops loaded their guns and advanced. At 12 M. the regiment formed behind our works and moved over them in a thick bushy place. The bushes had been cut down. The front line advanced. The Seventy-ninth moved to the left, nearly in front of the works we vacated in the early morning. The 1st Brigade of the 3d Division is in the front line charging the enemy's line of works. Rapid musketry and artillery firing. The 1st Brigade

carried the enemy's first line of works. The Seventy-ninth again moved to the left, and is on the extreme left flank. Advanced to the first line of enemy's works. Many wounded men are being carried to the rear. Third Brigade ordered to form on the rebel line of works, which faced our old line of works, vacated in the early morning, to hold the left flank. The Seventy-ninth was fortunate in being assigned to a position behind a stone fence, serving as breastworks, and made good protection. The men on the right and left of the 79th Indiana put up a temporary line of field works under a heavy fire from the enemy. Artillery kept up a continuous fire on the enemy. The latter were not firing much with artillery in our immediate front. At 1 P. M. it began raining very hard. Cannonading and musketry is heard on the right. Charge after charge is being made by the Union troops. Firing sounds nearer and nearer, indicating that the federal troops are successful and are driving the rebels. At 4 P. M. the right of the Union army is advancing and driving the enemy. A general charge on the rebel lines is ordered, and, after a severe fight, in which the Seventy-ninth takes part, the enemy takes flight and the works are in possession of the Union troops. The enemy is in full retreat and running in every direction. The Union troops are yelling for joy. The right is continuing its good work, and is advancing, following the retreating rebels. At dark the left of the army, where the Seventy-ninth is, advanced some distance to be in line. Moved about a mile to the front and right. Then to the left to the Granny White pike. Then to the right and formed in line with the other troops. Bivouacked for the night. At 8 P. M. the 1st Brigade captured a battery of four guns. A detail for picket was made from the regiment. Rained in the night.

16. Reveille 4 A. M. From all appearances the rebels are all gone. Some of troops are taking position. The bugle sounded "Attention" at 7 A. M. Skirmishing in front on the pike. The regiment marched to the left. Brisk firing of musketry and artillery on the right. Crossed the Franklin pike and the railroad. Saw the rebel works captured by the 1st Brigade of 3d Division, the day before. Lines of sharp stakes driven in the ground with a wide line of brush entanglement in their front. Marched toward Franklin. Recrossed the railroad. The rebel artillery opened on our line. Halted. 8 A. M. marched to the left and to the right to get in place in the line, the 3d Brigade was the left of the Union Army, except General Steadman division, one brigade white and one brigade of colored troops. Halted at 10:30 A. M. The line completely formed. Terrible fighting on the right. Moved a short distance to the right, to support that part of the line. Desperate fighting still continues on the right. Artillery is firing rapidly. 11 A. M. very heavy musketry is heard all along the lines, greater than ever. Then for a moment all was still. The firing began again more vigorously than before. The rebel artillery fired shells at our line with great accuracy, exploding among the men. The 3d Brigade held its position on the left. 2:30 P. M. the 1st and 2d Brigade of the 3d Division, 4th Corps, were massed and moved forward. The 1st Brigade deployed and charged the hill, the 2d and 3d in support. The hill was taken and the line established. The 79th Indiana was ordered to support the 6th Ohio Battery, to hold it at all hazard, if the troops in front were repulsed. The colored and white troops in front and left charged

the rebel line of works on the Franklin pike and were repulsed. The rebel artillery belched forth grape and cannister and the musketry was very heavy. 4 P.M. heavy fighting was renewed on the right. Seemed to be nearer and nearer. It sounded as if the whole line were advancing toward our line. The 79th Indiana, in support of the battery, had built a temporary line of field works. The rebel works could be seen in the distance as the fighting on the right became nearer. Our brigade was ordered forward to assault the rebel works. The regiment, with fixed bayonets, started at double-quick with a yell. As the regiment neared the works the enemy vacated their works and ran to the rear pell-mell, the regiment firing at them as they ran. This line of works was very strong and had a line of brush entanglements in front. There were many black and white soldiers killed near these rebel works. The rebels left a battery of four guns. Knapsacks, haversacks, broken guns, etc., scattered around. The rebels had been routed from their works all along the whole line, and they could be seen falling back very badly scattered and in disorder. The regiment moved forward several miles, until after dark and halted. The retreating rebel artillery fired an occasional shot without doing any damage. The 79th was ordered to the rear a short distance on line with the other troops and bivouacked for the night. This was the most crushing defeat of the war for the rebel army, and Hood's command never rallied.

17. Cannonading in the distance to the front. Cavalry in pursuit of the rear guard of Hood's army. Squads of prisoners marching to the rear. Three days' rations issued. Rain during the night.

18. Sunday. Reveille 4:30 A. M. Dried everything as well as could be done. Marched at 8:30 A. M.

Raining very hard. Waited for other troops to cross. Major Dunbar is detailed on the division staff as inspector of 3d Division, in place of Major Dawson, wounded on the 16th. Crossed the Harpeth river at 10 A. M. Marched through Franklin, the bands playing. Regiment in front of the division. The whole town was a hospital, filled with wounded of the battle of Franklin. The works where the rebels charged on the 30th of November—the entanglement of brushes in front of the works was shot to pieces and actually riddled. To the right there was a locust grove, the trees from two to four inches in diameter. Shot to pieces and cut down by musket balls. On the outside of the works the graves are very thick as far as can be seen from the road. Three pieces of artillery and a rebel flag, captured by the cavalry, passed to the rear. The cavalry deserve a great deal of credit for the good work they are doing. Cannonading occasionally in the front. Passed through Spring Hill. Rained all day. Halted at 6 P. M. to bivouac. Marched fifteen miles during the day.

19. Reveille 4:30 A. M. Rations and some beef issued. Raining hard at 9:15 A. M. Marched forward. Cannonading in front. Division formed in line on the left of the road. Cannonading ceased. Marched a short distance and halted. Heard yells in front gradually coming down the line. The men are cheering going to bivouac. Halted at 11:30 A. M. to bivouac. Marched three miles.

20. Reveille 4:30 A. M. It is very cold and windy. Drew shoes and socks. Some cannonading in front during the forenoon. Marched at 1:15 P. M. to Rutherford creek, turned to the right of the pike. Crossed Rutherford creek at 3 P. M. Cannonading ceased. It began to rain, and froze as it fell on the

clothes. Reached Duck river, turned to the left and went into bivouac. 4:30 P. M. marched four miles. The regiment furnished the pickets.

21. Reveille 5 A. M. Sleeting and snowing. Did not move. Some of the troops are across the river. Snowed nearly all day. Very disagreeable.

22. Reveille 5 A. M. Very cold and windy. Some cannonading, seemingly at the old bridge across the river. Rations and some beef issued. Marched at 6 P. M. down the river to the trestle bridge, and crossed Duck river. Marched through Columbia. Ordered to load. Fires are visible in front. Marched about two miles. Fires are seen on both sides of the road. The rebels disappeared. Moved to the side of the road and bivouacked for the night at 8:30 P. M., having marched five miles. The ground is frozen hard.

23. Reveille 5 A. M. The ground thawing under foot. At 11 A. M. ordered to get ready to march. Other troops are passing to the front. Marched at 3:30 P. M. Cannonading in front. Our brigade band played as the troops marched. Halted in bivouac at 5:30 P. M. Marched five miles during the day.

24. Reveille 5 A. M. Cold and clear. The cavalry began passing to the front before daylight. Marched at 11:45 A. M. The pike very muddy and much cut up. Some cannonading in front. Passed through a gap, where the rebels had put up barricades of rails against the cavalry, and had a fight. Saw several dead and wounded cavalrymen. Passed through Linnville and stopped to bivouac at 5:30 P. M. Marched sixteen miles. Heard cannonading all day in one position or another to the front.

25. Reveille 5 A. M. Christmas day. At 8 A. M. it began raining. We heard cannonading in front and cavalry skirmishing. Marched at 9:30 A. M. Marched

to Pulaski, band playing in front. Marched through town at 1:15 p. m. Musketry and cannonading in front. Cavalry engaged with rebel rear guard by the side of the road. The rebels being crowded, parked a portion of their train and destroyed a great deal of ammunition. Crossed Richland creek on a bridge which the rebels attempted to burn but which was saved for the infantry by heroic exertions of the cavalry in front. Marched through mud ankle deep. Hard fighting in front. Artillery ceased. Several dead rebels lying along the road. Moved close to the position of the fighting. Bivouacked at 5:30 p. m., having marched fifteen miles. Still raining. Last time the rebels were seen in line of battle in our front.

26. Reveille 5 a. m. Drizzling, chilly and foggy. Some beef. Three days rations' and some whisky issued. Bivouacked for the night. Quiet along the front, no firing.

27. Reveille 5 a. m. Still raining. Troops been passing since daylight. Marched at 8:30 a. m. Mud hub deep. Halted for bivouac at 3:45 p. m., having marched twelve miles.

28. Reveille 5 a. m. Marched at 9 a. m., the regiment in front of the 3d Division. Crossed Sugar creek. Crossed the Tennessee state line into Alabama. Passed swamps and wilderness and halted near Lexington, Ala., at 4 p. m. to bivouac, having marched twelve miles. The regiment ordered to make details for picket duty.

29. Reveille 5 a. m. Cold and clear. Pickets relieved and a detail of two men ordered from each company for forage. The foragers returned with a few good things. Some beef issued. Other rations very scarce.

30. Reveille 5 a. m. Raining. Three days' partial

rations issued. Ordered to be ready to march at 6:30 A. M. The rain turned to snow. Did not march.

31. Reveille 5 A. M. Marched at 8:30 A. M. in an easterly direction. The regiment in the rear of the 3d Division marched to Sugar creek and halted at 2:40 P. M., until the bridge is completed. Marched at 3:40 P. M. Crossed Sugar creek and halted to bivouac at 7:45 P. M., having marched sixteen miles.

JANUARY, 1865.

1. Reveille 5 A. M. Marched 2:30 P. M. Marched two miles to the river and halted at 4:30 P. M. to bivouac, as the bridge is not completed across Elk river.

2. Reveille 5 A. M. Two men from each company detailed to forage. The foragers brought in a lot of eatables.

3. Reveille 5 A. M. Began raining before 3 A. M. Marched at 1:30 P. M. Crossed Elk river on trestle-bridge built by Colonel A. D. Streight. Marched very fast. Ordered to call roll at every halt. Marched into Athens, Ala., at 6:30 P. M., having marched eleven miles. Marched one mile and went in bivouac 7 P. M.

4. Reveille 5 A. M. A cold morning. Marched at 7:30 A. M. The ground was frozen very hard. Marched through Athens out on the Huntsville road. Crossed Swan creek, two miles from Athens. Marched very fast. Crossed Piney creek, Limestone creek and stopped to bivouac near Indian creek at 3:45 P. M. Marched twenty miles during the day.

5. Reveille 5 A. M. Two days' rations issued. Marched at 9 A. M. to pike two miles from Huntsville, Ala. The regiment was equalized into eight com-

panies, and with flying colors marched into Huntsville, Ala., in column of companies. Halted at 12 m. At 3 p. m. marched about five miles from Huntsville on the pike leading south to the Tennessee river, and halted for camp on the left of the road, having marched eleven miles to-day.

6. Reveille sounded late. Raining. Roll-calls at regular hours.

7. Reveille late. Camp ordered to be pitched. Clapboard cabins to be built for four men each, to be ten feet long, seven feet wide, and five feet high, four feet apart, a door in one end. Streets ten yards wide.

8. Reveille late. Two men from each company ordered as foragers. Sergeant Kline of Company C appointed sergeant-major. Cold and stormy. Worked on cabins.

9. Reveille late. Worked on the cabins. Rained hard all day.

10. Reveille. Worked on the cabins. Brigade camp guards are established. Ordered to have roll-call three times a day. Raining all day.

11. Reveille. Worked on the houses. Cold and snowing.

12. Reveille. Routine duties.

13. Reveille. Routine duties.

14. Reveille and congratulatory order from President Lincoln read.

15. Reveille and company inspection.

16. Reveille. General inspection.

17. Reveille. The regiment made a good appearance. The 3d and 4th Michigan regiments joined the brigade.

18. Reveille. Routine duties.

19. Reveille. Routine duties.

20. Reveille. Routine duties. Rain.

21. Reveille. Routine duties. Rain.

22. Reveille. Company inspection. Ordered to be in readiness to march at 6 A. M.

23. Reveille. Marched at 7:30 A. M. with the 13th Ohio Volunteer Infantry. Foraging. Cold and freezing. Marched to Huntsville under command of Lieutenant-Colonel Parker. March five miles beyond Huntsville and north of it. We pass through Marcheyville and crossed Bar creek. When sixteen miles from Huntsville eleven wagons went to the left and loaded with corn two and one-half miles away from the road, where nine wagons had been attacked and burned by guerillas the week before and part of Company C, 86th Indiana, and teamsters had been captured. After the old iron of the burned wagons was loaded and all the teams loaded with fodder marched back and bivouacked at 8 P. M.

24. Reveille 5 A. M. Started at 9:10 A. M. Marched two hours and halted. Rested ten minutes and marched to Huntsville in one and one-quarter hours, and got back to camp at 3 P. M. Every one who went on this expedition came back loaded with eatables of all kinds—hogs, sheep, bacon, hams, turkeys, chickens, eggs, butter, milk, honey, dried apples and peaches.

25. Reveille. Policed camp and camp duties. Cold.

26. Reveille. Camp duties. Very cold.

27. Reveille. Camp duties. Cold.

28. Reveille. Camp duties.

29. Reveille. Company inspection. Camp duties. Cold.

30. Reveille. Camp duties.

31. Reveille. Ordered to be in readiness to march at 2 P. M. Marched at 3:30 in the rear of the 2d Brigade to the depot at Huntsville and boarded the

cars (open stock cars). So crowded for room could not sleep.

FEBRUARY, 1865.

1. Arrived at Stevenson, Ala., at 8:45 A. M. Sixty miles from Huntsville got off the cars and ate breakfast. At 11:50 A. M. passed through a swampy part of country with mountains on each side. Got to the tunnel through the Cumberland Mountains at 2 P. M., eighty-eight miles from Nashville. It took five minutes to pass through the tunnel. Stopped at Cowan Station a few minutes, eighty-seven miles from Nashville. Passed through some nice country. Stopped at Dechard, eighty miles from Nashville. Passed through Tullahoma at 5 P. M. Passed through Normandie, near Duck river, sixty-two miles from Nashville. Passed through Murfreesboro at dark. Arrived at Nashville at 2 A. M. Halted in the depot.

2. Awakened at 5 A. M. Got breakfast. Disembarked from the cars at 7 A. M. Marched out into the street; stacked arms in the mud. At 10 A. M. marched out to the Granny White pike. Went outside of the line of works where we lay in December last and camped on the right hand side of the road, where the regiment had driven the rebels out of their works December 15. Rain.

3. Still raining. Furnished the pickets.

4. Up late. Col. Kneffer in command of regiment and General Beatty the brigade. Very cold.

5. Ordered to be ready to march to-morrow at 6:30.

6. Marched to the Chattanooga depot and got on board the cars. Started toward Stevenson, Ala.; passed through Lavergne, sixteen miles from Nashville, stopped in Murfreesboro at 1 P. M., passed

through Fosterville, Bellebuckle, and reached Wartrace; on to Dichard, then Stevenson.

7. Very cold and several inches of snow on the ground. Reached Huntsville, Ala., at 9 A. M. and at 11 A. M. started for the old camp. On the way met some teams hauling in the cabins. Fixed bayonets and made them turn back with the lumber and fixed up camp again.

8. Up at day. Fixed up our camp. Colonel Knefler commands the brigade, Lieutenant-Colonel Parker the regiment. Colonel Parker started home on a leave of absence, Captain William A. Abbett in command of regiment.

9. Reveille. Clear and cold. Routine duties.
10. Reveille. Clear and cold. Routine duties.
11. Reveille. Clear and cold. Routine duties.
12. Reveille. Inspection companies.
13. Reveille. Cooler. Routine duties.
14. Reveille daylight. Cold and cloudy. Nothing important. Routine duty.
15. Reveille daylight. Warm, cloudy. Company drills. First Lieutenant Dan W. Hoadley mustered as captain of "K" company.
16. Reveille at daylight. Rain. General inspection at 2 P. M.
17. Reveille at daylight. Clear and windy. Nothing important. Routine.
18. Reveille at daylight. The regiment marched to the Tennessee river, went on board a gunboat down the river about thirty-five miles and drove off some bushwhackers. Back to camp.
19. Reveille at daylight. Nothing important. Routine duty.
20. Reveille. Policed the camp. Company drills and dress parade.

21. Reveille. Colonel Kneffer starts home on leave of absence of ten days. Colonel Dick in command of brigade. Company drills and dress parade.

22. Reveille daylight. Washington's birthday.

23. Reveille. Rained all night, still raining. Nothing important. Routine duty.

24. Reveille. Still raining. Nothing important.

25. Reveille. Still raining. Nothing important.

26. Reveille. Clear and cool. Company inspection and dress parade.

27. Reveille daylight. Policed the whole camp. Had dress parade.

28. Reveille daylight. Was mustered at 11 A. M. Drilled and had parade.

MARCH, 1865.

1. Reveille daylight. Raining. Nothing important. Routine duties.

2. Reveille daylight. Raining hard. Nothing important. Routine duties.

3. Reveille daylight. Still raining. Nothing important. Routine duties.

4. Reveille daylight. Cleared off. Nothing important. Routine duties.

5. Reveille daylight. Company inspection.

6. Reveille daylight. Company drills, and dress parade.

7. Reveille daylight. Policed camp. Brigade drill at 2 P. M.

8. Reveille daylight. Policed camp. Dress parade.

9. Reveille daylight. A detail is sent out to cut cedars to plant in streets to decorate the camp. Snow.

10. Reveille daylight. Cold. Brigade drill.

11. Reveille daylight. Cold.

12. Sunday. Reveille daylight. Lieutenant-Colonel

Parker returned to regiment. L. W. Munhall is commissioned and mustered adjutant. The train upon which Colonel Parker came was attacked by guerrillas. One man killed. Company inspection and dress parade.

13. Reveille daylight. Nothing important. Routine duty.

14. Reveille daylight. The 1st Division left for Knoxville to-day.

15. Ordered at 3 A. M. to have reveille at 5, and be in readiness to march at 6 A. M. Remained in camp.

16. Reveille 3:15. Raining hard. Started at 5:45 A. M. Colonel Parker in command of regiment. Arrived at depot at 8 A. M., and started in box or open cattle cars at 10 A. M. Cold. Arrived at Stevenson, Ala., at 3 P. M. Crossed the Tennessee river at Bridgeport. The river is very full. Passed Nicka Jack Cave. Crossed Whitesides bridge before dark. This bridge is 116 feet high, and connects two mountains. Arrived at Chattanooga, and stopped after 8 o'clock. So crowded in the cars could not sleep. Forty-seven men in one car. Henry J. Brattain mustered as First Lieutenant, "K" company.

17. Awakened at daylight. Before reaching Louden train met with an accident. Two or three cars off the track, and some of the boys were badly bruised and shaken up. The road was torn up for one hundred yards or more. At 4 P. M. the road was repaired, and the trains passed on. Started at 4:45 P. M. and crossed the Tennessee river on the continued long high bridge. Cars stopped in Knoxville at about 11 P. M.

18. Got up early and prepared breakfast. Left Knoxville at 4:30 P. M. Stopped before 6 P. M. for water and started again at 8 P. M. Passed the 1st

Division at Strawberry Plains and awakened to get off the cars at 11 o'clock P. M. Marched through New Market. Camped one mile from the depot.

19. Reveille sun-up. At 12 M. moved into woods one mile northeast of town. Camp and put up tents.

20. Reveille as usual. Colonel Kneffler returned to regiment and assumed command.

21. Reveille as usual. Rain and hail.

22. Reveille as usual. Cool and clear. Nothing important. On picket.

23. Reveille as usual. Dress parade witnessed by General Beatty. Sergeant Kline appointed sergeant-major.

24. Reveille as usual. Three men and sergeant for patrol and two men for picket from each company. Troops are passing going to the front.

25. Reveille at usual time. Policed camp. Dispatches read from General Sherman. Victories over the rebels caused cheers.

26. Reveille as usual. Cold and frosty. Company inspection and dress parade. Order is read that Alonzo McNeal, of Company "A," is to forfeit one month's pay ($16) for discharging his gun in camp.

27. Reveille as usual. Company skirmish drill and battalion drill. Dress parade.

28. Reveille as usual. Commissions came for the following officers: W. S. Cardell, E. M. Byrkit, captains. George G. Earl, captain on the staff of General Beatty. Charles J. Many, Henry Magsam, John B. W. Parker, Frank Hedderick, Ezra Buchanan, William H. Huntzinger to be first lieutenants. The sick and extra baggage ordered sent back. Battalion drill and dress parade. The 14th Wisconsin Regiment joined the brigade.

29. Received order in the night to have reveille at

3 A. M., to be ready to march at 6 A. M. Started after 6 A. M., the 3d Brigade in front. Stopped before noon for dinner. Marched again at 1 P. M., a little distance and camped for the night, having marched fourteen miles. Raining.

30. Reveille 3:30 A. M. Marched at 5:45 A. M. Passed through Morristown and Russelville. Halted at 12 M. for the night, having marched fourteen miles. Rained very hard.

31. Reveille at 4 A. M. Started at 6. Halted near Bull's Gap at 10 A. M., having marched six miles. Bivouacked.

APRIL, 1865.

1. Up late. Moved half mile to a better camp. George G. Earl mustered as captain "G" company. Henry Magsam mustered as first lieutenant Company "B." John B. W. Parker, first lieutenant "F" company. Charles J. Many, first lieutenant "C" company. Francis Herrick mustered as first lieutenant "B" company. E. M. Byrkit mustered as captain "I" company.

2. Sunday. Cold and frosty. Camp policed. Regimental inspection at 10 A. M. A rebel lieutenant and five men came to division headquarters and got General Wood's fine horses and two of his orderly's horses. The guard halted them. He had no load in his gun, and he bayoneted three of them. He was shot twice by the rebels, and one shot the lieutenant (Baxter by name), and broke his leg. He crawled away and was found with his papers buried under him. He proved to be one of General Vaughn's men. The others got away.

3. Nine men from each company for picket. Strict orders to allow no one to pass in or out without a pass.

The rebel lieutenant died of his wounds. Cannon firing is heard. Told it is because Richmond, Va., is ours. The boys are cheering.

4. Reveille early. Ordered to march at 7 A. M. The regiment, in front of the division, passed through Bull's Gap. Marched very fast and crossed Lick creek, and passed the 1st Division in camp. A dispatch is read that General Whitsell captured Richmond, and the enemy had left in confusion. It caused cheering from the boys. Passed through Blue Springs, where the 2d Division was in camp, and stopped for dinner at 11:30. General Beatty told us he would send our regiment in front to keep the bushwhackers out of the way. We loaded our guns, and at 1 P. M. started, and marched very fast, and reached Greenville at 3 P. M. Passed through town and camped on the other side at 3:30 P. M., having marched twenty miles. Laid off camp and pitched tents. This is the place where General John Morgan was killed as he was trying to escape from federal cavalry. Seventy-two men, six non-commissioned and three commissioned officers from the regiment to provost the town, furnished by the regiment.

5. Up late. A detail of sixty men was made for provost guards. Regular guard mount at 10 A. M. and at 11 A. M. Ordered to move at 2 P. M. Started. Guarding the train. Passed through Raytown. Bivouacked near the place for the night.

6. Reveille 4 A. M. Started at 6 A. M. Raining. Passed through Leesburgh. Halted at 12 M. for dinner. Started at 2 P. M. Marching slowly. The Colonel allowed the tired men to ride his horse; he walked. Halted near Jonesboro. Halted at 3:35 north of the town, having marched fifteen miles. Laid off camp

and pitched tents in regular order and sent out picket. Sixty men were detailed for provost guard.

7. In camp at Jonesboro doing provost guard duty. The first time since in service.

8. Cold and frosty. Bushwhackers are thick around this place. A detail is sent out after them. The provost guard's headquarters is in the court-house. The city is patroled after 9 P. M. Every soldier must be in camp at that time.

9. Sunday. All quiet.

10. A citizen reported where two rebels were in hiding, and Lieutenant Bratton and twelve men went out and captured them. Brought them to Colonel Knefler, provost marshal. They were armed with revolvers. At 3 P. M. received news of the surrender of General Lee and his whole army. Cheer after cheer went up from the boys. Drew rations and clothing.

11. Reveille usual time. A salute of anvils is fired by the citizens in honor of General Lee's surrender. The fire bells are ringing, the boys are cheering, the bands are playing and bonfires burning in the streets. All excitement prevails.

12. Reveille. Routine duties.

13. Reveille. A detail of the brigade is sent into the country to look for guerrillas.

14. Reveille. Cannons are heard firing at Greenville over the surrender of General Lee. Routine duties.

15. Reveille. Routine duties.

16. Sunday. The first lieutenants who received their commissions some time ago started to Greenville to be mustered in. They go well armed, on account of meeting bushwhackers. News of the assassination of President Lincoln. All soldiers confined to limits of the camps. Great excitement.

17. The first lieutenants returned to Jonesboro, having ridden fifty miles. They were mustered by Captain McIlvaine. The regiment is relieved from provost guard duty.

18. Reveille. Company "D" is detailed to convoy train to Greenville. One hundred men of Vaughn's command came in and surrendered. A citizen cheered for the man that killed the President and he was promptly knocked down by John Hoop, of Company "A." He was taken away and put under guard. The supply train was ordered back. The regiment had general inspection in the evening. A plot was discovered to hang the man that cheered for the man that killed the President. He was promptly taken out of town and sent under guard to Knoxville. Killed while attempting to escape.

19. Picket duty. All quiet.

20. Companies "E" and "C" go to town to guard the place. Some rebels came in. They were of Lee's army on their way home; had been paroled. The brigade started at 12 M. Pickets are stationed around the town. The regiment is the only one left in town.

21. Started at 10:15 and stopped at Leesburgh for dinner at 12 M. Wagons in the rear were fired on by guerillas. Started again at 1 P. M. Passed through Rayton and stopped to camp at 5:15 P. M., having marched sixteen miles.

22. Reveille 5 A. M. Started at 6:10 A. M. Marched into Greenville at 9 A. M., having marched the last two and a half miles in thirty-seven minutes; having marched nine miles in two hours and forty-seven minutes and rested thirty minutes. Drew three days' rations. Started at 11 A. M. and halted at 11:40 for dinner. Started again at 1 P. M. Marched through Blue Springs and crossed Lick creek and halted for

the night at 5 p. m., having marched twenty-four miles.

23. Sunday. Reveille. Marched at 6 a. m. through Bull's Gap. Halted at the same place as on the 3d, having marched four miles. Third Brigade all in camp. Started for the depot at 6:30. Three days' rations issued. Got aboard cars at 11 p. m., thirty-seven men in each car. Train left about midnight.

24. Crossed the Hollston river and stopped at 8 a. m. for breakfast and let other trains pass. Arrived in Knoxville before 10 a. m. Started again at 2:15 p. m. Crossed the river at Louden on the long bridge; three minutes crossing it. Sergeant William H. Hagerhorst mustered as first lieutenant of "A" company.

25. Arrived at Chattanooga at 5 a. m. Left Chattanooga at 10:15 a. m. Passed through Bridgeport and Stevenson. Passed through the tunnel at 6 p. m.

26. Awake at 6 a. m. Arrived at Nashville. The cars started on the Johnsonville railroad and went two miles and unloaded near the 2d Division. Ordered on the cars again and after 12 m. ran back and stopped in town. Got off the cars and marched out the Murfreesboro pike. Very dusty and warm. Halted three miles from the city at 4:10 p. m. and camped for the night. Camp established near Mill creek.

27. In camp. Police and routine duties.

28. Raining. Rations issued.

29. Raining. Moved after dinner to the brigade and pitched camp in regular style in a nice shady grove on a little hill four and a half miles from the city. Strict orders are issued about the men going to the city, and but five men will be allowed to go from the regiment each day. Camp guards are put out.

30. Regiment on camp guard.

May, 1865.

1. The regiment is mustered by Colonel Kneffer. Battalion drill at 2 p. m.

2. Reveille. Ordered to drill four hours each day.

3. Reveille. Sanitary stores and three days' rations issued. Company and battalion drill and dress parade. Camp is called "Harker."

4. At Camp Harker. Preparing for the review.

5. At Camp Harker. Working on muster-out rolls. The regiment takes part in the brigade review at 5 p. m. Major Dunbar reports to regiment. The order is that the general review will take place Monday and the 1862 troops will be mustered out at once.

6. At Camp Harker. Rations issued.

7. Sunday. At Camp Harker. Brigade review by Colonel Kneffer.

8. At Camp Harker. Grand review postponed until to-morrow at 10 a. m. on account of rain.

9. At Camp Harker. Preparing for the grand review. At 7 a. m. on the road to the reviewing place. The regiment on the right of the Brigade. Reached the reviewing place at 10 a. m. 4th Corps was closed *en masse*, and formed in line, the left of which was the 3d Brigade, resting on the knoll near Fort Negley, the line extending across the Granny White pike. At 11 a. m. a salute of thirteen guns was fired, the signal for the reviewing officers to start in front of the lines. Cheers are heard from each regiment, beginning on the right, and we saw the great commander, General George H. Thomas, coming. He rode in our front. Presented arms and gave three cheers. Generals Stanley and Wood accompanied him. Took their position in front. The corps changed direction by the left flank and passed in review. The whole corps passed the brigade. The day was beautiful. The troops

made a magnificent display. Witnessed by many people who came out to see the 4th Corps perhaps for the last time. Returned to camp.

10. At Camp Harker. Rations issued. An order read congratulating the division upon the fine appearance it made at the review.

11. At Camp Harker. Nothing important.

12. At Camp Harker. Battalion drill and dress parade.

13. At Camp Harker. Sanitary stores issued.

14. At Camp Harker. Working on the muster-out rolls. Dress parade.

15. At Camp Harker. Brigade inspection at 2 P. M. by Brigade Inspector. Captain William V. Burns, of "B," discharged—disability.

16. At Camp Harker. Dress parade.

17. At Camp Harker. Dress parade.

18. At Camp Harker. Sanitary stores issued. Rained. No parade.

19. At Camp Harker. Drew clothing. Rained.

20. At Camp Harker. Nothing important.

21. Sunday. At Camp Harker. Nothing important. Rained hard.

22. At Camp Harker. Battalion drill and dress parade.

23. At Camp Harker. Battalion drill and dress parade.

24. At Camp Harker. Company drill and dress parade.

25. At Camp Harker. Six days' rations issued. Battalion drill and dress parade.

26. At Camp Harker. Battalion drill and dress parade.

27. At Camp Harker. Battalion drill and dress parade.

28. At Camp Harker. Battalion drill and dress parade.

29. At Camp Harker. Battalion drill and dress parade.

30. At Camp Harker. Rations issued. Battalion drill and dress parade.

31. At Camp Harker. Battalion drill and dress parade.

JUNE, 1865.

1. At Camp Harker. Making out muster-out rolls. Battalion drill and dress parade.

2. At Camp Harker. Making out muster-out rolls. Dress parade.

3. At Camp Harker. Making out muster-out rolls. Dress parade.

4. At Camp Harker. Making out muster-out rolls. Rations issued. Dress parade.

5. At Camp Harker. Making out muster-out rolls. Dress parade.

6. At Camp Harker. Making out muster-out rolls. Dress parade.

7. At Camp Harker. The muster-out rolls are signed and forwarded to Indianapolis.

8. At Camp Harker. The records are boxed up, and the recruits and deserters sent to 51st Indiana to make up time lost. Ordered to have reveille at midnight and start at 1 o'clock A. M.

9. Took the train at Nashville, Tenn., and arrived at Indianapolis about 3 P. M. next day. The regiment was allowed to disperse until next Monday morning, this being Saturday.

Just before the regiment left camp at Nashville, and the other regiments belonging to the 4th Corps scattered for their homes, General Stanley, commanding our corps, issued the following order:

"HEADQUARTERS, FOURTH ARMY CORPS,
 "NASHVILLE, TENN., June 7, 1865.

"GENERAL ORDERS, ⸜
   "No. 21.   ⸝

"To the officers and soldiers of the regiments of 1862, who are about to leave us, the general commanding the corps desires to tender his congratulations upon their past proud career and good wishes for their future prosperity and happiness. Coming into service at a period of the war when success seemed doubtful —after all the illusions of excitement and first impressions, that war was all pomp and glory, had worn off —you, from the beginning of your service, pretty fully realized the stern, hard task before you, and well have you performed that task. In all that constitutes a veteran soldier, you are not one whit behind any soldier in our great army. In this army particularly, your regiments have passed through all the important battles fought by the Army of the Cumberland. How much influence these battles have had in destroying the great rebellion of this century, history must determine. Of the award, these regiments of '62 will have a full share. The rebellion is ended, and you leave us for your homes. Brought up, as our young men of the North are, to industry and self-exertion, you will find it no inconvenience or hardship to exchange the discomforts of camp and the vicissitudes of military life for the peaceful avocations of the citizen. We part with you in sorrow, and will, until the end of life, cherish you in our memories as our brave, amiable and constant friends and companions in arms.

"By command of Major-General D. S. Stanley.
"WILLIAM H. SINCLAIR.
"*Assistant Adjutant-General.*

"Official:
"———— ————,
"*Assistant Adjutant-General.*"

General Wood, commanding our division, also issued the following order. General Samuel Beatty, commanding our brigade, issued a like order for the brigade, but the original of this order we have not been able to find:

"HEADQUARTERS THIRD DIVISION,
"FOURTH ARMY CORPS,
"NEAR NASHVILLE, TENN., June 6, 1865.

"GENERAL ORDER)
"No. 47.   )

"*To the Officers and Soldiers of the 89th Illinois Vols., 93d and 124th Ohio Vols., 79th and 86th Indiana Vols.:*

"The order from the War Department, directing the muster-out of the troops whose terms of service expire before a certain date, will soon terminate the official relation which has so long existed between us. I contemplate the approaching separation with feelings of sadness, and I can not allow it to take place without expressing my warmest thanks and sincere gratitude for the noble conduct which you have ever displayed while under my command. Participation in common dangers, and in privations and hardships, has united us in the bonds of an indissoluble friendship. I will ever cherish, as among the brightest passages of my life, the memory of our past association. You have done your duty as good soldiers and patriots, engaged from the highest motives, in the holiest of causes. You can now return to your homes with the happy reflection that the mission which called you into the field, namely, the suppression of the armed resistance of treason and rebellion to the government, has been fully, nobly, honorably accomplished. Noble soldiers, your work is finished, now rest from your labors. Each one of you will carry home with you my highest esteem and kindest wishes for your future welfare. May happiness, prosperity, health and success wait on you throughout the remainder of your lives. May your future be as happy as your military life has been glorious! To each one of you, individually, and to all collectively, I bid a kind, a friendly good-bye. God bless you!

"TH. J. WOOD,
"Major-General Volunteers.

"Official:
"M. P. BESTOW,
"Captain and Assistant Adjutant-General."

FINAL SEPARATION.

Monday morning, June 11, 1865, the muster-out rolls had been signed and delivered, and the men of the 79th Regiment assembled at Camp Carrington, in the city of Indianapolis, to be paid off. They drew their pay for the last time, which is the last act they were ever to perform as members of that regiment. The officers and men are now in the same rank. No one is any longer subject to command or authority.

They are no longer soldiers, but citizens. The hour they had so long desired to see had come. They no longer had any guns, accoutrements, knapsacks, haversacks or canteens. They can no longer make requisitions or draw rations.

The situation at this moment was a little embarrassing. These men, who have drilled, marched, camped, associated and been in many battles together for a long time, must now separate. Crowding into the mind of every man were the recollections of past experiences of fun, hardships, hard services, dangers, dead comrades, warm regards for the survivors, the longed-for pleasures of home, civil life, of freedom and the anxiety for the future.

They stand about in groups for a few moments rather awkwardly, not waiting for the bugle to call them to drill, or to strike tents and break camp. They are well aware that no further duty is required of them. They can not stay there; they must be off, each man to what seemed to be almost a new life.

They are no longer under any conditions of war. This is peace—blessed peace, which they realized now as they had never done before in its full force. With moistened eyes and choking voices they closed the scene, mingled together for a moment, shook hands, said good-bye and were gone.

More than thirty-four years have passed since that day. Many of those men no longer answer to roll-call in our regimental reunions, and the rolls are rapidly becoming smaller. None of the men are any longer young or possess the vigor they once displayed; they can and are entitled, in advancing years, to enjoy the pleasure that comes from the reflection that, in their early manhood, they did their duty and took whatever hazard it involved in maintaining the government of the United States.

Their children can look with pleasure upon this record of their fathers' faithful service. They may not have the opportunity to do like service for the government, but there will come to them constant opportunities to show their fidelity and courage in protecting the interests of their government in many ways as important, patriotic and valuable.

www.ingramcontent.com/pod-product-compliance
Lightning Source LLC
Chambersburg PA
CBHW021834230426
43669CB00008B/964